The Near East, the Cradle of Western Civilization

Sema'an I. Salem
with
Lynda A. Salem

Writers Club Press
San Jose   New York   Lincoln   Shanghai

The Near East, the Cradle of Western Civilization

Published by Writers Club Press
an imprint of iUniverse.com, Inc.

For information address:
iUniverse.com, Inc.
620 North 48th Street
Suite 201
Lincoln, NE 68504-3467
www.iuniverse.com

ISBN: 0-595-00169-6

Printed in the United States of America

Contens

Introduction

Cultural and intellectual history is the true history of humanity. This is a history that deserves considerably more attention than has been ascribed to it, and a more careful consideration than it has received.

Conflicts wars and political upheavals divide nations and alienate societies; knowledge, culture, and scientific development unite these entities and bridge the gaps between them. True knowledge, the noblest of human attributes, knows no boundaries. It transcends social and natural confines to embrace the universal. It defies the imprisonment of space and time. A civilization may disappear from the face of the earth, but its intellectual contribution usually survives.

Civilization is the result of relationships and interactions, not isolation. It arises from the interactions of human beings not only with each other but also with their environment and with other living species. These interactions help fine-tune our evolution and shape our adaptation. They teach us how to cope with our environment and properly utilize its natural resources. The foundations of our civilizations rest on the proper utilization and protection of these resources, and prosper as the result of our interactions with one another as individuals and as groups and nations.

The key to the development of civilization is the ability of individuals to communicate, live together, and exchange ideas and material things. Civilization is enhanced by various forms of contact: migration, trade, wars, and occupations among them. It dies in isolation and grows and prospers with intercourse and interaction. Without these relationships, we would probably be still living in the stone age, waiting for the wheel to be invented.

Early humans realized that they were more successful in their hunt, especially of big game, if they hunted in groups rather than individually. This and other similar activities led to cooperation and the evolution of cohesion, culminating in permanent settlements and villages. This transition signaled the end of what came to be known as the Paleolithic (Old Stone) Age and the beginning of the Neolithic (New Stone) Age (10,000–8000 B.C.). Plants and animals were domesticated, and agriculture replaced gathering and hunting as a way of life, and permanent settlements appeared. Early on, these transitions took place in areas with permanent water sources and an abundance of plant and animal life; these were the centers of early civilizations in the Fertile Crescent, China, and possibly the Americas (1). People living in such settlements were able to produce enough food without involving every member of the community in its procurement, and they could accumulate more goods than they could carry. Professions other than farming and herding appeared; some workers became craftsmen producing tools and ornaments. In time, these artisans developed the skill to work with metal, to weave textiles, and to manufacture jewelry (2).

Writing, the most significant single step on the road to civilization, was invented in the lower valley of the Tigris and Euphrates rivers in the later centuries of the fourth millennium B. C. From there writing spread over the entire Fertile Crescent, and from the Nile Valley and Crete to the Indus Valley (3).

The excavations undertaken in the Middle East over the past century have proved that around 3500 B.C. that is about three millennia before the Golden Age of Greece, great civilizations had flourished in Mesopotamia, on the banks of the Nile and the Indus rivers, on the Eastern shores of the Mediterranean, and on Crete and other Aegean islands. These civilizations had many common characteristics, indicating the existence of a vast web of communication amongst them, and this is what raised them to their greatness.

The rise of European nationalism during the nineteenth and twentieth centuries, and the subsequent search for the roots of European civilization, led to an obsession with Greece as the cradle of all knowledge and culture. This was probably the result of the availability of Greek literature to European scholars. To a large extent, these nationalistic feelings obscured reality as European scholars fought with predilection to prove the purity of their culture and that it had never been contaminated by non-European thoughts.

In recent years the West came to recognize the debt owed by the Greeks to earlier civilizations of the Near East and this led to fundamental revision in the historical Eurocentric thoughts. With western scholars grudgingly and diligently working to obscure any such origin, it was not easy for the truth to surface, but it is now well established that through the mediation of Crete, Greece, and Rome, the Orient provided the West with all the foundations of civilization: the domestication of animals and plants, agriculture, the plow, irrigation and drainage, the horse and wagon, commerce, coinage, crafts, law and government, state and empire, architecture, glass, concrete, the vault, mathematics, astronomy, medicine, geometry, writing, the alphabet, paper and ink, books, libraries and schools, mythology and religion, literature, music, architecture, pottery, metallurgy and fine jewelry.

In honoring the Near East for these contributions, we are acknowledging "a debt long due to the real founders of European and American civilization." (4)

The Greeks and the Romans were well acquainted with the Near-Eastern world and its civilization, but about China and the Far East they knew very little, and what they knew was far from being accurate. Later, after the fall of the Roman Empire, almost all contacts between Europe and Asia were cut off, and with the rise of Islam during the seventh and eighth centuries A.D. East Asia and Europe were completely isolated.

In ancient times, the Western World was well separated from the early centers of Near Eastern civilizations; the gap, which involves time, geography, and language, made the Greeks and to a greater extent the Romans so much closer to the West, and therefore their achievements more accessible and less mysterious. Yet this huge gap and the countless significant differences between the people of the West and the early peoples of Sumeria, the Fertile Crescent, Egypt, and the Aegean should not make us forget the important role those early pioneers played in the development of western civilization and culture. Literally, the peoples of the Fertile Crescent invented civilization as we know it, and we owe them a great debt of gratitude for their immense contributions to all the fields of knowledge.

The centers of civilizations of China and the Far East, although having claim to antiquity, did not, due to their remoteness, contribute to Western civilization until modern times. The wool clothing of the mummies recently uncovered in Urunchi of the Tarim Basin of the northwestern corner of China was found to bear resemblance to the twill plaids of prehistoric Central Europe, and was acclaimed as proof that cultural contacts between Europe and China existed some 1500 years before the establishment of the Silk Road. But these contacts are relatively recent when compared with the rise of the civilizations of the Fertile Crescent, and their cultural significance is limited as herders moving at a pace set by their grazing sheep, which were domesticated in the Fertile Crescent several thousands years earlier, require close to a 1000 years to complete the journey from central Europe to northwestern China.

The first two chapters of the book deal with the development of cultures and civilizations; The first chapter is a brief summary of the history of civilizations in the Fertile Crescent from the domestication of plants and animals to the development of medicine, astronomy, and mathematics. The second chapter is a short account of the history of the civilizations and cultures that flourished on the Mediterranean shores and islands. Each of the remaining nine chapters deals in some details with one of the aspects of civilizations or cultures.

We acknowledge with gratitude the kind invitations by Ms Helaine Selin, the editor of the Encyclopaedia of the History of Science, Technology, and Medicine in Non-Western Cultures, and by Dr. Ghazi Brax, the Editor of Dahish Voice, to write about ancient civilizations for their respective publications. This activity led to the present work. We also thank Professor L. S. Lerner for reading parts of the manuscript and for his valuable comments.

---

(1). Martin, Thomas R. (1996:5).

(2). Ibid, (1996:11).

(3). Schmandt-Besserat, Denise. (1996:1).

(4). Durant, Will. (1935:116).

Chapter One

Early Development

Our progress from savagery to civilization has been defined by many nineteenth-century authors writing about the history of civilization as a series of occurrences, of which the most prominent are the developments of agriculture, metallurgy, writing, centralized government, and complex technology. The last entry in this list is broad enough to encompass many of the achievements of the present century. At the dawn of history, most of these advances took place in what became known as the Fertile Crescent.

Before settling in permanent dwellings, early humans lived in bands of hunter-gatherers. They endured in this state for millions of years; all our present development has taken place during the relatively short period of a little over the ten thousand years that followed. Hunter-gatherers, living often on the verge of starvation, were limited in their achievement by two main factors: being always on the move, they were limited to what they could carry, their weapons and their children. Their constant search for food and water left them little time to do anything else.

By the end of the Pleistocene Ice Age, the rainfall over Southwest Asia had begun to decrease and the deserts of the Near East began to expand, forcing the bands of hunter-gatherers to move into areas with reliable water sources. Game and hunters drifted towards the Fertile Crescent.

The region comprises most of present-day Israel and Jordan, all of Lebanon, northwestern Syria, southeastern Turkey, western Iran, and most of Iraq. It enjoys a Mediterranean climate, characterized by wet, mild winters and dry, hot summers. A plant, to survive in such a climate, must have rapid growth and must produce its seeds and bring them to maturity before the arrival of the hot, dry weather that causes it to wither and die.

The seeds remain dormant during the hot summer, ready to germinate and sprout with the return of the winter rains. The seeds of these annual wild plants are useful for human consumption; these are the cereals and pulses of the Fertile Crescent.

In addition to the proper climate, the region possessed a diversity of wild animals and plants, and mountains of various altitudes, which result in staggered harvest seasons of multifarious plant seeds. The harvests of these cereals and pulses were the precursors of the earliest domestications of plants, which was a magnificent leap in human development. This revolution enabled a few people, working for relatively short periods, to produce enough to feed a considerably larger population, thus freeing a segment of the community to engage in other occupations.

Plant domestication began in the middle of the ninth millennium B.C. in the Fertile Crescent and probably in one or two centers in China. What took place in China spread into Southeast Asia, the Philippines, and Indonesia, but not westward, leaving the produce and the technology of the Fertile Crescent to be diffused into Southwest Asia and Europe.

The earliest Fertile Crescent plants to be domesticated were primitive forms of wheat, barley, and peas. These choice candidates were domesticated around 8500 B.C. Aside from their nutritious value, they gave relatively high yields; they could be harvested in a few short months after being planted, and their crops could easily be stored. This was the simplest stage of domestication, and could have been accomplished by people who were not yet committed to a fully settled life style.

Within 500 years of the beginning of agriculture in the Fertile Crescent, eight crops, termed "founder crops", were domesticated. They are emmer wheat, einkorn wheat, barley, peas, lentils, chickpeas, bitter vetch, and flax. These are the main grains of most civilizations and the main source of calories to mankind (1). They are all self-pollinators, and are known collectively as founder crops because they were the foundation of agriculture in the Fertile Crescent and in most of the rest of the world.

It took over four thousand years from the domestication of cereals and pulses to the domestication of fruit trees. The probable reason for this long delay is the relatively long time required for a tree to bear fruit after being planted. Farmers cultivating fruit trees must have lived in permanent settlements, or dwelt in the same small area for extended periods.

In the Fertile Crescent, permanent settlements (villages) are known to have existed by about 9000 B.C. and in China by about 7500 B.C. While their appearance in England and at the western edge of Europe was delayed until about 3000 B.C.

The domestication of fruit trees also had its start in the Fertile Crescent. The earliest domesticated fruit trees were olives, figs, grapes, and pomegranates, each of which requires several years to reach maturity and produce fruits. Dates, also domesticated in the Fertile Crescent, require more than a decade. These trees can easily be propagated from cuttings (figs, grapes, and pomegranates), from basal knobs (olive), and from offshoots and seeds (dates).

The almonds of the Fertile Crescent, whose wild progenitors were either poisonous or bitter, were not domesticated until 3000 B.C. almost a thousand years after the domestication of the earlier fruit trees. Almonds, although easily propagated from nuts, were not domesticated until this later date because of the unpleasant taste or the toxicity of the nuts of the wild trees. Almonds were first leached in water to get rid of their undesirable properties before being consumed. This must have been the practice until a satisfactory strain of almonds was found and cultivated.

Except for the dog, the domestication of animals proceeded at roughly the same time as the domestication of plants, and several thousand years before the domestication of fruit trees. Archaeologists estimate that the dog was domesticated around 10,000 B.C. in the Fertile Crescent (Southwest Asia), China, and probably North America. In 1997, a team of biologists from the University of California at Los Angeles analyzed the DNA from wolves and from some 70 breeds of dogs and came to the conclusion that dogs and wolves split from each other almost 100,000 years ago, and that dogs were domesticated as soon as humans left Africa and entered the Near East. This is still a point of controversy between archaeological records and the findings of molecular biologists. A probable explanation that might reconcile the two opposing views is that dogs were domesticated from a breed of wolves that split off from other wolf lineages about 100,000 years ago, but domestication took place much later.

But the dog is of limited value to humans; although it is a useful hunter, guardian, and companion, it is not big or strong enough to be a useful beast of burden and in many societies its meat is considered repugnant.

Of the four large animals that are good sources of meat for human consumption, the sheep and the goat were domesticated in the Fertile Crescent around 8000 B.C., the pig was domesticated in the Fertile Crescent and in China also around 8000 B.C., and the cow was domesticated in the Fertile Crescent and in India around 6000 B.C. Thus the Fertile Crescent was the primary center where not only plants and fruit trees were domesticated but also the four animals preferred by many societies as sources of meat, milk, and clothing. This is the beginning of true civilization as human beings no longer had to spend most of their time in search of food, and could indulge in the development of a civilized way of life.

Now let us pose the question: Why did early domestication of plants, fruit trees, and animals proceed mostly in the Fertile Crescent to the near exclusion of other world centers? could it be because the region had dependable sources of water, the proper climate and topography and a large variety of plants, trees, and animal species? Was the process in any way assisted by the weather conditions that, in the middle of the ninth millennium B.C. forced a large population to move from arid areas into that region, and they had to find sources of food to sustain themselves? Is it possible that other factors were involved? Did the hunter-gatherers of the ancient Near East progress enough to search for better ways of life?

Probably all these factors came into play in elevating the people of the Fertile Crescent from their nomadic hunter-gatherer state to a life in permanent settlements where they depended on agriculture and upon their domesticated herds for food supply. With increased food production population grows, leading to a complex society. In turn, well organized complex societies generate public works such as large irrigation systems and long-distance trade, and help create new groups of specialists, other than food-producing farmers and herders. A surplus of food allows for a diversity of functions. This is how elaborate technologies and crafts had their beginning.

From the Fertile Crescent, food production spread rapidly west into Europe, east into the Indus Valley, and south into the Nile Valley; agriculture and animal domestication moved along these axes at an average rate of about one kilometer per year to become established in Egypt between 7000 and 6000 B.C. By this date, the Egyptians began their own domestication programs. They domesticated the sycamore fig, a local vegetable called chufa, and probably watermelon. By 4000 B.C.

they domesticated the donkey. And by 3000 B.C. the Egyptians had the world's most advanced society.

Although adequate food production may not be a sufficient condition for the evolution of civilization, it is a necessary condition. In the Fertile Crescent, food production was soon followed by other innovations. These include the wheel, writing, pottery, beer and wine production (2), and metalworking techniques (3). All these innovations spread east, west, and south from the Fertile Crescent, and were not independently invented by neighboring societies. For example, the invention of the wheel, which took place around 3400 B.C. somewhere north of the Fertile Crescent, or on its southeast, appeared within a few centuries over much of Europe and West Asia. All the old wheels found to date have the same design: two wooden planks fastened by a third to form a circle. This indicates a sole site of invention (4). On the other hand, pottery is known to have existed in China probably several centuries earlier than in the Fertile Crescent.

Experimenting with copper and tin and their alloys (bronze metallurgy) began in the Fertile Crescent and Egypt early in the fourth millennium B.C. and reached Europe a few centuries later, Iron smelting, which requires a much higher temperature than either copper or tin, became known around the middle of the second millennium B.C. but was not perfected until 1000 B.C. And the highly prized Damascene steel was refined several centuries before the European steel.

Civilization does not depend on technology alone. It manifests itself in the arts, in the formal establishment of centralized governments, and in the institution of laws, legends, myth, and religion. These aspects of civilization were also first developed in the Fertile Crescent and were diffused along the same routes as food production and technologies.

The environment in the Nile Valley is not very different from that of the Tigris-Euphrates Valley, but of the founder crops only barley grew wild along the Nile, and Egyptian agriculture had to await the arrival of the cereals and pulses of the Fertile Crescent. Once established along the Nile, the plants of the founder crops performed well, triggering the spectacular rise of the great Egyptian civilization. By the beginning of the fourth millennium B.C. Egypt became a contributing partner to the Near Eastern civilization.

By this date the Near East center of achievement and innovation encompassed Iraq, most of Anatolia, western Iran, Syria, Lebanon, Palestine, Egypt, and Crete. This center continued to be a leader in human development for some 3500 years, until the momentous rise of the great Hellenistic civilization.

The history of the ancient agriculture of the Fertile Crescent is the most studied and best known. On the southeastern tip of the Fertile Crescent dwelt the Sumerians, whose ancient history is the best documented and consequently the best known of all ancient culturally developed societies.

Based on the Sumerian language and the tools uncovered in Sumer, archaeologists believe that the Sumerian civilization had its beginning somewhere else, outside southern Mesopotamia, in a place one of their legends calls, "the Land of Tilmum", most likely located in southern parts of the Gulf area, in present-day Bahrain. An old Sumerian poems sings the beauty and the glory of the Land of Tilmum in Edenic terms:

"The Land of Tilmum is pure, the Land of Tilmum is clean,
The lion does not kill, the wolf does not touch the lamb,)

But regardless of their place of origin, the Sumerians came to and settled in a rather well developed region. Their earliest settlements in southern Mesopotamia may go back as far as the seventh millennium B.C., while a few of the early settlements in the Fertile Crescent are as much as 2000 years older. Permanently established villages are not the only signs of civilizations, and the Sumerians left written documents that prove without a doubt that they led all their contemporaries in all aspects of human development.

Were they the originators of everything they wrote about, or did they learn at least some of it from the indigenous people who settled the region before them? Those people who were the first to domesticate plants, fruit trees, and animals, and who built the first human settlements? These issues may never be settled. But we are sure that the Sumerians preserved that knowledge by writing every thing they knew on imperishable clay tablets.

Although they dwelt in separate city-states, the Sumerians built an elaborate irrigation system and used a common monetary system of weighted metal rings. Although their pottery remained crude, they are credited with the invention the potter's wheel, a significant technological innovation of the time. Through their interest in astrology, they laid the foundation of astronomy and mathematics, and established an adequate calendar.

Their most important contribution to humanity was the development of the art of writing. Around 3300 B. C., they invented true writing and the use of imperishable material to write on. In so doing, they ushered in true civilization and preserved its foundations. Because of the Sumerians many achievements, several historians are of the opinion that the southeast corner of the Fertile Crescent, the land of Sumer, is where human civilization and human history began.

To write, the Sumerians pressed the end of a reed blade onto the face of a soft clay tablet, making a wedge-shaped mark, and words were represented by various combinations of such marks (5). Once inscribed, a clay tablet was preserved either by being sun-dried or baked in a kiln.

The Sumerians also wrote and engraved various designs on cylinder seals, usually made of stones, backed clay, or ivory. When such a cylinder is rolled over soft clay, its inscription is transferred to the clay. Here one is tempted to say that the Sumerians invented a primitive printing press. Over half a million Sumerian tablets, fragments of tablets, and cylinder seals have already been uncovered, a testimonial to a highly cultured society and to its people's love for writing and learning. The tremendous amount of information found on these documents has made the ancient history of the Sumerian corner of the Fertile Crescent the world best known.

During the early period of their prominence as a civilized society, the Sumerians established trade and cultural contacts, primarily overland, with other settlements of the Fertile Crescent, the Indus and the Nile rivers. These early contacts had the positive effect of diffusing knowledge, augmenting and accelerating the progress of these early civilizations. However the highly sophisticated development of these centers failed to be further diffused, and societies outside these spheres remained for a time in a primitive, barbaric state.

On many Sumerian tablets, Semitic and Sumerian names appear side by side, indicating that the two groups lived peaceably together; There is no sign of any conquest, struggle, or racial tension. While the Sumerian settlements were confined to southern Mesopotamia, the Semites settled not only the land of Sumer but in all the areas with reliable water resources: the entire Fertile Crescent, Palestine, and the Nile Delta.

In contrast to the nomadic roaming of the early Semites, the Sumerians remained in their mud-covered huts, dwelling in cities like Ur, Eridu, Shuruppak, Larak, Bad-tibira, and Sippar, all located in the southern part of present-day Mesopotamia. In spite of the Sumerians trading activities, the art of writing remained confined to a small region for several hundred years. By about 2700 B.C., and at first for limited purposes only, the Akkadians of northern Mesopotamia adopted the Sumerian script for their own Semitic language (6).

Around 2380 B.C., King Sargon of Akkad subjugated Sumer and founded an empire that extended from the Mediterranean Sea to the Zagros Mountains and from Mount Ararat to the Persian Gulf. King Sargon, in building this extended empire, transmitted the art of writing and the Sumerian knowledge of mathematics and astronomy to various parts of this vast region, and by leaving inscriptions often written in both Sumerian and Akkadian, he unwittingly helped twentieth-century scholars decipher the ancient Sumerian script and uncover the oldest and one of the richest civilizations.

Later, the Babylonians, whose language was Akkadian, contributed to this endeavor by continuing the Akkadian practices and by compiling Sumerian grammars and lexica in their Akkadian tongue.

The Sargonic Empire lasted for about 150 years. Then, as a result of internal revolts, it disintegrated around 2230 B.C. During the hundred years that followed, Mesopotamia was governed by city-states later to be reunited under the supremacy of Ur. This reunification ushered in the beginning of the Sumerian Renaissance period, during which many Sumerian texts were written. Outstanding among them is the first known lawbook, which was promulgated by Ur-Nammu (r. c. 2111–2094 B.C.), the founder of the third dynasty of Ur. His son Shulgi improved on this code, especially in the areas of civic and business law, and imposed it upon the entire kingdom. During that period, the rulers of Mesopotamia acquired the title of "Kings of Sumer and Akkad", which helped establish the name "Sumer" and recognize the Sumerians as the inventors of writing (7).

The splendor of the Sumerian culture burst to light when, in 1920, Sir Leonard Wooley opened the royal tombs of Ur and uncovered artfully manufactured furniture, jewels, clothing, sculpture, musical instruments, and eating and drinking utensils. Two objects of exquisite workmanship, a ceremonial helmet of beaten gold and a harp inlaid with gold, silver, and lapis lazuli, were also uncovered. Thus, Sumerian art ranged from crude pottery to consummate jewelry.

It is well established that the Sumerians were not Semites, and so far it has been impossible to demonstrate any kinship between their language and any other language, modern or ancient. On the other hand, Akkadian is a Semitic language closely related to modern Arabic and Hebrew. Once the Akkadian script was deciphered, the decipherment of the Sumerian script, although fraught with difficulties, became possible.

The Akkadians and the Babylonians not only learned the art of writing from the Sumerians, but also absorbed the entire Sumerian body of knowledge. After conquering sumer, the Akkadians became the dominating political power in the Near East. But they were dominated by the advanced the Sumerian body of knowledge, mythology, and culture. They translated into their own language Sumerian legends, religious texts, and mathematical and astronomical tables. They adopted the Sumerian numerical system and the Sumerian calendar, weights, and measures. They learned the art of craftsmanship from the Sumerians, who were by far the finest craftsmen of their time. They worshipped Sumerian gods, after translating their names into their Semitic tongue, and admired and sang the praises of Sumerian heroes. In short, they absorbed the entire body of Sumerian knowledge.

The annals of history rarely if ever record many gentle conquests, where the conquerors, instead of imposing their ways of life on the vanquished, adopt the vanquished culture, religion, and literature. This rare happening had momentous effects on the development of Western civilization. The Sumerian body of knowledge was absorbed by the Semites and later by the Indo-Europeans, and for many centuries these peoples nurtured it, contributed to it, and transmitted it to whomever came in contact with them.

This is how far back we can trace many of our legends, fables, mythologies, cults, and certainly the roots of our religions. This is where the earliest creation and flood stories, the accounts of the fall of man, and the conflicts between Good and Evil were composed. This is where the earliest known lawbooks were written. This is how far back we can trace the roots of Judaism, Christianity, and Islam, and the origin of some of the laws that still govern our societies.

All of this was preserved not only because it was written on clay tablets but also because of the devotion to learning and writing, which began during the Sumerian period, became a Mesopotamian tradition, and was maintained during the Akkadian, Babylonian, Hittite, Hurrian, Assyrian, and Chaledean periods for a total of some two thousand years. During that long period, cuneiform was preserved mostly in temple schools, where young men, destined for the priesthood or for careers as professional scribes, were usually educated by writing new tablets. In addition to the cuneiform script and the literature written in it, these young men studied law, astronomy, mathematics, and most other forms of human intellectual activities. They lived in a complex, advanced society where such knowledge was a necessity. This knowledge was augmented and diffused east and west by armed conquests as well as trade.

Early in the third millennium a second wave of Semitic tribes penetrated the northern region of Mesopotamia and founded the city of Ashur (Assur), which continued to be an important religious and cultural center for over two thousands years. Soon after the establishment of Ashur, a strong wave of Semitic people moved from northern Arabia into the Fertile Crescent and settled most of Mesopotamia and Syria from its northeastern plains to the Jordan River Valley, the Judean hills, and the mountains of Lebanon. These people became collectively known as the Amurru or the Amureans, Those who entered southern mesopotamia established the great city of Babylon which became the capital of the immense Babylonian empire, while those who settled the Syrian planes imposed their name on that region. The Amureans who settled the sea coast became known as Canaanites and their land became the land of Canaan (8). Thus, the Babylonians of Mesopotamia, the Amureans of the Syrian plains, and the Canaanites of the coastal regions are genealogically the same people. While the Babylonians were able to form a unified state, the Canaanites and the Amureans, at times, formed as many as twelve city-states, and were known by as many different names.

By about 1500 B.C., another powerful wave of allied Semitic tribes moved from the northern region of the Arabian Peninsula into the Euphrates valley and thence west into Syria, Lebanon, and Palestine. These are the Aramaeans, whose political history in the region does not differ from that of their predecessors. They formed several tribal or city states, and the allies of old resorted to wars and conflicts.

But in spite of their quarrels, they were able to make significant cultural contributions. Early in the eighth century B.C., the Aramaic language began to displace other Semitic dialects from western Asia to become the dominant language of the region for almost 1500 years, and did not lose its prominence until the seventh century A.D. As a result of this dominance during that period, the biblical language was progressively Aramaized, and it is almost certain that Jesus and his disciples spoke Aramaic and not Hebrew. So did the early Christian pioneers, but they called it Syriac, as to them the word Aramaic came to mean pagan. Those early religious pioneers improved their script by introducing vowels in the forms of dots that they inscribed above or below the consonants. This is the system still used in modern Hebrew, and with some variation, in Arabic scripts.

Those early pioneers diffused their script eastward into central Asia, and the modern Mongolian script is a direct descendant of the Syriac. Several Oriental churches still have their gospels and part of their liturgies writing in Syriac.

All during that period when Semitic people were pressing against the Fertile Crescent from within, Indo-Europeans were pushing on it from the outside, mostly south form the central plateaus of Anatolia. Infiltrating perhaps through the Caucasus Mountains, Indo-European nomads began settling Anatolia in the waning centuries of the third millennium B.C. The new settlers, known to history as the Hittites, developed a fast-rising civilization primarily through their contacts with the inhabitants of the Fertile Crescent. Clay tablets uncovered in Asia Minor indicate that in their early correspondence, the Hittites used the Akkadian language and script. Then they adapted the cuneiform script to their own language, which was later classified as the Anatolian branch of the large Indo-European family of languages. Probably through the Hittites of Anatolia, the use of clay tablets for writing reached the Aegean, the first European center to taste the fruits of civilization.

The Hittites were followed by the Mitannians, who used the horse in their travel and their wars. The horse was domesticated around 4000 B.C. in the Ukraine and became known to the people of the Fertile Crescent by about 3000 B.C., but the Mitannians made full use of its services. Late in the seventh century, the Indo-Europeans Medes and Persians also entered the area, and built an empire that stretched from the Indian Ocean into central Anatolia.

While the Indo-Europeans were pressing south on the Fertile Crescent, another non-Semitic group made its presence felt in the amalgam of races of the Near East. These were the Hurrians (biblical Horites or Horims), who came down the Zagros mountains probably from Armenia, and settled in the northern planes of Mesopotamia. Although never a military power of significance, the Hurrians, whose language is neither Semitic nor Indo-European, were able to influence the culture and the literature of the Near East.

By the middle of the second millennium B.C., the Hittites successfully smelted iron and became a military threat to the region. Their soldiers penetrated the Fertile Crescent, and through a lightening military campaign in the sixteenth century B.C. they invaded Mesopotamia and the land of Canaan. They captured, plundered, and completely destroyed the great city of Babylon. They overthrew the last member of the Hammurabi dynasty, and returned to Anatolia carrying the spoils of their raid. This marked the end of the old Babylonian development and civilization. Babylonia fell into a state of complete stagnation that lasted for almost one thousand years, and was not revived until late in the seventh century B.C. when a new wave of Semitic tribes began to infiltrate southern Mesopotamia. The best known of these tribes is the Khaldi, who revived the Old Babylonian culture and built the great Chaldean civilization, and in time occupied the land south of the Fertile Crescent from the Persian Gulf to the Sinai desert.

The presence of the Hittites, Hurrians, Mitannians, Medes, and Persians on the Near Eastern political scene provided the ancient culture with multiracial elements and flavors, and significantly affected the magnitude and direction of its future evolution.

Egypt is linguistically, racially, and geographically different from Mesopotamia. In a burning desert that extends for several hundred kilometers on either side, the Nile flows through Egypt for some 3000 kilometers, from the Sudan to the Delta, without any tributaries or significant natural barriers. This geographical unity and isolation encouraged political unity and a strong central government. This gave rise to a unique civilization, which flourished early in the fourth millennium, and which in contrast to Mesopotamian development, had an aura of unity and permanence. The office of pharoah and pharoah-worship emerged, and a large segment of the country's resources were used for the glorification of the pharaohs. As their powers were believed to endure after death, their bodies were carefully preserved, and later artistic representations of them were made and buried with them. This gave rise to Egyptian mummification and monumental stone buildings and to Egyptian sculpture, painting, and architecture, which are among the world's finest.

Based on the belief that the soul would eventually return to the body, both Egyptian and Mesopotamian rulers were buried with their worldly possessions, food, drink, clothing, retinue, servants, vassals, and chariots. These customs have preserved a remarkably vivid picture of life in ancient Mesopotamia and Egypt. While the Mesopotamians were content with graves built with mud bricks, the Egyptians, by 3000 B.C., during the Old Kingdom, created the first architecture in stone. Imhotep (9), the royal architect, designed and built for his king, Zoser, a tomb in the form of a step pyramid sixty-one meters high, probably the world oldest surviving structure of stone masonry. Less than a century later, the Egyptians were building the great pyramids of Gizeh. It is estimated that the construction of one of the great pyramids required a minimum of 100,000 men toiling for some twenty years, not to mention the superb feat of planning and engineering. Such a project required great organization and a large number of well trained leaders. The pyramids were built to be everlasting, and they have already endured for five thousand years.

Aside from the pyramids architectural feat, the Egyptians have contributed generously to most other fields of knowledge. Their 365 day calendar, formulated towards the end of the fifth millennium B.C. is the world oldest. It remained unchanged until 46 B.C. when Alexandrian astronomers, began to add an extra day every fourth year and instructed the Romans to do the same thus establishing the Julian Calendar.

Isolated from Africa by the desert and the cataracts of the Nile, Egypt in its ancient culture and civilization belonged to Western Asia rather then to Africa. And it is natural to find elements of Western Asian cultures in the culture of Egypt and Egyptian cultural elements in Western Asia. Through the land of Canaan and north Sinai passed the busy road of ancient trade between Mesopotamia and Egypt. Thus the Egyptian, the Mesopotamian, and the Canaanitic cultural centers were closely associated in their development. There were almost always strong relations between Egypt and the coastal cities of Canaan; there were border crossings; there were Canaanitic settlements in the Nile Delta, and Egyptian settlements in southern Canaan. Recent excavation in northern Sinai, prompted by the construction of the Salam Canal (10), showed that, in ancient times, this coastal region served as a busy highway.

Contacts were also generated by armed expeditions. By the eighteenth century B.C. a conglomerate of people, mostly Canaanites, conquered the Nile Delta and ruled it for some 200 years. They introduced into Egypt the use of the horse and probably the chariot. During that period, the Egyptians called their rulers Hika Khasut (11) (Foreign Rulers). later the Greeks garbled the name into Hyksos and translated it to mean Shepherd Kings.

The earliest forms of contacts between Egypt and the land of Canaan were probably based on commerce; the rulers of Egypt, keen to commemorate their accomplishments in monumental architecture, were eager to procure good building materials, and there was simply none better than the cedar wood of Lebanon, which the Jbailys traded for gold, ivory, and ebony that the Egyptians brought forth from Sudan. Early in the third millennium B.C., the sea route between Jbail (Byblos) and the Nile delta was so well traveled by Jbaily ships that the Egyptians used the term "Jbaily ship" to mean an ocean-going vessel (12).

It is important to dwell somewhat upon the Egyptian-Jbaily relation, as it is probably through this channel more than any other that Semitic and Egyptian cultural exchanges took place. This relation, contrary to the general pharaohnic foreign policy of cruel subjection, was based on mutual respect and self-interest.

The merchants of the two trading partners became fluent in each others' languages, an essential step for concluding business transactions and for the transmission of knowledge. The Egyptians learned the Jbaily techniques of shipbuilding, and credited Hathor, "mistress of Jbail" for her skill in manufacturing oars. Recent excavations in Jbail have demonstrated that in the third millennium B.C., Jbaily architects adopted Egyptian building techniques and masonry in the construction of their temples. It is also believed that the Egyptian god of wisdom and writing Thoth and the Phoenician god of writing Taut or Taout are one and the same. And in all probability, a more practical scripts evolved as a result of the Canaanite-Egyptian cooperation in this matter.

In addition to Canaanite gods, Egyptian gods were worshipped in Jbail, and in recognizing Egypt's greatness, a Jbaily businessman prince is reported to have relayed to an Egyptian emissary: "All lands did

Amun (the Egyptian king of the gods) found, and he founded them only after he founded the land of Egypt whence you have come; but technical skill spread from there as far as (the) place where I am." (13). In an Egyptian myth, the Egyptian goddess Isis, searching for the body of her husband Horus, assassinated and thrown into the Nile by his monster killer Seth, sailed to Jbail where she found it inside one of the pillars in the king's palace.

Although among the Canaanitic cities, Jbail had the most prominent relations with the Nile Delta, other coastal cities shared in these ventures. The Ugaritic texts speak of Kothar-wa-Hassis, the Ugaritic (god of arts and crafts) as having his throne in Caphtor (Crete) but Hkpt (Egypt) is his original home:

> Then shalt thou surely set face toward all glorious Hkpt.
> Caphtor is the throne on which he sits,
> Hkpt is the land of his inheritance.

When a fire, probably the result of a violent earthquake, destroyed the city of Ugarit in 1358 B.C., Abimilki, the prince of Tyre, found it necessary to inform his ally, the Pharoah Amenhotep IV, of the disaster by sending him a letter that reads,

> Ugarit, the royal city, has been destroyed by fire,
> half the city has been burned down, the other half
> is there no more.

This letter was found in the Pharoah's archive in Tel Amarna.

Through all these frequent contacts and people's movements, the Near East became a great melting pot of races, civilizations and cultures. Although each segment of the vast region had its own traits and distinguishing characteristics, based primarily upon local needs and religious beliefs, the whole region had many common cultural features, cults, and mythologies. To be thoroughly understood, the ancient Near Eastern civilizations should be viewed and studied as the product of the entire region, from the valley of the Nile through the Fertile Crescent to Mesopotamia and the plateaus of Anatolia. Once viewed as a unit, its influence on Western civilization becomes clearer and more accessible.

In the almost always clear skies of the Near East, the view of the wondrous heavens led naturally to the study of astrology and subsequently astronomy. Early Near Eastern star gazers noted the positions of the stars and planets, and believing that what takes place in the heavens controls events on earth, they predicted what the gods decreed for the future. In time the art of star-reading developed into astrology, which in time led to the science of astronomy and became the main cultural legacy of Mesopotamia to the Greeks, Romans, and hence the Western World.

The definition of units is a fundamental step in the study of any science, and without well-defined units for measuring time and arcs, astronomy can not be perceived as a true science. By the middle of the second millennium B.C. the Babylonian unit of distance called beru (danna in Sumerian) came to mean the time needed to travel that distance, and the length of the day from sun-set to sunset was divided into twelve equal berus. This is the origin of our present units of measurement of time and arcs (14).

Early in their history, the Egyptians measured time using the clepsydra or water-clock, and attributed its invention to their handy god, Thoth. By the middle of the second millennium B. C., the Egyptians began to measure time using a "shadow" clock. They divided the time from sunrise to sunset into twelve equal time units. As the length of these units varied with latitudes and seasons, these units are now termed "seasonal hours". A combination of the Babylonian sexagesimal reckoning of time and the Egyptian seasonal hours produced the day 24 equal hours used in Hellenistic astronomy and which we continue to use today (15).

But complex societies require more practical knowledge to regulate public affairs, such as commerce, farming, irrigation, health, and the construction of roads, canals, temples, and dwellings. Most if not all of these activities requires some knowledge of mathematics. We know, from the many uncovered tablets, that the early Mesopotamian scientists were interested in the need of their society. They worked diligently on the practical side of science and mathematics; many of their mathematical tablets were prepared for the training of scribes and deals primarily with administrative accounting and the balancing of accounts. There were also tables of multiplication and "reciprocals" (16).

The knowledge of mathematics in the advanced and complex Mesopotamian society was so important and highly regarded that several Mesopotamian kings boasted of their mathematical accomplishments. Furthermore, there are indications that Mesopotamians differentiated between the educated and the uneducated by their relative mathematical ability. "A mind which does not know accounting, is it a mind that has intelligence?" Says a Babylonian proverb (17).

By the time of Hammurabi, the middle of the eighteenth century B.C. Babylonian scribes were instructed about rectangles, triangles, trapezoids, circles, and pyramids.

In describing the contents of the cuneiform mathematical texts, Nemet-Hejat writes, "By virtue of the variety of the inscribed topics and the depth of the knowledge therein, these texts provided rigorous training for scribes seeking posts available in the advanced and complex society." (18).

As human beings are graced with inquisitive minds and a love for discovery and adventure, they are also adorned with a passion to diffuse their knowledge and transmit whatever erudition they possess. They acquire knowledge to satisfy their curiosity and transmit it to please themselves and satisfy the curiosity of others. Most ancient rulers of the Near East encouraged these traits by inviting learned scholars into their courts, providing for them and for the institutions of learning. Knowledge in itself was highly regarded by the average citizen as well as the rulers, and kings often boasted of their own scholarly accomplishments; Apophis (Epafos) (c. 1615–1577 B. C.), the powerful Hyksos ruler of Egypt, left inscriptions calling himself "a scribe of Re, taught by Thoth himself..."; and added that "he could read faithfully all the difficult passages of the writings, as flows the Nile" (19).

The great Ashurbanipal, King of Assyria (c. 669–626 B.C.), whose library contained 30,000 classified and catalogued clay tablets, left inscriptions describing his vast knowledge; "I understand the craft of wise Adapa (20), the secrets of all scribal arts...I explained the heavens with the learned priest, recited the complicated multiplications and divisions that are not immediately apparent. The beautiful writings in Sumerian that are obscure, in Akkadian that are difficult to bear in mind, it was my joy to repeat..." (21).

It is difficult to overestimate the effect of such royal declarations on the education of the average citizen.

In both Mesopotamia and Egypt, statements praising knowledge and learning were uncovered. A tablet uncovered in a Babylonian school house contains the proverb, "He who shall excel in tablet-writing shall shine like the sun." And from Egypt an enlightening papyrus reads, "Give thy heart to learning, and love her like a mother, for there is nothing so precious as learning." And a second papyrus reads, "Behold, there is no profession that is not governed; only the learned man rules himself." And a third reads, "The only happiness is to turn thy heart to books during the daytime and to read during the night." (22). These sentiments must have encouraged many youths to study and to learn.

Two relatively recent but exceedingly important centers of Near Eastern civilizations are the Ugaritic and the Hebrew centers. Ugarit, a phoenician settlement in Northern Syria, came into prominence in the middle of the second millennium B. C. as a port city through which copper from Cyprus passed to the mainland. The accidental discovery of the ruins of Ugarit led to its 1929 excavations, which revealed clay-tablets inscriptions of choice literary value. Their contents proved that the scholars of Ugarit had inherited much of the ancient cultures of the Near East. The Ugaritic texts contain elements of Sumerian, Babylonian, Assyrian, Hittite, and Egyptian origins. They also provided a link between the ancient Greek epics and the Old Testament literature, and helped in understanding many biblical passages and obscure expressions that had puzzled biblical scholars for centuries (23). Many Ugaritic tablets were written in four parallel columns with a different language in each column; the highly literate Ugaritic scribes wrote in Ugaritic, Sumerian, Akkadian, and Hurrian and in four different scripts: Sumerian-Akkadian syllabic, Egyptian and Hittite hieroglyph, and the native alphabetic cuneiform (24). In so doing, they simplified the task of decipherment and rendered their fine literature more accessible.

The labor of the scholars of Ugarit points to their great ability and to a high degree of literary sophistication. The effect of the Ugaritic texts on the great classics of ancient Greece is evident in the general concepts and the many specific points shared by Homer's Iliad and the Odyssey on the one hand and the epics of Ugarit on the other. "The Ugaritic-Homer parallels are simply too numerous to be coincidental" (25).

The main language of the Ugaritic texts is Semitic and is closely related to biblical Hebrew; indeed they have the same vocabulary, the same word morphology, and the same literary style and phraseology. The texts of Ugarit and the Bible contain a large number of related stories written in the same relaxed, repetitive style. The contribution of the Ugaritic scholars to the content of the Old Testament is immense and is surpassed only by the Hebrew tradition. This and the tremendous effect of the Ugaritic literature on the epics of ancient Greece prompted some modern scholars to refer to Ugarit as "the cradle of Western civilization." (26).

Some two centuries after the destruction of Ugarit, Semitic tribes established their presence in southern Canaan, the land of milk and honey. They may have entered the region considerably earlier but did not establish themselves as a historic entity until the final years of the second millennium B.C. Their second and renowned king David conquered the old city of Jerusalem around 1000 B.C. (27).

In their early history, the Israelites did not differ from other Semitic tribes that dwelt in the area; they roamed with their cattle in southern Canaan searching for water and pasture, quarreled with their neighbors, and worshipped primitive gods such as caves, hills, snakes, and calves. A special relation between Canaan and Israel was established, and was manifested in a common language, history, folklore, and literature; the two civilizations had similar practices, rituals, and poetry and were so interwoven as to allow for only minor differences. The Israelites were attracted to the Canaanite religion and worshipped the Canaanite gods (Jud. 2:2,3). They worshipped El and Asherah (the mother goddess and the tree of life, whose name appears as "the grove" in the modern English version of the Bible). They also worshipped Baal and his sister and consort, the Virgin Anath ('nt), and Salem or Shalem (Slm), the son of El; and also the Babylonian god Tammuz. Even when they proclaimed Yahweh as their god, they viewed him as a local, tribal god; "There is no God in all the earth, but in Israel." (2 Kings 5:15).

The Hebrews were later distinguished from other Semitic tribes by their monotheistic views, by Yahwism, and by the zeal of their many prophets. This and certain world political events transformed the Hebrews, to the exclusion of other Semites, into a great cultural power that exerted tremendous influence upon the development of world religion and world history.

The authors of the Old Testament borrowed much of their poetry and their terminology from the Canaanites, and many of their legends and their calendar from Babylon. They oversimplified the Hammurabi code of law and recast it into the Mosaic code. Many of their psalms are of Canaanite origin or are translations of old Egyptian hymns; Psalm 24 is a Hebrew version of Akhenaten's Hymn to the Sun Disk (28). The Old Testament is thus the product of the Near Eastern civilization and culture.

Probably all of this is of little consequence, considering what the Hebrews were able to accomplish with the material they had collected and blended together. They provided the Western World with the Old Testament, which is not only a code of law; it is history, poetry, theology, and philosophy of the highest order. They gave the Western World its Bible, which has inspired and comforted countless people, and will continue to do so for centuries to come. It is the resource book that cultured the Western mentality; its Mosaic code is the foundation of the laws and the political systems of the Judeo-Christian world. Of this code, the prudent George Sarton writes: "Its importance in the history of institutions and law cannot be overestimated." (29). How was this most honored of all literary works put together? When and where was it written? And who are the authors? Attempting to answer these simple questions, Will Durant, in 1935, stated that some fifty thousands volumes have already been written (30), and the press is not about to slow down.

Why all the interest and the great devotion? It is because the Old Testament alleviated the great fear from human hearts, and provided passionate form to the final longing of the mind. It filled a void in human souls by providing a simple answer to humanity most vexing question, what is there after death? And Daniel spoke of life beyond the grave when all wrongs will be righted; the wicked would be punished and the just would inherit the infinite reward (Dan. 12:2,3). This calming thought was carried into Christianity, and carried both Judaism and Christianity to victory.

This brief outline indicates that many diverse peoples have contributed to the civilizations of the ancient Near East; no one group or race can lay claim to these contributions. From each of the many peoples that dwelt in the Near East for many centuries came the threads, the colors, and the patterns that fashioned the tapestry of the great

Near Eastern cultures and civilizations. Thus, the ancient Near Eastern civilization is not the child of a race, but the product of a homogeneous people that was formed by the intermarriage and gradual assimilation of different stocks. It developed over thousands of years and in dozens of places. It spread overland as far as the Indian subcontinent and into Europe across the Mediterranean.

---

(1). Zohary, Daniel, and Hopf, Maria. (1988:13,14).

(2). The recent discovery of a jug in Hajji-Firuz, Iran, containing wine residue and terebinth resin proves that by the middle of sixth millennium B.C., the people in that region did not only knew how to make wine but also knew that terebinth resin inhibits the turning of wine into vinegar. The Sumerians, a few centuries later, produced another brew spiced with cinnamon instead of hops, and they called it 'sikaru'. This word is still used in the Middle East, and means "drunk".

(3). Diamond, Jared. (1997:178,182).

(4). Ibid. p. 255).

(5). The Sumerian script, which dominated writing in most of the Near East for over 2500 years, became known as the cuneiform script, from the Latin "cuneus", meaning wedge. This designation probably came about as a result of a paper entitled "Dactuli Pyramidales seu Cuneiformes", written in 1700 by Thomas Hyde of Oxford.

(6). Garraty and Gay (1972:60).

(7). Based solely on the royal title "king of Sumer and Akkad", commonly used by the kings of Mesopotamia during that period, Jules Oppert correctly attributed the origin of the cuneiform script to the Sumerians. The word "Sumer" could itself be of Semitic origin, as the Sumerians referred to themselves as the Black-Headed people and the Semitic word "sumr" has a similar connotation.

(8). It was thought that Canaan meant low land, but this is probably incorrect. Canaan means purple, and in the Old Testament, it is taken to mean merchant. And Phoenicia is likely the Greek translation of the Semitic word Canaan.

(9). Imhotep, a true genius, was a statesman, an architect, and an astronomer, and was revered as the father of medicine some 2500 years before Hippocrates was born.

(10). The Salam (peace) Canal is an Egyptian project designed to bring the water of the Nile to the arid Northern Sinai.

(11). The vocalization of the ancient Egyptian language is still speculative.

(12). Redford, Donald B. (1992:38).

(13). Ibid, p. 40).

(14). Rochberg-Halton, Francesca, "Babylonian Seasonal Hours" Centaurus 1989: Vol. 32: P. 146.

(15). Ibid. pp. 146-147.

(16). Based on their sexagismal system of counting, they defined the "reciprocal" (igi) of a number as being 60 divided by that number. Thus the reciprocal of 5 is 12 and the reciprocal of 6 is 10. The reciprocal of, say, 7 is approximated by two numbers one smaller and one larger than the true value of 8.5714...

(17). Nemet-Nejat, Karen Rhea (1993:10).

(18). Ibid. p. 24).

(19). Redford, Donald B. (1992:118–122).

(20). To the ancient Mesopotamians, Adapa, like the biblical Adam, symbolized the fall of man.

(21). Durant, Will. (1935:227).

(22). Ibid, p. 170.

(23). Pfeiffer, Charles F. (1962:58–61).

(24). Gray, John (1965:3).

(25). Gordon, Cyrus H. (1965:101–112).

(26). Gordon, Cyrus, H. (1966:13).

(27). Before David's conquest, the city bore the name Ubus (the name of the tribe that occupied it). David called his city Urusalem (the environs of the Canaanite god Salem). The name was changed to Jerusalem during the Roman period.

(28). Redford, Donald B. (1992:387–389).

(29). Sarton, George. (1930:63).

(30). Durant, Will. (1935:328).

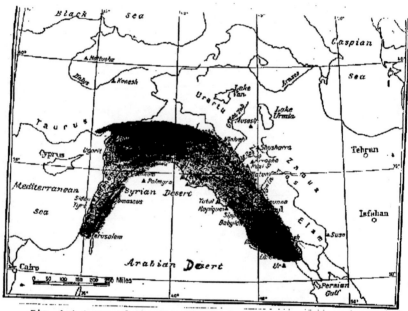

Fig. 1-1 A map of the Near East, showing the Fertile Crescent (shaded Area) and ancient ▲ and modern o cities.

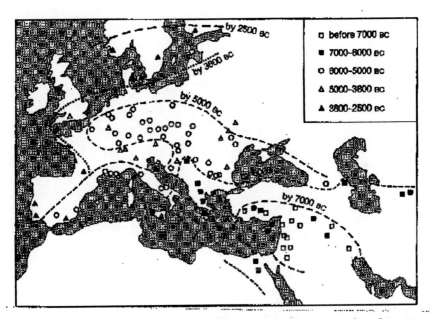

Fig. 1-2. This map shows the diffusion of the domestication of
plants. Note that dates become progressively later as one moves
farther from the Fertile Crescent. The map was originally
produced by Zohary and Hopf [Ref. 1. p. 210]. Its radiocarbon
dates were later calibrated by Diamond [Ref. 2. p. 181].

Chapter Two

Across the Mediterranean

The Mediterranean, this body of water that connects three continents, knew the foot steps of men since time immemorial. On its shores and islands, early dwellers left monuments and signs that go back in time for tens of thousands of years.

In 1985, a bulldozer opening a road in the prehistoric site of 'Ain Ghazal (Arabic for "spring of the gazelle") near Amman, Jordan uncovered pieces of lime plasters, which were soon recognized as fragments from ancient sculptures. Too fragile to be excavated at the sight, the entire block of earth in which they were entombed was dug up and shipped to the Smithsonian's Conservation Analytical Laboratory, where all the pieces were painstakingly reassembled. A process that required about ten years to complete and resulted in eight of the oldest human form statues ever found in the Middle East. Two full size statues and a two-headed bust about one meter in height were almost fully restored, and were dated at about 7000 B.C. Hence, they belong to a prehistoric culture known as Pre-Pottery Neolithic B (c. 8500–5500 B.C.), which has been identified at many sites in present-day Jordan, Lebanon, Israel, and Syria.

The statues were made of mixture of limestone powder and lime plaster, which proves that the people of that era were using advanced stone tools, and firing technique that produced temperatures above 600 degrees Celsius. Such high temperatures are needed to extract calcium oxide from calcium carbonate. The oxide is then mixed with water to form the durable and water-resistant lime plaster, which was used extensively in 'Ain Gazelle in making various vessels and in covering the walls and floors of houses.

The figures, now on display at the Arthur M. Sackler Gallery, perhaps represent gods, goddesses, heroes, or rulers. What they represent, we will never know, but they have already provided us with considerable information about the people who lived in the Jordan Valley, and parts of the Near East, some 9000 years ago (1).

Malta

Half way across the blue waters of the Mediterranean sailing westward from the Jordan valley, the tiny rocky island of Malta rises up. Malta and its neighboring islets are adorned with what may be the world's oldest freestanding stone monuments. In 1972, Colin Renfrew demonstrated that these monuments were erected early in the fourth millennium B. C., predating the great pyramids of Egypt by about one thousand years.

It is believed that these monuments form the southern end of the gigantic structures that extend in an arc along the western coasts of Europe from Denmark to Malta, and of which the best known is the Stonehenge of England.

Some thirty such structures may still be found on Malta and the neighboring islet of Gozo, and it is believed about as many are buried under new developments: city streets, towns, and villages. The most impressive of these structures are the Tarxien, Mnajdra, and Hagar

Qim (probably Phoenician for "Standing Stone") on the island of Malta, and the Giant's Tower, whose walls still stand some twenty feet tall, on Gozo. The major monuments are not single structures but elaborate complexes surrounded by massive walls; Hagar Qim covers some ten acres and was probably designed as a temple with a highly decorated alter. These structures are not merely massive stone walls; many of them are highly decorated with stone carvings. In addition to human busts and heads, there is a variety of statues of a fertility goddess, a sow suckling its piglets, and a stone frieze of rams and deer. The female statuettes, called fertility goddesses, and scalped with extra-large breasts, abdomens, buttocks, and thighs turned up in many Mediterranean islands, in Africa, and in many Paleolithic sites scattered over Europe (2).

Not all the great Maltese monuments are above ground. Adjoining the temple complex of Tarxien, the prehistoric builders had dug down eighteen feet in lime stone to create a three-story network of 33 intricately interconnected chambers and chapels. Most of these chambers were used for burials, as they were found to contain in addition to scattered human remains as many as 7000 complete skeletons (3).

The presence of these magnificent monuments on isolated islands in the middle of the Mediterranean, and the discovery of traces of ancient civilizations, statues, pottery, and symbols that bare some resemblance on many of its shores led some historians to speculate that this body of water was crisscrossed by shipping lanes as early as 5000 B.C. (4).

Undoubtedly there was some sort of human movement over the waves of the Mediterranean as early as the sixth millennium B.C., but these were confined to short distances between neighboring coastal villages and off shore islands. International shipping lanes did not get established until the early centuries of the third millennium B.C., and these were still somewhat confined to the coastal regions (5). In this fashion, the ships of the coastal cities of Canaan sailed south to the Nile Delta, and north to the southern shores of Anatolia. Those who sailed south came in contact with the advanced civilization of Egypt, but those who sailed north encountered native inhabitants in a primitive state of development. By the third millennium B.C. the inhabitants of Anatolia have already populated many of the Aegean islands as far south as Crete.

Crete

This island that stretches east to west, as if designed to serve as a breakwater to the Aegean, was destined to play an important role in the history and the development of European and Near Eastern civilization. The earliest arrivals in Crete were neolithic people, who must have reached it between 6000 B.C. and 4000 B. C. island hopping from Anatolia. Their main settlement was at Knossos on a mound in a hilly region. They also lived in easily defensible caves in the east and center of the island. A second migration came into the island sometime before 3000 B.C. probably from the Near East (6). These were farmers who brought with them the cult of the fertility, or mother, goddess. They left behind figurines which represent her as hugh-buttocked, heavy-thighed, and large-belied. These are basically the same figurines found around the Mediterranean basin and parts of Africa.

The culture of these people bares some similarity to Near Eastern culture and is characterized by black and grey burnished pottery. The fact that they chose to settle the eastern parts of the island over the better irrigated and more fertile land to the west indicates that they reached the island from the east (7).

Egyptian records indicate that, during the same period, sea worthy ships were sailing the Eastern Mediterranean between Jbail and the Nile Delta. The Egyptian commercial fleet established its shipping lanes between Egypt, Crete, and Jbail only a couple of centuries later.

The Cretans began their early development towards the middle of the third millennium B.C. During that period, houses, hamlets, and small villages began to appear on their island. Around 1950 B. C. a sudden urban revolution took place. This is the beginning of the great Minoan civilization (8), whose rapid development on the Aegean soil led to the view that it must have received its impetus from outsiders- a powerful sea-going people, who entered Crete and established a government based on their past experience and maritime supremacy. The Minoan civilization developed in the Aegean from the twentieth to the fourteenth century, reaching its peak around 1600 B.C. During that period, the Minoan commercial fleet ruled the Eastern Mediterranean from the western shores of Italy and Sicily to Greece, Anatolia, Canaan, and Egypt, and with their commerce they widespread their knowledge, culture, and highly advanced civilization. They brought back to Crete the products of these countries and the Minoan settlements in eastern Crete around the Messara plain became rich and prosperous centers.

European archaeologists, excavating the Aegean sites, put forth a concerted effort to show that the Minoan civilization was independent of external influences; they wanted to preserve the purity of western culture free from Semitic contamination. The discovery of magnificent structures, highly decorated palaces, usually erected around a central courtyards, and intricately connected labyrinth on the island was hailed as a proof that the Minoan civilization bears no relation to Near Eastern culture where such elaborate structures did not exist. As we shall see, the presence of overwhelming evidence linking the Minoan culture to Near Eastern traditions makes this argument exceedingly limp.

The Minoan civilization, the first truly great civilization on European soil, exhibits much of the traditions of the peoples of Egypt and the Fertile Crescent. By the end of the third millennium B.C. the Eastern Mediterranean had become the focal point of culture and civilization. Along its shores, Egyptian and Mesopotamian cultural influences had already mated and Canaan inherited the best of both. In addition to the two great civilizations, a host of various ethnic peoples were intermingling in the region adding their traditions, diversity, virility, and impetus to its cultural complexes. Trading among the coastal cities of Canaan, Anatolia, Egypt, and Crete was heavy, and with it, elements of the various cultures of the Near East, including the rich cultures of Mesopotamia and Egypt, spread over the entire eastern Mediterranean, and this is what lifted these civilizations, including the Minoan civilization, to greatness. This heavy trading caused much of the Near Eastern traditions to be transplanted into the Minoan culture.

The earliest Cretan writings are scratches on clay tablets dating to about 2000 B.C. These are commonly called Cretan hieroglyphs, and could have been introduced from Egypt or developed locally. As Greek and Near Eastern historians neglected to mention anything about the language of this great civilization, knowledge of this language remained latent and the discovery of what became known as the Linear A script did not satisfactorily resolve the problem. This script written on clay tablets between 1750 and 1400 B.C. and uncovered in the Haggai Triad area of southern Crete remained undeciphered; In 1965, Cyrus Gordon put a strong effort but was unable to prove that the language of the Linear A script is mostly Western Semitic (9). Probably the most interesting word in the Haggai Triad script is "ku-lo", which is the Canaanite word for "all". "Ku-lo" appears thirty-six times in these texts, and its enunciation and meaning suggest that it could be the origin of one of the most widely used Greek word, "kilo" (a thousand).

The Minoan religion and form of government had many of the Near Eastern features. As in the land of Canaan, the kings and queens of the Minoans had priestly as well as royal functions. The head of the Minoan pantheon is the god Yashashalam. Although not much is known about Yashashalam's functions and attributes, his name is West Semitic and means "he who causes peace". The Minoan also worshipped the god

Danuga (Dagon), the god of the Philistines and, according the epics of Ugarit, the father of Baal, the Canaanite god of fertility.

By far the best known of the Minoan divinities are the snake goddesses, whose statuettes have virtually become the symbol of the Minoan civilization. Although they are collectively called snake goddesses because they appear with snakes in their hands and around their legs and bodies, they had various functions including that of a mother goddess, a house goddess, and a goddess of wild animals. The snake cult and snake worship had their origin in Mesopotamia and Egypt. They entered into the land of Canaan and Anatolia then the Aegean, Greece, and Western Europe-(see chapter seven, "The Snake, The Symbol Of Healing."

Probably second in popularity only to the statuettes of snake goddesses are the symbols and paintings of bull-jumping that decorated the walls of Minoan palaces and Minoan ceremonial vases. What started in Mesopotamia as a mere sporting event became a religious or a mythical ceremony in the Aegean. The danger involved in facing the charging bull elevated the event to new heights. Here young men and women would stand in front of a charging bull and grab its horns; when the bull tossed its head up, the young athlete would somersault off the horns, execute a handspring on the bull's back and land upright behind it. Motifs of such daring activities were found only in Minoan ruins. (See Chapter Six, The Bull Cult).

In a similar fashion, the Minoans far eclipsed all their contemporaries, not only in bull-vaulting, but also in the lively expressions in their art, and palace building. They built immense structures, several stories high, rambling over several acres, with walls decorated with the most lively forms of art work. The Minoans also surpassed their contemporaries in the production of fine jewelry and exquisite and functional pottery.

The intimate relation between the Phoenician and the Minoan civilizations is also supported by the Homeric tradition. Homer in his own way informs us how the Phoenician culture was intertwined with the Minoan civilization. The Iliad 14: 320–322 reads;

> Illustrious Persus' mother, or Europa
> Daughter of Phoenix, world-renowned, who bore me
> Minos and magnificent Rhadamanthys.

Thus making Phoenix, the ancestor of the Phoenicians, the maternal grandfather of King Minos. In ancient times, this was the common way used to indicate close relation between two civilizations. This relation is also retold in one of the Greek legends that states that King Minos was the son of Zeus and Europa, the daughter of Agenor, king of Phoenicia.

For several centuries, the Minoans dominated the sea, keeping northern primitive people boxed inland. During that period, the Eastern Mediterranean was crisscrossed by heavily travelled shipping lanes, along which material goods, knowledge, and culture were exchanged.

Important information about these trading routes was recently revealed while salvaging a shipwreck off the southern coast of Turkey, just south of the tiny peninsula known as Ulu Burun. The ship sank late in the fourteenth century B.C. and the diversity of the items in its cargo provides a clear picture of the routes and trading methods of the period. Among what was salvaged there was copper and tin from the land of the Hittites, and 149 Canaanite amphorae (10), one filled with glass beads, several with olives, but most contained terebinth resin which was widely used to inhibit the growth of the bacteria that turned wine into vinegar. There was also logs of Lebanese cedar and African black wood, a whole elephant tusk, a dozen hippopotamus teeth, some ostrich eggshells, a few tortoise shells, and various kinds of jewelry.

By far the most interesting items found on the ship is a gold scarab (11) inscribed with the name and picture of Nefertiti, the stunningly beautiful wife of the Egyptian Pharoah Akhenatun, and the well preserved figure of a nude female holding a gazelle in each hand. This is undoubtedly the figure of Asherah, the Canaanite fertility goddess, and probably the ship's protective deity. If true, the ship's home port must have been one of the Canaanite cities, and most likely neighboring Ugarit.

The End of the Minoan Civilization

Early in the nineteenth century, Greek-speaking peoples moved south through Macedonia and into present-day Greece. The first of these migrating people to come in contact with the Minoans became known as Mycenaeans. Before this contact, the Greeks lived a nomadic tribal life, knew no agriculture and certainly no industry. By about 1600 B.C. these contacts assumed a large scale that caused radical and rapid changes in the life of the uncivilized Mycenaeans, who, by about 1400 B.C., moved into northern Crete and took control of Knosos. For a short period, Crete became the homeland of the Minoan-Mycenaean culture. The Linear B script was written during this period (12).

By the middle of the fifteenth century B.C., a series of powerful earthquakes (13), the most notorious among them is the eruption of Santorini on the island of Thera north of Crete, devastated the region. Thera was reduced to a sickle rock around the hole made by the volcano, which threw out an estimated ten cubic kilometers of ejecta and produced tsunami tidal waves, poisonous ash, and acid rain, that weakened the Minoan society. By the middle of the fourteenth century B.C. the Mycenaeans displaced the Minoans as the dominant power in the region, and the great Minoan civilization came to a tragic end.

The Mycenaean civilization continued to flourish for a short period to be completely crushed by the uncivilized Greek-speaking Achaeans and later Dorians. This led to a period usually referred to as the Greek Dark Age (c. 1000 B.C.–750 B.C.), that settled over Greece and the Aegean.

The intelligentsia, the able, and the powerful fled the darkened region, leaving behind the illiterate, the poor, and the weak to contend with the uncivilized invaders. Many sailed to the Canaanite coastal cities and the Western parts of Anatolia, while other fugitives sought new homes in Egypt and other Mediterranean shores.

For a period, Egypt was host to two historically important groups: the Cretan Philistines and the Etruscans. Egyptian monuments also indicate that two other groups landed on Egyptian soil; they are the Sardinians and the Sikels. Many of the youths of the settlers served as Egyptian mercenary, but all were later driven out of Egypt. The Philistines sailed east, settled in South Canaan, and gave their name to the land they occupied. Later they warred with the Hebrews, and their god Dagon fought with Yahweh, the god of the Hebrews. Because of this enmity and the Hebrew influence on western culture, the word "philistine" acquired its English prosaic meaning.

The Sardinians, the Sikels, and the Etruscans also took to their boats, but sailed west, The Sardinians settled in Sardinia, the Sikels in Sicily, and the Etruscans after roaming the Mediterranean for a while settled the west coast of Italy north of present day Rome. Probably they were attracted to the then sparsely populated region by its rich metal deposits; Etruria and Tuscany had, and in many areas still have, a wealth of copper, iron, tin, and lead. The Etruscans worked their mines extensively, extracting their riches for local use as well as exportation. This, and their commerce, provided their rulers with immense wealth, enabling them to live a life of splendor.

The Etruscan language, although not completely deciphered, is known to be related to the Eastern Mediterranean group of languages and is definitely non-indo-European (14). The traces of the Etruscan inscriptions found in the Aegean, in Egypt, and the more than ten thousand inscriptions, mostly on the walls of tombs in Etruria and Campania, make use of the Phoenician alphabet, which they later taught to the Romans. The Etruscan culture incorporates so many

Near Eastern elements, leaving little doubt that they have migrated from this region.

If speculation persists as to the ultimate origin of the Etruscans, their ample contribution to the history of civilization and the art, and the important role they played in the early development of the western Mediterranean are well known. Caere and Veii, their two most southern cities (15), were highly progressive, civilized centers at the outskirts of Rome, and to them, Rome owes much of its early development. We can not be sure that Rome itself fell under Etruscan political domination, but the Etruscan knowledge and culture did penetrate and enrich the Roman social structure.

For several centuries, the Etruscans, unable to form a unified state, were organized in a loose federation. They allied themselves with the Carthaginians, shared in their trade and exploration, and later the two allies defended the western Mediterranean against the invading Greeks.

The appearance of the Mycenaeans on the Eastern Mediterranean scene came about when the Egyptian civilization was about 2500 years old. It corresponds to the beginning of a period known in Egyptian history as the New Kingdom (1539–1075 B.C.). During that period, the Egyptian capital city of Thebes became one of the great urban centers of the ancient world, and the immense temple complexes of Karnak and Luxor were built. Their massive obelisks, second only to the pyramids in splendor, were hewn from the pink granite quarries of Aswan, decorated and inscribed, then transported north to Karnak where they were erected to adorn the Great Temple of Amun-Re.

Around 1250 B.C., the great Pharoah Ramesses II reopened the canal that links the Eastern branch of the Nile River to the Red Sea, allowing the Egyptian navy to sail freely between the Mediterranean and the Red Sea (16). With the death of this great Pharoah, the Egyptian clergy gradually took control of the power in Egypt. They emptied the Egyptian treasury, starved the people, and slowly brought to an end one of the greatest civilization the world has ever known. They forced Egypt into a state of despondence from which it never fully recovered (17). As a result, the Egyptian fleet, like the Minoan fleet, lost its presence, leaving a maritime vacuum in the Eastern Mediterranean.

Phoenicia

The Canaanite coastal cities, free from Egyptian influence, hemmed by high mountains to the East, and weary of their aggressive neighbors, looked west and proceeded to fill this vacuum. They took to the sea with vigor, and a zeal for trade unmatched in history. Allured by the safety of their ships and their love for trade, they tried whenever possible to detach themselves and their communities from the mainland. They built their cities on islands and peninsula that they sometimes severed from the mainland with wide trenches. In so doing they altered the function of the Mediterranean from a body of water that separates three continents to a multi-lane maritime bridge that links them.

About this time, the Greeks bestowed the name Phoenicians on these traders, who transported their goods to the Aegean and to the Greek shores on ships with purple sails. To the West and later to the rest of the world, these Canaanite traders became known as Phoenicians.

To carry their goods over long distances, the Phoenicians introduced significant changes in the design and construction of ships. By about 1000 B.C. they developed sturdier, faster, and larger vessels than had ever been constructed before. In addition to rowing slaves, the motive power for these ships was provided by sails; the Phoenicians usually fitted each of their ships with a single, large, rectangular, often purple, sail, and turned the inward-curving bow of the old design into an outward pencil-sharp beam, constructed right under water level. This design was later copied by Greek ship builders. With these long sharp beams, the Phoenicians plowed the water and, when needed pierced enemy ships. For some six hundred years, their fleet ruled the seas of the known world.

They built an empire different from all others; there was no military conquests, and no invading armies. They sailed their commercial fleet and settled the then sparsely populated, wild regions of the Mediterranean. They founded trading-posts that either remained small settlements and dissolved, or developed into prosperous metropolises that served as springboards for further explorations. They spread their language and culture in Southern Anatolia, built colonies in Cyprus of which the most prestigious was Kition or Citium (Qart-Hadasht), situated on the Southeast bay of the island. Classical Greek historians referred to the city as Belos Kition, Belos being the Greek adaptation of Baal, the name of the Canaanite god of fertility. Archeological finds in Ugarit show that contacts between Cypress and Canaanite coastal cities go back to the Middle and Late Bronze Age (18). Ugaritic texts state that Kothar-wa-Hassis (the god of arts and crafts) came from Caphtor (Crete) to build a palace for Baal, and to fashion the composite magic bow for Aqhat. In classical times, the Cretans were famous for bow-making and for being great archers.

The Phoenicians also settled Rhodes, and established colonies on several Aegean islands; they had trading-posts in Thasos, Kythera, Melos, Thera, and most importantly Crete, where they taught the Greeks and probably the Etruscans how to manufacture bronze artifacts.

Able to sail the open seas by day and night (19), they had settlements in Ritab in the Nile Delta where their distinctive purple ornaments and pottery were uncovered, they colonized the North African coast and founded Utica (c. 1100 B. C.), and probably Auza and Hadrumentum (Souse). They sailed through the pillars of Melqart (Hercules) and founded the city of Gadir (Phoenician for powerful or able). Later the name was changed to Cadiz and Gades. They built Gadiz, which later became their springboard into the Atlantic, on a small island off the

Atlantic coast of Southern Spain, south of the region that the Bible calls Tarshish (probably hill of marble).

On the African side of the Atlantic, on the coast of Morocco, they founded the city of Lixus (Arzila). Both Cadiz and Lixus, considered the earliest Phoenician colonies in the far west, were founded almost a decade before the foundation of Utica.

Of the Mediterranean islands, the Phoenicians had a presence in Sicily, where they established the settlements of Motya, Palermo, and Solunto before being driven off by the invading Greeks. South of Sicily, they settled Malta, Gozo, and several other islets, which they used as bases for their fleet. Moving farther west, we find that both ancient tradition and modern archeology indicate that the Phoenicians had a presence in Sardinia, founding the cities of Nora, Bythia, and Sulcis on its Southern shores and Tharros on the tip of a small bay on its Western coast. And in Southern France, Phoenician inscriptions detailing what percentage of a sacrificed animal went to the priest and what was left to the offerer were uncovered in Marseilles (20) indicating a probable phoenician presence in that region.

All these colonies were founded before the Tyrians established Carthage (814 B.C.), by far the most important of the Phoenician colonies. In a very short period, Carthage extended its dominance, formed its own sphere of influence, and began to build its own empire and settlements (21). Trading posts founded after this period could have been founded by either the Phoenicians of the Near East or their Carthaginians cousins, and possibly used by both.

Until the seventh century B.C. all Egyptian manufactured goods were circulated throughout the Mediterranean by Phoenician traders. The ambitious pharoah Necho II (610–594 B.C.), to expand his trade in tropical goods, commissioned around 600 B.C. a Phoenician fleet to sail south in the Red Sea and circumnavigate Africa. Of this daring venture, Herodotus wrote, "When autumn came, they went ashore, sowed the land, and waited for harvest; then, having reaped the corn, they put to sea again. When two years had thus passed, in the third, having doubled the pillars of Hercules, they arrived in Egypt." (22). The Phoenicians accomplished this astounding feat, one of the most magnificent achievements in the annals of seafaring, more than two thousand years before the famed Portuguese explorer, Vasco de Gama, sailed around the Cape of Good Hope in A.D. 1498.

The Phoenicians, better known for their trade and their alphabet, should also be remembered for their great contribution to the wide diffusion of Near Eastern civilization. They were responsible for the large population movement, that proceeded from the old civilized centers of the Near East to the wild world of the Western Mediterranean, North Africa, and the Eastern shores of the Atlantic, and which brought to the primitive inhabitants of these regions the best that the advanced culture of the Near East could offer. They built cultural centers and trade-posts in the midst of the native inhabitants, who were still living under very primitive conditions. For some 600 years, they bound the East and the West in a commercial and cultural web that freed much of Western Europe from barbarism; They planted the seeds of the ancient Near Eastern civilizations in the virgin land of the West. Their commerce brought unity to the peoples of the Mediterranean; no other chapter in world history better illustrates a close and active relation between commerce and culture exchange.

As early as the Bronze Age, Near Eastern craftsmen began to settle some of the Aegean islands. They traveled west looking for new markets for their skills. They brought with them not only their technological expertise but also a repertory of myths that influenced the peoples with whom they interacted. In this way they became indirect agents of cultural change. Treasures found in a woman's grave in Athens that dates back to about 850 B.C. include gold earrings and rings, and a necklace of glass beads. This jewelry had either been imported from the Orient or made locally by artisans who came from there, and reflects the ongoing contact between Greece and the prosperous civilizations of the Near East and Egypt (23).

The Greeks and the peoples of the Aegean are not to be viewed as passive recipients of Near Eastern skills and traditions; their entrepreneurs did effectively participate in the diffusion of oriental culture; they sailed all over the Mediterranean, and to them, the ports of Egypt and the Near East were favorite destinations. Thus, sea travel played a central role in the development of Greek culture and civilization; the sea lanes that linked Greece with Egypt and the Near East worked in both directions and put the Greeks into contact with the older civilizations, from which they learned new technologies, religious ideas, sciences, and much more (24).

What knowledge the Greeks took from Egypt and the Near East, they adapted and interpreted according to their own culture and system of values. By putting their stamp on what they learned, they made it their own (25).

All the Phoenician activities, sea travel, explorations, and art work were designed to improve their trade. They were skilled workmen, and they used that skill to manufacture not only cheap trinkets that they sold, but also some true art work. Their artistic ability was recognized and utilized by several of the rulers of the Near East. The Old Testament mentions that carpenters and masons came from Tyre, "and they built David an House" (2 Sam. 5:11). The Tyrians also helped king Solomon build the richly decorated, stone temple of Jerusalem (1 Kings 5:18 and 6:13,14), and King Hiram of Tyre helped Solomon build his merchant fleet. Their business partnership brought Solomon the wealth that enabled him to acquire "many strange women" and live in luxury and splendor.

The kings of Assyria also employed Phoenician artisans to build the furniture and the metal art work for their palaces.

They manufactured various objects of glass and metals; they made vases, weapons, ornaments, and jewelry; they had a sort of monopoly on purple dye, which became known as Tyrian purple, and which they extracted from mollusk that abound on their shores and used it to stain their highly prized fabrics. They exported their art work and that of Egypt to wherever their ships could take them. They loaded their ships with cereals, wines, textiles, precious stones, and manufactured goods and with spices and perfumes imported from India and South Arabia by their cousins, the Arameans. They sailed the seas to trade their wares for copper from Cyprus, gold, lead, and iron from the Southern region of the Black Sea, ivory from Africa, silver, tin, and lead from Spain, tin from Britain, and slaves from wherever they could get them.

In many of their colonies and particularly in Spain, they enslaved the natives, shipped some to the Near East where they were sold and made others work long hours in the mines. In the 11th, 10th, and 9th century B.C. Spain was to the Phoenicians what Mexico and Peru were to the Spaniards in the 16th century A.D.

The lack of political organization, and the fact that many Oriental chieftains and heads of clans, who could afford to acquire sea-worthy ships and transport goods, became merchants, and were all called Phoenicians, provided the Phoenician trading practices with a high degree of non-uniformity. While most Phoenicians exhibited their merchandise from their ships, or in their trading posts, and bargained with their customers, others had different approaches. About the Carthaginians traders, Herodotus writes:

"Hither they came and unload their cargo; then having laid it orderly by the waterline they go aboard their ships and light a smoking fire. The people of the country see the smoke, and coming to the sea they lay down gold to pay for the cargo and withdraw away from the wares. Then the Carthaginians disembark and examine the gold; if it seems to them a fair price for the cargo, they take it and go their ways; but if not, they go aboard again and wait, and the people come back and add more gold till the shipmen are satisfied. Herein neither party defrauds the other: the Carthaginians do not lay hand on the gold till it matches the value of their cargo, nor do the people touch the cargo till the shipmen have taken their gold" (26).

Although there is no documented proof, one may speculates that this method may also have been used earlier by the Phoenicians. Wherever they went with their goods, the Phoenicians carried with them pieces of pale yellow sheets with black markings that many of their early customers mistook for good luck charms or amulets. On these sheets of papyrus, they kept records of their business transactions and at the same time used them to teach the known world the use of the alphabet. Papyrus is more convenient than heavy clay tablets for keeping and carrying business accounts, but it certainly lacks the durability of clay tablets. This is why most of the Phoenician body of knowledge and literary work, except that of Ugarit (written on clay tablets), was lost; Papyrus survived in the dry climate of Egypt, but did not in humid Phoenicia and its coastal colonies. Thus, most of what came to us about the Phoenicians was written by their enemies, the Greeks and the Romans. The loss was so complete that the Phoenician language itself became a dead language and the Ugaritic texts were deciphered by comparing their phraseology with ancient Hebrew and Syriac.

The traders of antiquity, the Phoenicians, were in contact with Lydia and Phrygia and knew the Babylonian and Egyptian cultures. They were clever navigators and businessmen with diligent observations of weights and measures. Their lyric and poetry became epics, and their highly developed critical faculty was the prelude to the era of scientific research. Across the waves, they carried their goods and their knowledge; they traded their goods and gave freely of their knowledge (27).

The Greeks came into the picture towards the middle of the eight century B.C. As their number increased on the mainland, they found it necessary to migrate first into the Aegean and western Anatolia, then it became very common for Greek traders to take residence in Phoenician settlements all across the Mediterranean (28). These cohabitations generated the proper contacts and introduced the Greeks to the rich Near Eastern civilizations, mythologies, cultures, sciences, and literatures. But most of all, the Greeks learned from the Phoenicians the art of trading, which in time led to bitter competition.

Trade brought slaves, riches, and prosperity to Phoenicia; its coastal cities, with their high rise buildings and bustling ports became the envy of their neighbors. Towards the end of the sixth century, Zechariah wrote, "Tyrus did build herself a strong hold, and heaped up silver as the dust, and fine gold as the mire of the streets." Zech. (9:3). He and other prophets foretold its destruction and that of other Phoenician cities (Zech. (9:4), Isa.(Chap. 23), Jerem. (25:22), Ezek. (Chaps 26-28), Joel (3:4), and Amos (1:9-10)).

These prophecies were made several centuries after the Greeks began their maritime expansion, which led to hundreds of years of Greco-Phoenician competition. The two rivals competed in establishing trade posts and spheres of influence that stretched from the western shores of Anatolia through the Aegean islands and southern Greece to the western shores of Italy. At times, these competitions turned into full scale wars, but also resulted into stronger associations between the two rivals, allowing the Greeks to acquire more of the knowledge of the ancient Near East. They learned astronomy and mathematics from Mesopotamia, medicine from Mesopotamia and Egypt, the use of coinage from Lydia, the use of stone for architecture and sculpture from Egypt, and the luxury and splendor of oriental bronzes and oriental fabrics from Egypt and Phoenicia (29). Also during this period many Greek youths served as mercenaries in the army of the pharaohs and were exposed to the vast body of Egyptian knowledge. The Greeks passed much of that body of knowledge to the Romans, who in turn, passed it to the rest of the Western world.

Rome came into the picture when the Greco-Phoenician conflicts were still brewing. For a brief period, Rome allied itself with Carthage against the Greeks and checked their advances into the western Mediterranean. With the Greeks no longer a concern, the Romans and the Carthaginians turned against each other, and the long and costly Punic wars began in 264 B.C.

While the Mediterranean powers were competing for trade, resources, and spheres of influence, the Assyrian kings were collecting clay tablets building a library that preserved the knowledge and the literary works of ancient Mesopotamians. Late in the seventh century B.C. the royal library at Nineveh contained some twenty-two thousand clay tablets.

Persia

During that same period, but farther east, the Persian tribes were reuniting under the leadership of Cyrus, the founder of the Persian Empire (530–330 B. C.). He defeated the Assyrians, conquered Mesopotamia, Anatolia, and Canaan, but fell in battle south of the Caspian Sea. His son, Cambyses conquered Egypt in 525 B.C. to give the Persian Empire complete control of the entire civilized Orient.

Cambyses' attempt to march against Carthage did not materialize because the Phoenician cities refused to have their fleets participate in a venture against their sister city. Cambyses, after profaning Egyptian temples, was stricken with a severe illness, lost his thrown, and probably committed suicide.

Our main interest in the history of the Persian Empire is in the diffusion of knowledge and civilization that came at the hands of its emperor, Darius the Great (522–486 B.C.). This wise ruler selected the most convenient and valuable achievements of the great civilizations under his rule, and popularized them in his vast empire. He perceived the practicality of the Egyptian calendar with its twelve thirty-day months and adopted it for his empire. Recognizing the value of Egyptian medical knowledge, Darius freed the Egyptian High Priest and instructed him to return to the western Delta and restore the

Egyptian medical school/hospital that had fallen into ruin. Darius provided the funds necessary to operate this school, making it the first known government endowed institution of learning. An inscription upon the statue of the High Priest, now in the Vatican collections, reads: "His majesty (Darius) did this because he knew the value of this art (medicine), in order to save the life of every one having sickness." (30). The well-equipped school had its own library and enrolled students from the best Egyptian families.

Darius also encouraged the great Chaldean astronomer Naburimannu to continue his observations, and almost a hundred years later, his successors offered the same curtsey to another great Chaldean astronomer, Kidinnu. The observations of both Chaldeans astronomers were performed under Persian rule.

The Great Emperor also recognized the convenience of metal coinage, which he put in general use, and whose value he guaranteed by the effigy of the administrator. Some experiments in this direction had been made in earlier times, for there are traces of primitive monetary systems in the shape of stamped ingots far back in Egyptian antiquity. And, in the middle of the first millennium B.C., monetary coins spread in the Hellenistic area, the Aegean, and Ionia to be later elaborated upon in Lydia (31). But the true starting point of monetary organization was the silver shekel (86.4 grains, about 17.3 grams) of Darius and his successors. In both Persia and Lydia, gold coins appeared little later (32). The use of coined money instead of produce in commerce and taxation remarkably simplified both operations.

To further facilitate business transactions, he adopted the language of the land merchants of that period, the Arameans, who were using the Phoenician alphabet in their business interactions. All documents, including those dealing with the collection of taxes, were written in Aramaic with ink on papyrus, and clay tablets and cuneiform script began to slowly disappear (33). The Persian Empire had two main languages, the official language, Persian, and the financial language, Aramaic, used to conduct business and collect taxes.

Recognizing the importance of maritime power, Darius completed the digging of the Suez (Darius) Canal, and left inscriptions that read: "I command to dig this canal, from the stream flowing in Egypt, called the Nile, to the sea which stretches from Persia." And, knowing that he needed the Phoenician war fleet for further expeditions, he treated the Phoenician cities with respect and kindness.

Darius, and later his son, Serxes, made use of the Phoenician fleet, which comprised several hundred war ships to fight their common enemy, the Greeks, and in their attempt to conquer Europe. The Greco-Persian war was a conflict between the two most advanced and progressive societies of the time. This conflict came to its climax with Alexander of Macidon defeated Darius III at Issues, in southern Anatolia and led his forces down the Phoenician coast and into Egypt. The Phoenician cities received him peaceably, but upon reaching the city of Tyre, which then consisted of a continental city and an island fortress, he announced that he intended to offer a sacrifice in the temple of Melkart, the city protective deity, but the Tyrians refused him access to the temple, which was on the island. Not willing to leave the island city alone and knowing that his war fleet was no match to the Tyrian fleet, he asked and subsequently received the help of the Phoenician cities of Byblos, Sidon, and Aradus. Only Carthage sent a fleet to assist Tyre against the invader. Realizing that the island fortress was impregnable from the sea, he ordered the construction of a causeway some 800 meters (about half a mile) long, connecting the mainland to the island.

For this undertaking, timber was brought from the mountains of Lebanon, and Alexander ordered the destruction of the continental city and used the rocks from its buildings. Finally, Alexander's soldiers marched on dry land, pushing along assault machines and catapults that were developed by Alexander's father and employed them to breach Tyre's formidable walls. This sounded the death knell of walled city states as settlements impregnable to siege. Alexander conquered Tyre, and laid it to ruin. Many of its citizens fled to North Africa, then he marched his troops into Egypt where the Egyptian High Priest called him "son of Amun", thus proclaiming him a god.

With the construction of Alexandria west of the Nile Delta, one of over half a dozen cities upon which Alexander bestowed his name, the destruction of Tyre was complete. The wealthy, the notables, and the achievers of Tyre migrated to Alexandria, and this included Euclid, the greatest geometer of all time (34). Infused by Tyrians as well as others, Alexandria, under the rule of the Ptolemies, flourished and became a great center of knowledge and scientific research.

Alexander the Great, after reaching India, returned to Babylon to begin his truly important work, introducing Greek culture into the Orient, intending to put to practice the views advanced by Greek philosophers, concerning a world-wide idealized state, whose citizens are not of a country or a city, but of the universe. Alexander died before fulfilling his dream.

As in the East, it was in the West; The costly and bitter Punic wars lasted well over a century and resulted in the complete destruction of Carthage in 146 B.C. After being the center of commerce, culture, and civilization for some 700 years, Carthage was savagely turned into ashes. Alexander's conquest the East and the destruction of Carthage in the West left the Orient-except for the center of Alexandria, which was the product of the wise policy of the Ptolemies-in a culturally dormant state, from which it did not awake until the advent of Islam in the seventh century A.D.

This cultural intercourse across the Mediterranean which involved practically all the peoples of the region led to the most spectacular rise in human cultural development. It gave birth to the Hellenistic Golden era and to the greatness of Rome. The Greco-Oriental relations, which, for a millennium, engaged the participants in commerce, cultural exchange, competition, and war, led to the Hellenistic Golden era. And the Carthaginian-Roman relations and engagements gave rise to the glory and the greatness of the Roman Empire. Thus across the Mediterranean, the West received from the East the precious seeds of civilization.

---

(1). Simthonian, Vol. 27, No. 7. Oct. 1996. PP 108–109, and Carolyn McGhee, private communication.

(2). Martin, Thomas R. (1996:8).

(3). Wernick, Robert, Smithsonian, Vol. 27, No. 6. Sept. 1996. pp 62–73. The name Malta (shelter) is Phoenician and so are the names of many of the islets around it and some of the old monuments found on them.

(4). Durant, Will. (1963:105).

(5). Redford, Donald B. (1992: 210).

(6). Colliers Encyclopedia. (1994:331).

(7). Marinatos, Spyridon and Hirmer, Max. (1960:14,15); and hopkins, adam. (1977:28–31).

(8). Homer's Iliad mentions the great king Minos as the ruler of the city of Cnossus (Knossos) and the British journalist-archeologist Sir Arthur Evans gave the name of the great king to the great civilization.

(9). Gordon, C. H. (1965:216–217). And (1966:33–34). In spite of Gordon's effort, many archaeologists still believe that the linear A script is yet to be deciphered.

(10). In a desk dictionary, the word amphora stands for an ancient Greek jar with a large oval body and a narrow cylindrical neck. The amphorae salvaged were used in Canaan several hundred years before the Greeks set foot in Greece and they are still used in Syria and Lebanon as containers for olive oil and wine.

(11). The scarab or a precious stone in the form of the scarab was used in ancient Egypt as a talisman, an ornament, and a symbol of resurrection. According to an ancient Egyptian myth, the scarab propels the sun across the sky.

(12). When the Mycenaens were using their Linear B script, the people of Ugarit were writing their great epics using a fully developed alphabet.

(13). The Aegean are located on the geological fault between the African and the European plates. As a result, they experienced several devastating earthquakes; the first occurred around 1700 B.C. and leveled the Cretan palaces, but the Minoans rebuilt on a grander scale. The notorious Thera eruption followed several hundred years later.

(14). Bloch, Raymond. (1958:72).

(15). Scullard, H. H. (1967:59).

(16). Probably this canal was first opened as early as 2000 B.C. And we know for certain that it was in existence in 1470 B.C. It required continuous maintenance as the shifting desert sands kept encroaching upon it. Necho II, the ambitious pharoah, was the last of the Egyptian rulers to undertake the project, which was completed by Darius, the Persian king (522–486 B.C.), hence the name, Darius Canal.

(17). For a short period, the ambitious Pharoah Nicho II (610–595 B.C.) lifted Egypt out of doldrums, but his efforts were short lived.

(18). Moscati, Sabatino. (1968:104).

(19). The Phoenicians were probably the first seafarers to make use of fixed stars in navigation. Because of their dependance on the North Star in their nocturnal sailing, the classical Greeks named it the Phoenician Star.

(20). Moscati, Sabatino. (1968:143).

(21). Ibid. (1968:98–100).

(22). Herodotus, IV, 42.

(23). Martin, Thomas R. (1966:23, 41).

(24). Ibid. (1996:2).

(25). Ibid. (1996:22).

(26). Herodotus, IV, 196.

(27). Krumbhaar, E. B. (1985:116).

(28). Martin, Thomas R. (1996:56).

(29). Richardson, Emeline Hill. (1964:45).

(30). Breasted, James Henry. (1935:271).

(31). At about the same time, the Carthaginian government issued money in the form of stamped pieces of leather. This is the precursor of the paper money used to day.>

(32). Weill, Raymond. (1940:189,190).

(33). The latest known cuneiform tablet belongs to the Chaldeans astronomical records, and was inscribed in 7 B.C.

(34). Euclid Nuqatrus Barniqus, the father of modern geometry, was of Greek ancestry, but was born in Tyre, where he worked as a carpenter. He moved to Alexandria, and acquired the designation Euclid of Alexandria. Here he did most of his scholarly work, writing fifteen books, of which the most famous is Al-Astrushia [the Foundation of Geometry]. [Al-Andalusi. (1991:93)]

Fig. 2-1. A sculpture found near Amman, Jordan, (c.7000 B.C.).

Altar from Hagar Qim

Fig. 2-2. A decorated altar from Hagar Qim, Malta (c. 3500 B.C.)

Fig. 2-3. A Phoenician trench near 'Amfeh, Lebanon (c. 1000 B.C.)

Chapter Three

The Alphabet

As early as the late Stone Age, some 20,000 years ago, cave dwellers were decorating the walls of their shelters with the pictures of their preys. With great fidelity, they incised the images of deers, antelopes, bisons, lions, tigers, and of human hunters bearing down on their prey with pointed spears. These were the earliest human thoughts expressed in picture forms, and bear no relation to the language of the people who drew them. This picture writing-pictography-primitive as it may be, preserved some information about early cave dwellers and opened avenues for further development.

By about 5000 B.C., the dawn of history was ushered by the introduction of ideography. Ideograms, written during and after that period, exhibit a link between the spoken and the written words and this, in many instances, provided some intelligible and informative human records. This was the first notable improvement on pictography in about 15,000 years. True literacy appeared around 3200 B.C. some 2000 years after the introduction of ideography.

Most archaeologists are of the opinion that the earliest people to have left written symbols are the Sumerians, followed, a short time later, by the Egyptians and other Near Eastern societies. The 1998 discovery of clay tablets with primitive form of hieroglyphic writing that dates back to the later centuries of the fourth millennium B.C. may prove that writing in Egypt began at roughly the same time it did in Sumer, and may provide hieroglyphs with the missing development stage.

The earliest clay tablets unearthed in the southern parts of Mesopotamia are picture writings which have not yet been deciphered. Those written after 3200 B.C. are clearly Sumerian and their contents are well known. Their subject matter includes groups of words, accounts of deeds of sale, and some fragments of early literature. The Sumerians wrote primarily on clay tablets, producing wedge-shaped characters which became known as cuneiform script, from the Latin "cuneus" meaning wedge. The Sumerians took several centuries to develop their system of writing. A couple of centuries later, hieroglyphic writing appeared rather suddenly and in nearly full form; except for the few tablets uncovered in 1998, there is no evidence of any gradual development of the Egyptian way of writing. Early experiments in hieroglyphic writing either never existed, or have not been preserved.

After the rise of Sumerian and Egyptian writings, and within a few centuries, there appeared other apparently independent forms of writings, such as the proto-Elamite writing in Iran, the Hittite hieroglyphic in Turkey, and the Cretan pictographs in Crete. Although each of these systems has its distinctive set of signs that are different from those of Sumer and Egypt, it is reasonable to assume that the Elamites, the Hittites, and the Cretans were aware of the development of writing of their neighbors and trading partners. This leads to the belief that the Sumerians were the true inventors of writing and their neighbors learned of the important discovery and formulated their own.

The Egyptian system of writing consists of picture word-signs that only their priests used. They called it m-d-w-n-t-r (speech of the gods) and which is now known by its Greek name hieroglyphs (sacred, carved letters). This form of writing is usually found carved on the stone walls of Egyptian temples. There is also the hieratic (sacred) writing, which is a simplified version of the hieroglyph, and which was used to write on papyrus, wood, or cloth. Later on, when the common Egyptians, not only the priests, learned to write, they used a highly simplified syllabic form of writing, which became known also by its Greek name, demotic (popular), and which may be considered a first step towards alphabetic writing .

By about 2000 B.C. other forms of writing began to appear in various parts of the Near East. The Hittites, who lived in the hill country south of the Black Sea and north of the Fertile Crescent, introduced a new form of hieroglyphs. It consisted of some seventy signs, each of which stood for a simple syllable, plus about one hundred word-signs. Similar forms of hieroglyphs, consisting of word-signs and syllable-signs, were also used in Crete, Cyprus, Lebanon, Palestine, and Syria. A study of the various script uncovered in Crete is necessary to dispel the claim that the art of writing originated on the island.

The oldest script uncovered on Cretan soil is in the form of pictograms, which was probably introduced into the island by Egyptian merchants late in the third millennium B.C.

In addition to the Cretan pictograms, the island had two distinct forms of syllabary scripts, where each character represents a whole syllable. The two scripts became known as the Minoan Linear A and Linear B, and were widely used in various regions of the island early in the second millennium B.C. The two scripts, although not identical, are quite similar; most of their signs are alike and have the same phonetic sounds .

The Linear B script, uncovered mostly around Knossos, was decoded in 1952 by Michael Ventries, who determined that its language is mostly pre-Homeric Greek, and that it contains vessel-inventories and administrative records, dealing mostly in produce issued from, or received by, the palace stores.

The Linear A script, which predates the Linear B by a few hundred years, was used mostly in Southern Crete, and more specifically in the

Hagia Trida (H.T.) area. Through a series of publications that began in 1956, Cyrus Gordon, an authority on ancient Semitic languages, proved that the two scripts, the Linear A and the Linear B, were the same script used in writing two different languages, and showed that the Linear B scripts is only a modification of the Linear A, adapted for writing pre-Homeric Greek. By decoding several Phoenician words that often appear in the H.T. script, such as "qiryat" (city), "ku-ni-su" (wheat), "ku-lo" (all), and a-ga-nu (bowl), he determined that the language of the Linear A script is mostly Western Semitic (Phoenician), and concluded that "the Greeks learned both their systems of writing from the Phoenicians; first the Minoan syllabary, and then the alphabet." (1). Gordon's conclusion was not widely accepted.

Further study of the Cretan syllabary scripts established the Near Eastern influence on the early development of civilization on the island. The H.T. contains Phoenician names such as ka-du-ma-ne, the Phoenician (kdm) "Cadmus", mi-na-ne, the Phoenician (mn) "Minos", da-na-ne, the Phoenician (dn) "Dan", and ki-re-ta, the Ugaritic prince (krt) "Kret".

The H.T. also contains almost twenty personal names that end with the name of the Egyptian god Re. Most, if not all of these names, are Egyptians and their presence in Southern Crete indicate that early Egyptians could have migrated to the island, or some of the Semites, who lived on the island emigrated from the Nile Delta, where Semites are known to have lived. Egyptian personal names that appear in H.T. include ne-tu-ri-re, the Egyptian ntry-re "Re is divine" and ra-na-re, Egyptian rn-re "name of Re".

But in spite of the mounting evidence, not all scholars are in agreement as to the language and origin of the Linear A script; recently T. R. Martin wrote, "This script, used during the first half of the second millennium, is today called Linear A. Its language remains largely undeciphered, but recent scholarship suggests that it may have been Indo-European." (2).

What is well established is that with the fall of the Mycenaean civilization around 1200 B.C. the Linear B script disappeared, and the region returned to an age of pre-literacy. It remained in this state for almost four hundred years until the Phoenician alphabet entered into Greece and the Aegean.

The best preserved script found in Crete is the world famous Discos of Phaistos. The beautifully made clay disc, sixteen centimeters in diameter, was discovered in the ruins of a Minoan palace in 1908 by the Italian archeologist Luigi Pernier. It is stamped with 45 different symbols that include a variety of human beings, human heads, human hands, human breasts, animals, insects, fish, flowers, tree branches, and other symbols indicating that the the script is syllabary. The most fascinating feature of this Disc is that all the imprints of the same symbol are identical, indicating that they are actual imprints and not free-hand scripts. This means that the scribes have developed forms that they would press in the clay to make such imprints, and that, in all probability, the disc is not a unique fixture. It is hard to believe that a scribe would go into the trouble of etching 45 different symbols just to write one such short document.

On both surfaces of the Disc, the symbols run spirally from the rim to the center in a well planned design leaving no gap either at the end of the spiral or between the words. The author seems to have separated the various words by straight lines normal to the script.

Gordon, in an effort to prove that the Disk is of Phoenician origin, used a complex and risky approach to decipher its contents. He examined the two lower sections of the second surface, and came up with boat-mouth-barley-ti and corner-man-te-breast-da. the signs for ti, te, and da are similar to symbols found in the Linear B and deciphered by Ventris. He then used the first syllables of some Phoenicians words, such as "si" for "sipinatu" (ship) and whole words such as "pe" for mouth and included some Egyptian and Hebrew .words and came up with si-pe-'i-ti bi-bu-te-ha-da, and translated it to mean "I have eaten [my ceremonial meal] in the house of Haddad". Such a statement appears often in Ugaritic texts (3). This combination of Phoenician, Western Semitic, and Egyptian words, and syllabary symbols in a single script is not as far fetch as it seems; as it reflects, to a certain degree, the multi-cultural nature of the Minoan civilization. But Gordon's effort did not receive the proper acceptance, and has been generally neglected. The importance, the origin, and the date of this artifact are still points of contention. The signs on the famous Disc may not be related to any other script, making their decipherment next to impossible. Speculations that the Disc was left on Cretan soils around 1200 B.C. by the invading Sea People, have recently been advanced (4).

By the middle of the second millennium B.C., other syllabary ways of writing gained popularity in the Near East and the Aegean. The Akkadian syllabary had 285 characters, the Mycenean linear B had about 80, and the later Cypriot Greek syllabary had 56. Also around this time, the people of Jbail dropped their old Egyptian hieroglyphs in favor of a simpler script consisting of eighty syllabic signs and several characters depicting simple objects in a stylized fashion.

All the word-sign and the syllabary methods of writing are complex and difficult to learn, and only professional scribes were able to read and write. To write a letter, keep an account, check a legal document, or read a will, an ordinary person had to rely on the services of trained scribes.

This monopoly on reading and writing, held by the few professional scribes, persisted until the advent of the alphabet, whose invention is one of the most important and most useful inventions of all time. Its value lies in its elegance and simplicity and in its ability to express all the vocal sounds needed in any language in about two dozen symbols. This great invention simplified the process of reading and writing to a degree that enabled a common person to master the art, thus freeing him from the need for professional scribes. It is considered by many as one of humanity's greatest discoveries, and certainly the greatest improvement between the invention of writing and printing.

There has always been speculation as to the origin of the alphabet, beginning with the early Greek and Latin authors who credited the invention of the alphabet to practically every Near-Eastern country. Diodorus Siculus states that, "The Syrians are the discoverers of the letters, and the Phoenicians having learned them from the Syrians and then passed them to the Greeks." Pliny, on the one hand, claims that "the invention of the letter is a Phoenician feat," and speaks also of a Mesopotamian origin. Tacitus maintains that the alphabet is of Egyptian origin, and adds that "the Phoenicians took all the credit for what they received before passing it on to others." (5). The various views of the classical authors are mere speculations that demonstrate their awareness of the problem, and their cognizance of the importance of the discovery.

Opinions as to the origin of the alphabet are still voiced. There are those who still believe that the alphabet is of Mesopotamian origin. They base their opinion on the Ugaritic script which dates back to about 1400 or 1500 B.C. and which consists of thirty symbols representing thirty consonant letters written in cuneiform script. The existence of an alphabet in a cuneiform script does not imply, in any way, that the idea of an alphabet originated in Mesopotamia, where there is no evidence that it ever existed. Of the half million or so cuneiform tablets and fragments of tablets uncovered in Mesopotamia, there is not one that bears a sign of an alphabet.

By about 2000 B.C. the Mesopotamian cuneiform system of writing was used throughout the Near East and particularly in Canaan, where the rulers were using it in their correspondence even with the pharaohs of Egypt. All the 360 tablets uncovered in Tell Amarna were written in the Canaanitic language and cuneiform script.

When the Ugaritic scribes were writing their alphabet using the wedge-shaped cuneiform signs, the Mesopotamians were still content with their word-symbols.

The discovery of Minoan hieroglyphs and other Minoans pictograms in the beginning of this century suggested to the archeologist Sir Arthur Evans that the Phoenician alphabet was itself derived from Crete. On the basis of Evans' statement, and in spite of the fact that excavations on the island revealed no alphabetic signs, Glasgow wrote: "We now know, for instance, that the art of writing came from Crete, Phoenicia being the medium" (6). We now know that early in the second millennium B.C. Crete became a prosperous Phoenician center, and the Linear A script is a Phoenician syllabery, and the Linear B is a mere adaptation of the Linear A to the pre-Homeric Greek language.

There are also contemporary scholars who believe that the alphabet is of Egyptian origin; they base their views on the Sinaitic inscriptions uncovered in 1906 by Sir William Flinders Petrie in the Sinai Desert, and which date back to about 1500 B.C. (7). This discovery was hailed by many as the missing link between the alphabet and the Egyptian hieroglyph, and led to the belief that the Canaanites learned their method of writing from their contact with the Egyptians. A recent discovery in the land of Canaan showed that the so called Proto-Sinaitic inscriptions were in use by Semitic people as early as 1700 B.C., which demonstrates that the Proto-Sinaitic script instead of being an attempt at the development of an alphabet from the hieroglyphic, or more precisely the demotic scripts, is an Egyptian version of an already existing Semitic script. This and the presence of prayers to the goddess, Baalat of Jbail, on a wall in one of the Sinaitic mines, support the Canaatic origin of the Sinaitic script.

There are those who support an Egyptian origin of the alphabet, basing their claim on the presence of simple symbols in the Egyptian hieroglyphs. Around 2000 B.C. Egyptian scribes, like most other scribes in the region, introduced into their writings, 24 signs which stood for simple sounds and which represented the 24 Egyptian consonants. Thus began the development of the Egyptian alphabetic system of pictures, where each picture stood for a simple sound; but the

Egyptian scribes failed to discard all their logograms and other complex signs, and the use of their alphabet remained limited to writing names and foreign words. None of the pictures in the Egyptian alphabetic system looks remotely like the symbols in the early Phoenician alphabet. The inclusion of simple symbols in the Egyptian hieroglyphs resulted in a pseudo-hieroglyph script, which has so many signs that it can hardly be considered alphabetic. In reality, this inclusion, instead of simplifying the Egyptian way of writing, added to its complexity. The ultra-conservative priests, who were the only scribes in ancient Egypt, were determined not to introduce a simple writing system that could be readily apprehended and used by the average citizen. They realized if that ever happened it would mean the end of the privileged priestly class and do away with the presumed sanctity of the complex script. Thus, through their trickery and the complexity of their script, the Egyptian priests were able to maintain, to a certain degree, their monopoly on writing, and to preserve their complex picture word-signs of "heavenly origin" practically unchanged from about 2900 B.C. to about A.D. 500.

As may be deduced from earlier statements, by about 2000 B.C. the development of writing moved from the land of the Nile to the South Western corner of the Sinai Peninsula, an area rich in turquoise, copper, and gold. To mine these precious commodities, the Egyptian lords hired Canaanite shepherds and engaged criminals and prisoners of wars into force labor. The Canaanite tribal chiefs became the foremen of this labor force, and were assigned the duty of preparing written reports for their Egyptian masters.

The chieftains-foremen did not have the patience to master the complex Egyptian script and certainly felt no qualm about its religious aspect. They relinquished all its redundant, complex ideograms and Egyptianized their own "alphabetic" form of writing, producing 40 syllabary symbols. This did not translate into an ideal writing system, but served exceptionally well for keeping the records of the Sinai mines.

One may speculate that in Canaan, where simplified versions of both hieroglyphic and cuneiform methods of writing came in contact, a new form of writing, simpler than both, emerged. Peoples' movement and the advancement of commerce, mining, and other activities, provided the need for it.

There are supporters of non-Canaanitic origins of the alphabet, who point out that some of the sounds assigned to the signs that make up the Phoenician alphabet do not correspond to the Canaanite names represented by these signs. As a matter of fact very few of the alphabetic signs do not correspond to any known objects. But as we shall see, most of them do, and this should be taken as a proof that the final form of the alphabet is Canaanitic and probably Phoenician. The variations that exist may be attributed to the whim of a scribe or scribes, who forsook fidelity in favor of beauty or simplicity. The alphabet may have evolved for several centuries before being perfected by the Phoenicians of Jbail. Here it should be mentioned that none of the simple characters found in the Egyptian hieroglyphic writing phonetically sounds like the Phoenician name of the object represented in the alphabet. The Egyptian language is completely different from Semitic languages, and there are letters in the Phoenician alphabet that are not found nor needed in the Egyptian language.

Although, towards the middle of the second millennium B.C., various forms of the alphabets were used in the Near East, the one that was adopted by the Greeks and later by the rest of the western world is the one that originated in the land of Canaan and most probably in Jbail (Byblos). There a scribe conceived of the idea that a language may be written without the numerous signs used in Babylonian cuneiform, Egyptian hieroglyphs, or the various syllabary scripts. It took a great deal of effort and insight to realize that complex words may be broken down into simple sounds, and that it does not take many of these simple sounds to write an entire language. This led Cyrus Gordon to point out that ancient Phoenicians seem to have preempted modern linguists by almost four millennia, and discovered what modern day linguists call the phonemic principle, according to which any language may be broken down into a limited number of distinctive sounds-usually around thirty. This is tantamount to saying that the large number of words that form a language are made up of various combinations of a relatively small number of sounds. Thus it may be assumed that the discoverer or discoverers of the alphabet had a highly sophisticated knowledge of linguistics. The Phoenicians, the traders of the ancient world, through their contacts with their many trading partners, may have acquired such a knowledge.

It should be noted here that early in the second millennium B.C. several forms of writing, with varied degrees of simplicity, mushroomed in the land of Canaan. These include the 40 symbols of the Proto-Canaanitic-Sinaitic script in the extreme south, and the 30 cuneiform alphabetic symbols of Ugarit in the north, and many others in between. Chief among them are those unearthed in Jbayl and ascribed to the middle of the second millennium B.C. (8).

The symbols found in various locations are some what different, indicating that the often competing Canaanite clans extended their competition to the formulation of the alphabet. Many of these early stages of the evolvement of the alphabet are lost.

The giant step came about in the middle of the second millennium, when a true genius, most probably a Phoenician living in Jbail, conceived of a marvelous scheme. He dropped many of the cumbersome symbols and retained only 22. He assigned to each of them the name of simple, common object, thus formulating the simple Phoenician alphabet, the foundation of all known alphabets. Each of the simple sounds was represented by the picture of a familiar object whose Canaanitic name phonetically corresponds to the sound. Thus, for example, the simple picture of a "beit" (house) stood for the "b" sound, and the simple picture of a "daleth" (door) stood for the "d" sound. This should be emphasized, because this is the beauty of the

Phoenician alphabet; the pictures stood for simple sounds and not for word-signs. In this fashion all the consonants that form the language were represented. For reasons yet unknown, the vowels were not considered important enough to play a role in this scheme. As we shall see, in the later development of the alphabet, a few of these consonants became vowels.

Except for the Ugaritic alphabet, which was written on clay tablets, the few early alphabetic signs found in the land of Canaan, were scratched on stones or rocks. Toward the middle of the second millennium B.C. the land of Canaan was under the influence of Egypt, and the Canaanite scribes were writing on Egyptian papyrus. Unfortunately, in the relatively damp soil of Canaan, papyrus did not prove to be a durable material, and the early development of the alphabet, written on papyrus, is lost, and the real inventer may never be known. The Phoenicians themselves attributed the discovery of the alphabet to their god of writing Taut (Greek Taoutus). Many believe that the Phoenician Taut and the Egyptian god of writing Thoth are one and the same. Or could Taut be the name of the Phoenician genius who invented the alphabet, and as a result became the Phoenician god of writing?

The earliest known "alphabetic" signs are the proto-Canaanaitic scripts found in Southern Canaan and in the Sinai Desert, and they may be considered a first attempt in a long process that led to the alphabet. But, on the whole, they do not suggest true alphabetic designations as a large number of the Sinaitic signs are syllabic rather than alphabetic. Although there are a few similarities between the Sinaitic and the Phoenician (Jbaily) signs, many are different indicating that radical changes had taken place.

The alphabet in its entirety, but not the alphabetic signs, could have been invented around the fifteenth century B.C. in Ugarit. The Ugaritic literature, written on clay tablets, is the earliest, most comprehensive alphabetic script that has survived. Furthermore, the order of the first few letters of the alphabet support this contention; the head of the Ugaritic pantheon is El, whose epithet is "Thor" (Bull). It is most appropriate to put the head of the pantheon at the head of the alphabet, hence aleph, the first letter of the alphabet, means an ox-head. The myths of Ugarit often speak of the house of god; they frequently mention the abode of El, and the construction of a house for Baal receives lengthy, detailed description. Building a house for the lord was an indication that the god had grown in stature and required an impressive dwelling. Thus the second letter of the alphabet, b, is represented by "beit" (house).

Some scholars believe that the origin of the first two symbols of the alphabet is the Egyptian hieroglyphic symbols for eagle and foot. But the aleph does not resemble an eagle nor does the symbol for beit resemble a foot, and they are clearly simple representations of an ox-head and a house.

Now what is a house without a "daleth" (door), thus "d" is the fourth letter of the alphabet, followed by "hah" (window). There are other similar groupings of related objects in the Phoenician alphabet of Ugarit and of Jbayl; there is "yad", "kaff", and "lamed" (hand, palm, and staff), and also "mem", "nahir", and "samkeh" (water, river, and fish), and there are two conjugate pairs: "'ain" and "feh" (eye and mouth), and "rosh" and "shin" (head and tooth). Thus the order of the symbols of the alphabet makes some sense, and is not as strange as claimed by those who believe that the invention of the Phoenician alphabet and the order of the letters in it were accidental and not deliberate.

If, on the basis of what we know now, one is to assign credit for the invention of the alphabet, the credit would go to the pre-Phoenicians Canaanites and to the people of Ugarit. The Phoenicians of Jbayl would get the credit for putting the alphabet in its basic, now familiar form, replacing the old Canaanitic symbols and the cumbersome Ugaritic cuneiform signs with simple, easy to reproduce characters.

The most recent discovery of alphabetic symbols in Wadi el Hol (Valley of Terror) in the Egyptian southern desert might have pushed back the invention of the alphabet as much as two hundred years and confirmed its Canaanitic origin. The uncovered scratches on a rock are unmistakably the Canaanitic letters P, L, T, M, and W corresponding, respectively, to the Canaanite words mouth, staff, cross, water, and hook. They could have been left for posterity by one of the Hyksos soldiers.

There are indications that the scribes of Ugarit, in their later writings, wrote from right to left and dropped a few of the consonants symbols. The scribes Jbail continued the process of converging sounds to accommodate sound variations in their standard language and in so doing reduced the total number from thirty characters to twenty-two (9).

The simplicity of the Jbaily-Phoenician signs rendered them more accessible than all others, and towards the end of the second millennium, this simple alphabet displaced all others and became firmly established in the entire land of Canaan (10).

As discoveries related to ancient scripts were made in the various regions of the Near East, archaeologists hastily and carelessly accredited these regions with the invention of the alphabet. The recent discovery of an alphabetic script on the tomb of king Ahiram of Jbayl convinced most recent authors that Phoenicia and more precisely Jbayl is the place where invention of the letters has taken place.

Other than the few words that survived on some coins, the oldest surviving script, written in Phoenician alphabet was chiselled on a rock on the tomb of king Ahiram of Jbayl. It dates back to the late thirteenth or early twelfth century and reads as follows; "This tomb was built by 'Itu Baal son of Ahiram king of Jbayl for Ahiram his father to be his eternal dwelling.

If a king from among kings, or a governor from among governors, or a general from among generals, after conquering Jbayl, dares to open this grave, the thrown of his kingdom be destroyed and the crown of his kingdom fall,"

If any doubt persists as to the origin of the invention of the alphabet, it is absolutely clear that the Phoenicians taught their letters to the Greeks, the Romans, and to the rest of the known world. If there was any other alphabet, developed in any other part of the world, it must have died in its place of birth, allowing the Phoenician alphabet to become the mother of all known alphabets.

While the Phoenician traders and seafarers of the ancient world carried their alphabet with their goods and deposited both all over the Mediterranean world, Western Europe, and North-West Africa, their cousins, the Arameans moved with it inland into Persia and the Indian subcontinent. Thus the Phoenician alphabet displaced most of the cuneiform script on its way down the Euphrates, into Persia, and penetrated the western frontiers of India, furnishing the Indians with their Sanskrit alphabet.

Many authors recognize the importance of this step and do not speak so much about the invention as about the diffusion of the alphabet. Herodotus is one such author and in one often quotedpassage, he wrote:

These Phoenicians who came with Cadmus...among other kinds of learning, brought into Hellas the alphabet, which had hitherto been unknown, as I think, to the Greeks (11).

Later Greek authors and poets wrote about Cadmus with reverence and gratitude; Nannus, a fifth century A.D. poet states that Byblos must be Cadmus's home;

That must be his home, beside the river of that enchanting Adonis, for that lovely young man came from Lebanos (Lebanon) where Cythereia dances. No, I was wrong! I do not suppose any mortal womb bred Cadmus; no, he is sprung from Zeus and he has concealed his stock (12).

Whether the Phoenicians brought the alphabet to a settlement on mainland Greece, as claimed by Herodotus, or its adaptation took place in one of the communities co-inhabited by both Phoenicians and Greeks, is not historically well established or of great significance.

What is certain and important is that the Greek adaptation of the Phoenician alphabet was almost mechanical with only few minor changes. As soon as the Phoenician alphabet entered into coastal Greece its diffusion through the mainland was rapid and easy.

Early Greek scribes, not familiar with the art of writing, sometimes wrote from right to left, sometimes from left to right, and sometimes both ways in a single text. These scribes at times wrote from the bottom to the top of the page instead of the other way around. To compound the reader's difficulty, they left no spaces between the words. By 403 B.C. when the alphabet was officially adopted by Athens, all these troubling features were eliminated (13).

The similarities between the old Phoenician and modern Greek alphabets are apparent; the order of the letters are basically the same and the names, assigned to most symbols, which have no significance in Greek, are taken from Phoenician words. In the fifth century B.C., the Greek scribes altered the shape of their letters mostly by changing them into their mirror images, thus moving them a step further from the original Phoenician symbols. In general minor changes took place whenever the alphabet was introduced into a new language, but all European alphabets have, to a large extent, preserved the order of the Ugaritic alphabet and the shapes of the Jbayly's characters.

The early Greeks expressed their gratitude to their benefactors by referring to their letters as "phoinikeia" (Phoenician objects), and an inscription unearthed in Crete contains a verb "poiniazein" (to write) and a title "poinikastas" (a scribe).

The vowels, sometimes erroneously referred to as a Greek contribution, were arrived at either by sheer misunderstanding or because some of the Phoenician consonants were not part of the Greek language, and were not needed in it and the Greeks themselves were having difficulty pronouncing them. Thus the Phoenician aspirate or breathy "hah" became the short "e" or epsilon in Greek, the aspirate "heth" became the long "e" or eta, the semi-consonantal "yad" or "yod" became an "i" or iota (14), and the throaty "'ayn" became an "o" or omicron.

By the early seventh century B.C. alphabetic writing became wide spread in Greece, and soon after the alphabet spread into the Mediterranean region, or more precisely wherever Phoenician trading posts were established. The alphabet was soon borrowed from the Greek by their sometimes friends, the Etruscans, who occupied the Northwestern region of Italy. The Romans, expanding their empire, became familiar with the Etruscan alphabet, adopted it to their language and eradicated the Etruscan kingdom and civilization. And with little modification (the Romans added the letters y and z), the Phoenician alphabet became the writing tool of the Roman Empire. Within a thousand years from its development, the Phoenician alphabet spread west to the Phoenician and Carthagenian colonies on the shores of the Atlantic Ocean and east to the Indian subcontinent. The diffusion of the Jbaily alphabet provided the proper tool to fuel one of the greatest cultural explosions, the world has ever known.

The Phoenician alphabet, language, and culture continued to develop as they were transplanted from East to West. During the early period of expansion, the Phoenician script was characterized by broad massive signs, especially on the islands of Malta (15) and Sardinia. But as Carthage rose to power, the Punic (16) script with its slightly curved, elongated characters came into prominence and continued its dominance in the Punic empire until the middle of the second century B.C. It should be noted that various lines of the alphabets evolved leading to modern Arabic, Hebrew, Indian, and Southeast Asian alphabets. But the alphabet used in most European and American languages is the one that the Phoenicians taught to the Greeks and the Etruscans early in the eighth century.

Speculations

There are a few scholars, Cyrus Gordon among them, who believe that the signs of the alphabet originally stood for numbers and were used in a lunar calendar. Thus the words aleph, beit, and gamma (or gimel-camel) also meant one, two, and three, respectively and the ancient scholars, by assigning a simple object to each day of the lunar month, arrived at a system of thirty words (the number of letters in the Ugaritic alphabet) originally used as a calendar and a number system (see Chapter eleven, The Development of Mathematics).

There is no doubt, the letters of the Phoenician alphabet were used to designate numbers. I recall as a youngster studying my Arabic alphabet in Lebanon, that older men in the village-not the young teachers-were trying to teach us the Arabic alphabet in the same order as the Phoenician alphabet, then assigning a number to each letter, and showing us how to add and subtract (17). This system could have been used in the Near East up until the discovery of the Arabic numerals and the decimal system.

Were numerical values assigned to the letters, or the alphabet was originally used as a number system? What sense does it make to call "yod" (hand) ten, "kaff" (palm) twenty, and "lamed" (staff) thirty? These simple objects were chosen because of their association with the simple sounds Y, K, and L. Furthermore, the best known and the best preserved of the Semitic numbers is sabi' or shabi' (seven), and phonetically, it is not remotely related "zayn", the letter that corresponds to seven in the Phoenician alphabet.

There are also those who entertain the possibility that the letters of the alphabet were extracted from ancient zodiacal signs. The orientalist, Hugh Moran, claimed that there are numerous parallels between the symbols of the Phoenician alphabet and those that form an ancient Chinese calendrical zodiac. He further speculated that the zodiac, which was once widely used in the Far East, was invented by the Sumerians, and the Phoenician drew their alphabet from that lunar zodiac.

David Kelley, of the University of Calgary, in Alberta, Canada, expanded on Moran's theory. By comparing symbols of the zodiac-based calendars of the Old World and those of the New World with signs in the Phoenician alphabet, he claimed to have found broad similarities (18). Is it possible that if one looks intently at two sets of thirty symbols, one could always come up with some similarities? Or did the ancient Chinese, or the Phoenician traders establish cultural contacts with the pre-Columbian New World? Lacking any tangible evidence, the answer to this question remains in the realm of speculation .

---

(1). Gordon, C. H. (1965:216).

(2). Martin, Thomas R. (1996:24).

(3) Gordon, C. H. (1966:33)

(4). Zangger, Eberhard, "Who were the Sea People?" Aramco World; Vol. 46, No. 3. May-June, 1995.

(5). Moscati, Sabatino (1965:88).

(6). Glasgow, George (1923:85).

(7). Most of the inscriptions found on the walls of the Sinai mines are prayers.

(8). The Canaanite name Gubla, or Jebel (present day Jbayl), means either a mountain or a foundry of glass ornaments. It was transcribed into Egyptian hieroglyphics as Kpni, Kpn, and Kbn. The Assyrians called the city by its Canaanite name, Gubli. The Merchant of Gubla transported papyrus from Egypt to Greece and the early Greeks named the city after the product, Papyrus, hence the word, "paper". In all his writings, either intentionally or erroneously, Herodotus, in spite of the fact that he visited Phoenicia, called the city Bublos instead of Papyrus. Herodotus designation was later transformed to Byblos, hence the Greek word for "book" (biblos) and the English word for the Scripture, "Bible". [Freyha, Anis (1992:47)].

(9). 'Abbudi, Henry H. (1991:32–37).

(10). Alexander, Pat (1986:39).

(11). Herodotus (V:58). The word Cadmus (Kadmus) has its origin in the Canaanitic word "KDM" (kedem), meaning East. It was first used to denote the edge of the flat land east of the Lebanese Mountains. The Egyptians heard it and subsequently adopted it as a toponym. [Redford, Donald B. (1992:43)]. Greek tradition attributes to Cadmus, not only the teaching of the alphabet, but practically everything they have learned from the East: the building of cities, the use of the plough, the smelting of metal, etc.

(12). Jidejian, Nina (1968:128–129).

(13). de Cruz, Daniel, "Writing from A to Z"; Aramco World; Vol. 17. No. 5, Sept.–Oct. 1966.

(14). Murray, Oswyn (1983:93).

(15). Malta is one of the few Phoenician names, given to a place away from Phoenician mainland, that survived unaltered. Malta means hideout or harbor, and the word is still in use in Lebanon and parts of Syria.

(16). Some scholars believe that the word "Punic" is the Roman corruption of the Greek word Phoenician, and that it was used to degrade the sworn enemies of Rome, the Carthagenians. The word Punic is similar to the Semitic word "FNK" which means (High Living), or (Easy Living). The "P" and the "F" are the same letter in the Phoenician alphabet, and the Semitist Professor Freyha entertains the possibility that "FNK" is the origin of the word Phoenicia. If true, there is nothing degrading about the name "Punic". And as we have seen above, the early Greeks began the word Phoenicia with the letter P rather than Ph.

(17). In the Phoenician order, the Arabic letter corresponding to number eight, appears as eight in the Indian (Later Devanagari) numerical system.

(18). James, Peter and Thorpe, Nick (1994:504).

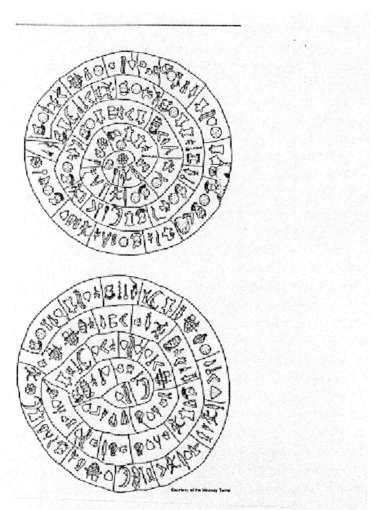

Fig. 3-1. The two sides of the Discos of Phaistos.

THE UGARITIC ALPHABET AND TRANSLITERATION

Symbol	Translit.	Symbol	Translit.
	'a		m
	'e		n
	'u		s
	b		ṯ
	g		‛
	d		ġ
	ḫ		p
	w		ṣ
	z		q
	ḥ		r
	ḫ		ṯ
	ṭ		ẓ
	y		t
	k		ı̇
	l		ı̣

The thirty symbols that constitute the Ugaritic alphabet and their pronunciations. [For further clarification, see Bull. American School of Oriental Research, May 1986, No. 262. p. 3.]

THE DEVELOPMENT OF THE ALPHABET

Phoenician c. 1200 B.C.	Picture represents	Meaning	Greek Character	Greek Name
⋉	alef	ox head	Λ	alpha
𐤁	beit	house	B	beta
𐤂	gamma	throw-stick	Γ	gamma
Δ	daleth	door	Δ	delta
𐤄	hah	window	E	epsilon
Υ	waw	hook		
I	zayn	----	Z	zeta
目	heth	----	H	eta
⊗	teh	----	θ	theta
𐤉	yad or yod	hand	I	iota
⋎	kaff	palm	K	kappa
∠	lamed	staff	Λ	lambda
⋈	mem or myi	water	M	mu
M	nahir	river	N	nu
⧻	samkeh	fish	Ξ	xi
O	'ayn	eye	O	omicron
𐤐	feh or peh	mouth	φ or Π	phi or pe*
ш	sad	---	Σ	sigma*
Φ	quof	----		
𐤓	rosh	head	P	rho*
Ш	shin	tooth		
X	ta	cross	X	chi or tau*
			Υ	upsilon*
			Ψ	psi
			Ω	omega

* The Greek letters are not in their proper order

Chapter Four

The Sanctity of Seven

The sanctity of the number seven is well rooted in Mesopotamian, Canaanite, Hebrew, Arab, Greek, Indian, as well as other ancient cultures. To these early civilizations, the number seven was of great significance: it was frequently used in their prayers, literature, myths, and legends. Although, over the years, the reason for its sanctity and importance was long forgotten, its frequent use endured.

The Semitic word for seven has its roots in the words "sabi'" or "shabi'" which means perfection, completeness, or fullness. Probably this is also the root of the English word "seven" and the words designating the same number in several other Indo-European languages (1).

Later on in Semitic literature the word was used to indicate a very large number, or a very large quantity, and sometimes poetically in junction with seventy or even eighty for added emphasis.

The Semitic word "sabuttu" or "sebittu" (iminbi in Sumerian), meaning a group of seven, was the collective name given to the seven beneficent gods and also to a group of seven demons. According to Babylonian tradition, there was also the group of seven sages (apkallu) who lived before the Babylonian flood (2).

Ancient Mesopotamians associated diseases with harmful demons, and to invoke the seven gods or expel the seven demons, magical incantations had to be repeated seven times. One such incantation reads:

> Seven, they are they seven,
> In the deep they are seven,
> Sitting in heaven they are seven,
>
> Neither male nor female are they,
> Destructive whirlwinds are they,
> They have no wife, they produce no offspring,
> Mercy and pity they know not,
> Prayer and petition they hear not,
> Horses raised in the mountains are they,
> Hostile to Ea are they,
>
> Evil are they, evil are they,
> Seven are they, they are seven, twice seven are they (3).

The Babylonian underworld had seven gates and the heavens were seven in number. Later Chaldaean astronomers divided the world into seven regions, each governed by one of the seven planets, the five naked-eye planets plus the sun and the moon.

In ancient societies, the power of seven influenced daily practices; to be properly attired, a Babylonian maiden should grace her neck with a seven-cylinder necklace; and a The Tel-Amarna inscription states that the pharaoh, to properly propose to a foreign princess, had to propose seven times, and the Egyptian cubit equals seven palms, and there are four fingers to a palm.

The common use of seven was not confined to the Near East nor to ancient times; the seven celestial spheres of Aristotle's astronomy have their origin in Mesopotamian mythology, and also the Ptolemaic seven-climatic scheme according to which the inhabited portion of the earth was divided into seven climatic zones. A similar but more fanciful arrangement is given by the Persian seven-kishvar system which divides the inhabited world into seven circular regions, of which the seventh (containing Persia) is at the center and is completely surrounded by the other six.

The old mystique of the seven still lives; we still use the phrase, "I am in seventh heaven", and the wonders of the world are seven in number. In the Roman Catholic Church, the deadly sins are seven: sloth, lust, anger, pride, envy, gluttony, and greed; and the sacraments are seven and the order of the ministry are also seven.

Although many ideas have been advanced in an effort to explain the reason or reasons for the importance of number seven, the most plausible ones exhibit some connection between deities and heavenly bodies.

Ancient civilizations had great interest in astrology, thus making it a very popular "science" and causing it, along with the mystique of the seven, to spread to may cultures beyond the borders of Mesopotamia, The idea of associating what happens on earth with what exists or takes place in the heavens, and believing that events on earth are controlled by heavenly bodies, or gods who resides in the heavens, has fascinated and captivated the human mind since the dawn of civilization. Over the years, our views of the nature of gods of God have undergone tremendous changes, but we still look up to the heavens as their residence, and we still pray to "Our Father which art in heaven."

One of the prominent concepts, explaining the importance of seven, associates divinities with Pleiades, a cluster of stars in the constellation Taurus. An old Mesopotamian myth equates the "seven beneficent gods" with the stars of Pleiades of which, under good observational conditions, seven may be seen with the naked eye.

The association of the sanctity of the number seven with the seven stars of Pleiades was later re-enforced by a Greek myth according to which the Pleiades were the daughters of Atlas, and the attendants of Diana. When Orion saw them he fell in love with them and pursued them. To avoid being captured by Orion, they prayed to the gods to change their form, and Jupiter, hearing their distress, felt pity and turned them into seven pigeons. He then arranged them into the group of stars known as Pleiades. Probably the Greek astronomers-astrologers were unable to see but six stars in Pleiades. But not willing to tarnish the sanctity of seven, reconciled the difference by stating that the daughters of Atlas were actually seven, and only six stars are visible in Pleiades, for Electra, one of the seven daughters, left her place in the constellation so that she might not behold the destruction of Troy, which was founded by her son, Dardanus (4).

Ancient Arab tradition adds to the mysticism of the seven gods who reside in Pleiades by associating the disappearance of the cluster from the heavens with harmful winds, head cold, and other illnesses (5).

A second and probably a more plausible explanation for the sanctity of seven came about after the discovery of the five naked-eye planets and thus goes back to the dawn of the development of astronomy. The early inhabitants of Mesopotamia were ardent astrologers and astronomers, and were first to identify the five classical planets: Mercury, Venus, Mars, Jupiter, and Saturn. The apparent motion of these planets on the celestial sphere clearly differentiated them from fixed stars. These five celestial bodies, together with the sun and the moon became seven important divinities to the exceedingly religious people of ancient Mesopotamia. The identification of the five planets was a big step in the development of astronomy, and their association with the seven gods certainly strengthened the concepts of astrology.

As the seven-planet-divinity cult spread westward into Canaan and Palestine, it became customary to pray for and chant the praise of one of the seven gods on a given day. And a seven-day cycle of worship was thus established. In time, the name of the god was bestowed of the day of his worship, and the seven day week came into being (6).

The ancient peoples of Canaan and Mesopotamia worshipped their gods in the following order: Shamas or Shapas (the Sun) on Sunday; Nannar of Sin (the Moon) on monday; Nergal, whose planet is Mars, on Tuesday; Ea or Nabu, whose planet is Mercury, on Wednesday; Marduk or Bel (7), whose planet is Jupiter, on Thursday; Ishtar or Belitz, whose plane is Venus, on Friday; and Ninib or Ninurta, whose planet is Saturn, on Saturday (8). Just for convenience, the Babylonians, later, tried to divide each month into six weeks of five days each; but the mysticism of the seven was too powerful to be dislodged by human convenience.

In Mesopotamia, and later in Canaan and Israel, the mystique of the seven transcended the seven-day cycle to encompass a seven-year cycle, and what became a well established seven-year agricultural cycle in Canaan and in Palestine may well have originated in Mesopotamia.

When Ishtar, the Babylonian goddess of love, threatened to open the door of the underworld and cause the dead to rise and eat as the living, her father, the great god Anu, retorted;

101. Anu opened his mouth and said,
102. Speaking to great Ishtar:
103. "If you do what thou desirest of me,
104. There will be seven years of empty straw.
105. Hast thou gathered enough grain for the people?
106. Hast thou gathered enough fodder for the cattle?
107. Ishtar opened her mouth and said,
108. Speaking to Anu, her father,
109. "I have heaped up grain for the people,
110. I have grown fodder for the cattle.
111. It there will be seven years of empty straw,
112. I have gathered enough grain for the people,
113. And I have grown enough fodder for the cattle."
(The Gilgamesh Epic, Tablet I)

This exchange between Ishtar and Anu could be the origin of the narrative of the seven years of plenty and the seven years of famine that befell the land of Egypt (Gen. Chap. 14). It could also be the prelude for the seven-year agricultural cycle later adopted by the Canaanites and the Israelites.

The Ugaritic literature clearly describes the Canaanite's seven-year agricultural cycle as a duel between Baal, the valiant god of weather and fertility and his brother, Mot, the god of death, drought, and sterility. Mot is dethroned but re-emerges in the "seventh year" to challenge Baal again. When Baal loses and Mot kills his brother, their sister Anath comes to the rescue and avenges the death of her good brother. Here the text provides a most graphic description of the battle in which Anath, the Canaanite goddess of love and war, cleaves Mot with a blade,

> She (Anath) seized El's son, Mot.
> With a sword she sliced him;
> With a sieve she winnowed him;
> With a fire she burned him;
> In the field she scattered him
> So the birds may eat his remains.

By scattering Mot's remains in the field for the birds to eat, Anath denies him a burial. To the canaanites, this was considered the ultimate punishment fit for the god of sterility. The duel between the two brothers and their death and subsequent resurrection provided the mythical reasoning behind the seven-year agricultural cycle in Canaan. It is also a continuation of the fight between Good and Evil.

This septennial ritual was later adopted by the Hebrews who created an artificial situation to satisfy or exhaust the power of sterility; during the sabbatical year, they left their land fallow, giving evil powers free rein to exhaust or satisfy themselves so they might leave the Hebrew farmers to enjoy a six-year cycle of plenty.

Thus the religious and the agricultural septennial cycle found in the Old Testament was a regional cultural concept that the Hebrews adopted from the older cultural of the Canaanites, who in turn may have adopted it from the people of Mesopotamia (9).

With the advent of monotheism, the Hebrews began to worship a god whose power transcend the powers of the seven planetary gods, but they were unable to rid themselves of the underlying symbolism of the seven. In the Hebrew tradition, the seven powers are still represented in the seven-branched menorah, in the seven Sounding Shofrot (horns) played during the Rosh Hashana Rituals, in the seven pillars of Wisdom (Prov. 9:1), and in the seven gifts of the holy ghost: wisdom, understanding, council, fortitude, knowledge, piety, and the fear of the Lord (Isaiah 11, 2). In the Old Testament, the number seven appears some 400 times, and seventh about one hundred times, while six appears 173 times and eight shows up only 53 times (10). In Revelation Chapter 13, number six represents imperfection, falling short of the perfect number seven; "…count the number of the beast; for it is the number of man; and his number is six hundred three score and six." Rev. 13:18. The number 666 is thus a triple or superlative form of evil.

Traces of the frequent use of seven are also found in the New testament; There are seven wicked spirits (Mat. 12:45), and when Peter asked, "How oft shall my brother sin against me and I forgive him? Till seven times? Jesus saith unto him, I say not unto thee, until seven times, but until seventy times seven" (Mat. 18:21,22). Also the Hellenistic men of good repute were seven (Acts 6:2,3), and the golden candlesticks were seven (Rev. 1:12). Revelation 3:1 speaks of "the seven Spirits of God, and the seven stars;" and Revelation 15:1 recalls the sight of "great and marvelous seven angels having the seven last plagues."

Many early christian thinkers tried to reconcile between astrology and christian doctrine stating that the soul is the creation of the seven planets, or the soul is "from the Seven".

In Canaan, the mystique of the seven did not remain confined to the seven-day of the seven-year cycle, but transcended these limits to practically dominate the Canaanite's way of life. It shaped their culture, literature, mythology, and the way they ran their daily affairs and the affairs of the state.

Recent excavations of the royal library of Ebla, in northern present-day Syria, have uncovered tablets dating to the middle of the third millennium B.C. The texts of some of these tablets are documents that attest to the dominant influence of number seven, not only on the running affairs of the kingdom but also on the daily life of the citizens. The texts of these tablets state that the people of Ebla had adopted a lunar calendar which was a monthly account with a repetitive cycle that extends over a seven-year period, and that they "elected" their king at the beginning of each cycle (11).

As a reflection on the Mesopotamian "seven beneficent gods" and their relation to the seven stars of Pleiades, the Ugaritic texts relates how El, the head of the Ugaritic pantheon, sired the seven good gods upon two human wives. To the people of Ugarit, those seven good gods came to symbolize the seven-year cycle of plenty.

> "O sons I have begotten!
> Lift up, make preparations
> In the midst of the wilderness of Kadesh (12)
> There you would be clients
> Of the stones, and of the trees,
> Seven complete years
> Yea eight cycles" (13).

The Ugaritic texts further demonstrate that, at the death of a hero, there was a seven-year mourning period,

> From days to months,
> From months to years,
> Until the seventh year,
> He weeps for Aqhat, the hero,
> He sheds tears for the child of Da'el (Daniel), Man of Rp'.

In seven years, Da'el, Man of Rp' declares,

...

"Depart, weeping women, from my palace,
  Wailing women, form my court Pzgm Gr! (14).

Likewise, when a grave injustice, or a serious crime, is committed, and the god curses the land, his incantation covers a seven-year period,

Seven years may Baal afflicts thee,
Eight, the Rider of the Clouds!
Let there be no dew.
Let there be no rain.
Let there be no surging of the two deeps (15).

And the seven invaded the world of music of ancient Ugarit. A clay tablet, uncovered in Ugarit in the early 1950's and dates back to around 1400 B. C. was found to be a hymn accompanied by musical notations. This hymn was composed of harmonics, and was not a simple melody of single notes. In describing the find, the eminent musicologist Richard Croker said it is "The oldest 'sheet music' known to exist." What is fascinating about the highly praised hymn is that it is constructed in a seven-note scale, just like modern day musical scale (do, re, mi,...) (16).

From the Near East, the mysticism and the sanctity of the seven spread into Indo-European countries, and many of its features became culturally dominant worldwide. According to Indian mythology, the heaven, where Vishu reigns, is made up of gold and its palaces of precious stones, and from it the crystal waters of the sacred river Ganges fall down to earth. To prevent the immense water from completely drowning the earth, the water of the sacred river falls on the head of Druva, the protective god, and splits into seven Rishis (watercourses) allowing them to make their way to the sea (17).

Greek astrologers became aware of the divine powers bestowed on the seven planets by their neighbors to the East, and not to be outdone, they awarded the seven planets to their deities. Helius acquired the Sun, Slene the Moon, Ares acquired Mars, Hermes or Apollo acquired Mercury, Zeus dislodged the Babylonian supreme god Marduk and acquired Jupiter, Aphrodite replaced Ishtar as the goddess of love and acquired the planet Venus, and Cronus acquired Saturn.

As the Romans followed in the footsteps of the Greeks, and extended their empire eastward, they came in contact with Near Eastern and Greek astrology, and gave Latin names to the seven powers of the week. In certain cases they gave additional meanings and functions. The Sun became the symbol of illumination and the first day of the week was given the name Dies Solis (Day of the Sun). When Christianity became the religion of the Roman Empire, Dies Solis became Dies Dominicus (Day of the Lord). But Christianity was unable to dislodge the remaining powers: the Moon became a symbol of enchantment, but retained the second day of the week, Dies Lunae; and Mars, the Roman god of fertility and later of war, became a symbol of growth and the third day of the week was named Dies Martis; and the protector of business and businessmen, Mercury, became a god of wisdom and his name was bestowed on the fourth day of the week, Dies Mercurii; this was followed by Dies Jovis (Day of Jupiter), Jovis-Pater (Father of Light) became the symbol of law. She is the goddess of love whether you call her Freya (18), Inana (19), Ishtar, Aphrodite, or Venus, and the Romans bestowed her name, Dies Veneris, on the sixth day of the week. Dies Saturni, the last day of the week was named after the planet Saturn, the symbol of peace (20).

These Latin equivalent to the Babylonian names still designate the days of the week in all Romance languages, and with some modification in many others.

The following table shows how the modern European names of the days of the week were derived from the Ancient Babylonian names of the planets-gods.

Planet Ancient Days-Gods Modern Names

	Babylonian	Roman	Anglo-Saxon	Italian	French	English
Sun	Shamas	Sol	Sun	Domenica	Dimonche	Sunday
Moon	Sin	Luna	Moon	Lunedi	Lundi	Monday
Mars	Nergal	Mars	Tiw	Martedi	Mardi	Tuesday
Mercury	Nabu	Mercurius	Woden	Mercoledi	Mercredi	Wednesday
Jupiter	Marduk	Jove	Thor	Giovedi	Jeudi	Thursday
Venus	Ishtar	Venus	Freya	Venerdi	Vendredi	Friday
Saturn	Ninurta	Saturnus	Saturn	Sabato	Samedi	Saturday

In spite of its mathematical inconvenience, the Mesopotamian-Canaanite seven-day week has been adopted worldwide. Owing to the power of the myth associated with the seven heavenly bodies, it dislodged the more functional ten-day week from the Egyptian solar calendar, and the five-day week from the Babylonian calendar. With some modification, the ancient Sumerian-Egyptian calendar, and the seven-day week, are the basis of the modern Western calendar (21).

The mysticism and the sanctity of seven are further illustrated by its frequent use in ancient literature; important dates and events are often associated with number seven. We have already stated that seven is commonly used in the Canaanitic literature of Ebla and Ugarit, and it appears some thirty times in the Gilgamesh Epic, while six appears half as often, and eight only a few times.

At the conclusion of the flood story, as narrated in the Gilgamesh Epic, Utnapishtim, the hero of the Babylonian flood, offers sacrifices to the gods,

The following table shows how the modern European names of the days of the week were derived from the Ancient Babylonian names of the planets-gods.

Planet Ancient Days-Gods Modern Names

Babylonian	Roman	Anglo-Saxon	Italian	French	English
Sun	Shamas	Sol	Sun	Domenica Dimonche	Sunday
Moon	Sin	Luna	Moon	Lunedi Lundi	Monday
Mars	Nergal	Mars	Tiw	Martedi Mardi	Tuesday
Mercury	Nabu	Mercurius	Woden	Mercoledi Mercredi	Wednesday
Jupiter Marduk	Jove	Thor	Giovedi	Jeudi	Thursday
Venus	Ishtar	Venus	Freya	Venerdi Vendredi	Friday
Sarurn	Ninurta	Saturnus Saturn	Sabato	Samedi	Saturday

In spite of its mathematical inconvenience, the Mesopotamian-Canaanite seven-day week has been adopted worldwide. Owing to the power of the myth associated with the seven heavenly bodies, it dislodged the more functional ten-day week from the Egyptian solar calendar, and the five-day week from the Babylonian calendar. With some modification, the ancient Sumerian-Egyptian calendar, and the seven-day week, are the basis of the modern Western calendar (21).

The mysticism and the sanctity of seven are further illustrated by its frequent use in ancient literature; important dates and events are often associated with number seven. We have already stated that seven is commonly used in the Canaanitic literature of Ebla and Ugarit, and it appears some thirty times in the Gilgamesh Epic, while six appears half as often, and eight only a few times.

At the conclusion of the flood story, as narrated in the Gilgamesh Epic, Utnapishtim, the hero of the Babylonian flood, offers sacrifices to the gods,

...I poured libations,
I set sacrifices on the mountain peak,
I fixed twice seven sacrificial vessels.

Using the expression "twice seven" instead of "fourteen" demonstrates the importance of seven in an impressive way.

The Babylonian Epic of creation is narrated in seven tablets, and Marduk, the supreme god of babylon, in the traditional fight of Good versus Evil, created the seven winds to help him defeat the powerful forces of Tiamat, the evil goddess.

The seven also invaded early Greek literature; the tribute that the Athenians were forced to pay every year to Minos, the legendary king of Crete, was seven youth and seven maidens, who were devoured by the minotaur. Also in Greeks ritual contexts, as in Babylonian tradition, "dis hepta" (twice seven) often replaces fourteen (22). Number seven was also sacred to Apollo and to Dionysos, and held a conspicuous place in the teaching of Pythagoras, who provided it many distinctive apprehension.

There is also the "Seven Sages of Greece" or the "Seven Wise Men of Greece": Solon of Athens, Thales of Miletus, Pittacus of Mitylene, Bias of Priene, Chilon of Sparta, Cleobulus of Lindus, and Periander of Corinth; they lived between 620 and 548 B.C.

In the early narration of the conflict between Good and Evil, the Evil power was usually represented by a seven-headed monster. The seven heads represent strength, and in order to defeat a seven-headed creature, Good must be exceedingly powerful.

Legends narrating such conflicts are common in Near Eastern literature, mythology, and religion. One of the earliest is a cylinder seal unearthed in Mesopotamia and dates back to the twenty-second century B.C. (23). The seat impression clearly shows two horned gods engaged in a fight with the seven-headed creature while men watch. Four of the seven heads are dead and hanging low while the remaining three are still fighting. The body of the creature has caught fire, and the outcome of the battle is no longer in doubt. The good gods shall kill the evil monster.

This old Mesopotamian legend gained popularity and was retold by the Canaanites, the Hebrews, the Greeks, and the Indians among others. In most versions, the all-important seven is retained, but the credit for destroying the evil monster is invariably given to the god of the people narrating the story.

From Mesopotamia, the legend moved to Canaan, where Baal, the valiant god of fertility, smite lotan, the seven-headed serpent. In a tablet uncovered in Ugarit, Anath, in a prelude to Baal's resurrection, addresses him, saying,

> Because thou didst smite lotan, the evil serpent;
> Didst destroy the crooked serpent,
> The mighty one of seven heads...

in a similar episode, the Lord of Israel "brakest the head of Leviathan (24) in pieces" (Psa. 74:13). And "A beast rises out of the sea, heaving seven heads and ten horns" (Rev. 13:1) (25).

The legend moved East as well as West. The people of the Indus basin knew about it from their early contact with the Sumerians. And according to an Indian narration written almost a millennium after the Sumerian version, a seven-headed dragon came out of a and was killed by the Indian god, Krishna.

The Ancient Greeks were most probably introduced to the myth of the seven-headed dragon through their contact with the people of Canaan. This myth was in existence when the Greeks were still in a primitive state, and before they set foot in Greece. According to Greek tradition, Hercules was compelled to perform a succession of twelve desperate adventures that became known as the "Twelve labors of Hercules." In the second of these adventures, Hercules had to kill the multi-headed Hydra that dwelt in a swamp and ravaged the land of

Argos. To destroy the creature, the hero began to knock off its heads with his club, but every time he severed a head, two new ones grew forth in its place. Finally, with the help of his servant Iolaus, he destroyed the Hydra by fire (26). Thus, the Greek Hydra, like the Sumerian monster was consumed by fire.

In literature there is the famous Christian legend of the "Seven Sleepers" and the tales of the "Seven Wise Masters". The latter was introduced to the West from the Orient through the Crusades. Since then, this collection has been translated into almost all Western languages.

From our more recent literature we mention the "Seven Lamps of Architecture" by John Ruskin, published in 1847, and the "Seven Seas" by Rudyard Kipling, published in 1896.

Centuries of varied cultures reduced the power and the significance of the seven, but were unable to completely eradicate its use; we still rise into the seventh heaven and believe that a broken mirror signals seven years of bad luck. And in the age of air travel, we still sail the seven seas.

In the Middle East, in anticipation of abundant spring rains, farmers often say, "March, the thunderer, brings seven great snow storms." And to describe one who has no regard for law and order, they say, "He devours the seven and its holiness." Farmers in Southern Arabia believe that seeds planted at the rising of the seventh star of Ursae Majores produce better crop.

Other Sacred Numbers

In addition to the seven, Middle Eastern tradition shrouded four numbers with some mysticism: they are the three, the four, the twelve, and the sixty.

The Sumerians, in a effort to establish order in their religious hierarchy, assigned numbers to their prominent gods. Thus Anu, the god of Heaven, was allotted number sixty; his son Enlil, the warrior, the number fifty; Enki, the wisest among the gods, was assigned forty; and the Moon god, Nanar or Sin was assigned thirty. In time these numbers became sacred and temples were built for the numbers as well as for the gods.

Sixty also became the basis of the Sumerian numerical system; they used sixty the same way ten is used to day. The Sumerian unit of weight, the talent was set equal to sixty minas, and the mina was set equal to sixty shekels. This system dominated the Near East for thousands of years. With the discovery of silver during the Assyrian period, the precious metal replaced grains in making business transactions, and the Sumerians units of weight passed through Asia Minor to the Ionions, who, in turn, passed them to the Aegean and mainland Greece. The Athenians divided the mina of silver into 100 drachmas (handful) and spread its use in most of Europe. It still survives as the franc in France, the lira in Italy, and the krone in Austria.

By about 3000 B.C. the Sumerians put forth the earliest calendar of which we have a written evidence. It was regulated by lunar observation, and according to which the year was divided into twelve months of twenty-nine or thirty days each. To correct for accumulated difference between the lunar and the seasonal year, they simply added a month-an intercalary month-every few years or whenever they felt it was needed.

In the twenty-first century B.C., during their renaissance period, the Sumerians regulated their old calendar by rounding off each lunar month to thirty days, and introducing what they called a national year of 360 days. This new calendar, although five days shorter than the seasonal year, fits well into the Sumerian sexagismal mathematical system, as 360 is neatly divisible by 60. A unit for measuring arcs was later devised, and the sky and all geometrical circles may be divided into 360 such unit that we now call degree. This innovative approach strengthened the Sumerian sexagismal system as it linked their calendar to their astrological and astronomical systems.

The Mesopotamian civilizations that followed adopted the use of the sexagismal system, and it is still in use, the world over, at the present time.

The significance of the three has its origin in Babylonian mythology, according to which the world was divided into three superimposed regions, or layers, designated as heaven, earth, and the underworld. Also the world eastern horizon was divided into three bands, the ways of the three gods, Anu, Enlil, and Enki. Thus, the concept of a triad became a part of the Babylonian religious practices to be later adopted by other Near Eastern religions, and number "three" acquired special meaning.

Early in the first millennium B.C. the concept of a triad was introduced into Canaan, resulting in the restructuring of the pantheons of most Canaanite cities. These restructured pantheons almost always included a triad made up of a supreme god, guardian of the city, a mother goddess, and a young god who annually dies and gets resurrected. With some modification, this concept was later adopted into Greek mythology (see ADONI HAS RISEN), and in Christian teachings where the trinity is viewed as one of the foundation of the Christian faith.

As a result of early Sumerian mythology, number four also acquired a special meaning. The ancient Sumerians viewed the earth as a rectangle with its corners pointing in the directions of the four winds, the south, the north, the east and the west wind. The ancient Egyptians also viewed the world as a great rectangular box, with the earth as its bottom and the sky stretches over it as a cover. The sky is supported by four exceedingly high mountain peaks, one at each corner (27).

If the earth has four corners, then four must be a special number, and in the eighth century B.C. Babylonian astronomers divided the zodiacal belt into four segments. In addition to all his inherited titles, King Shulgi (c. 2093–2064 B.C.), the son of Ur-Nammu, the founder of the third dynasty of Ur, acquired the title of king of the four corners of the world. Later such a title was adopted by the kings of Assyria, who became known as the kings of the four quarters of the world.

The four acquired a place of eminence when Hippocrates advanced the concept that the human body is composed of four liquids or humors: blood, phlegm, black bile, and yellow bile. A balance of the four humors is good humor, that is good health. This view was extended to describe the inanimate world as being composed of four elements: earth, air, fire, and water, having the distinctive qualities: hot, cold, wet, and dry.

In time the classical Greeks added the four ages of man, the four mental states (temperaments), and the four seasons (28).

Running a distant second to number seven, but more important than either three or four, is number twelve, whose mysticism is also associated with heavenly bodies. The ancient Mesopotamians , for astrological purposes, drew an imaginary belt in the heavens and divided it into twelve segments or constellations. They assigned a sign to each constellation and came up with the twelve signs of the zodiac. These signs had their roots in the Sumerians astronomy, and led both the Sumerians and later the Egyptians to divided the year into twelve equal periods in the formulation of their calendar.

For designing the time of the day or night, Mesopotamians cuneiform texts indicate that a homogenous time-scale evolved, in which the period from sunset to sunset was divided into twelve equal units called "beru" (danna in Sumerian). As this unit of time is almost equivalent to two of our hours, the word "beru" is usually translated as "double hour".

The idea of applying number twelve in designating the time of the day entered into Egypt early in the second millennium, when the Egyptians built the "merkhet", probably the world first solar wooden clock (sun dial). This clock, now in the Berlin Museum, consists of a across mounted at the end of a long plank. In the morning the clock was oriented so that the shadow of the cross beam fell on the marked long plank to give the first six hours from sunrise until noon, when the wooden clock had to be turned to measure the remaining six hours of the day. Thus the period from from sunrise to sun set was divided twelve equal hours regardless of the duration of daylight. An "hour", being one twelfth of the period between sunrise and sunset, varied in length over the course of the year. These "hours" are now referred to as "seasonal hours".

The Egyptians also devised a water-clock, a container shaped like a truncated cone, which allowed the water to escape through a small hole in its base. The interior of the cone is marked to show the elapsed time on the basis of the quantity of water that escaped. The Egyptian water-clock is the forerunner of the Greek clepsydra used during the Hellenistic period, when Greek scientists combined the Egyptian "seasonal hours" and the Babylonian reckoning of time to produce the 24 equal hours used today (29).

The association of sixty and twelve with the measurement of time led to dividing the year into twelve months, the day into twelve "double hours", and each hour into sixty minutes, and each minute into sixty seconds. Reminiscent of the power of twelve are the watches and clocks that run from one to twelve instead of the more convenient one to twenty-four.

The significance of number twelve is further demonstrated in its association with the tribes of Israel, the disciples of Christ, and the common use of the words dozen and dozens. Let us not forget that American courts require exactly twelve jurors to reach a verdict, and of course there is the "twelve labors of Hercules" that many historians associate with Samson's exploits.

In reality such stories may be found in the literature of many cultures, but they are exceedingly common in Near Eastern mythologies, especially the Sumerian. Going back to the early Sumerain period, one finds the myth of the "Slain Heroes", which credit the god warrior Ningisru or Ninurta for killing a bizarre group of monsters. Among

Ninurta's victims, the myth mentions the six-headed Wild Ram, the seven-headed Snake, the Dragon, the Palm-tree King, the Gypsum, the Strong Copper, the Kuli-ana, the Magillum-boat, Lord Saman-ana, the Bison-bull, and the Imdugud-bird. Some of these so called monsters were in reality minors deities.

In time, other trophies were added to the list of slain heroes, and other deities were accorded the honors of being the monsters' killers. Among the Mesopotamian gods accredited with such achievements, the legend mentions Zababa, Lugalbanda, Nergal, Marduk, and Nabu (30).

Greek mythology, like that of ancient Mesopotamia, is saturated with such fables. Practically every Greek hero, god, or man slew his dragon. Of course Hercules and Persus stand out for being the most renown Greek dragon killers (31).

---

(1). Waddle, L. A. (1983:241).

(2). Black and Green (1992:145, 162).

(3). Jastrow, Morris, Jr. (1915:243).

(4). Bulfinch. (1979:206).

(5). Varisco, Daniel. (1944:97).

(6). Breasted, James H. (1935:211,212).

(7). Marduk, the supreme god of Babylon, to demonstrate all his powers, was given fifty names. Bel is one of them.

(8). Many different theories have been advanced in an effort to explain the history that led to the importance of number seven. Although associating seven heavenly bodies with seven gods could be the starting point, other advances have strengthened the myth.

(9). Gordon, Cyrus. (1966:21).

(10). Ellison. (1984).

(11). Pettinato, Giovanni. (1981:71,72).

(12). In many Semitic dialects, the word Kadesh (QDSH) means sacred. Kadesh or Kadesh Barnea is a wilderness on the southern border of Judah. There is also a valley in northern Mount Lebanon called "Wadi Qadisha", and there was an ancient but important city, by that name in central Syria. The Arabs refer to Jerusalem as "al-Quds" (the Holy City).

(13). The "eight" is introduced for added emphasis.

(14). These verses were extracted from the legend of Dn'el (El is my judge, or the judgement of El), which was uncovered in Ugarit and dates back to the fourteenth century B.C.

(15). This curse is repeated in the Old Testament (2 Sam. 1:21), where as a result of poor translation, the phrase, "No surging of the Two Deeps" is replaced by "Nor fields of offerings".

(16). Kilmer, A. D.; Brown, R. R.; and Crockerm R. I. (1986:37).

(17). New Larouse Encyclopedia of Mythology, p. 378.

(18). Freya is the Norse goddess of love and beauty, hence the sixth day of the week, Friday.

(19). Inana is the Sumerian most important female deity. She was replaced by Ishtar during the Babylonian period.

(20). Freyha, Anis. (1991:117).

(21). Late in the fifth millennium B.C. the ancient Egyptian formulated their calendar, dividing the year into twelve thirty-day months plus a five year-end, feast days. Each month was then divided into three ten-day weeks. [Al-Andalusi (1991:95)].

(22). See for example Herodotus I:86. Also note the similarity between the Semitic word "sabittu" and the Greek word "hepta".

(23). Gordon, Cyrus. (1957:84,85).

(24). Lotan, the Canaanite name given to the evil creature is the Latinized Hebrew Leviathan.

(25). Note that the horns, the symbol of divinity in ancient Mesopotamia and Canaan, appear on the heads of evil monsters and devils in Christian-dominated literature.

(26). Bulfinch, Thomas. (1979:144).

(27). Selin, Helaine. (1997:112).

(28). The Egyptians divided the year into three seasons of four months each; first Akhnet (Flood of Inundation), coinciding with the overflow of the Nile, second was Peret (Emergence or planting), and third was Shomu (Harvest).

(29). Rochberg-Halton, Francesca, "Babylonian Seasonal Hours" in Centaurus 1989: Vol. 32: pp. 146-170.

(30). Black, Jeremy and Green, Anthony. (1992:164,165).

(31). Kramer, Samuel Noah. (1961:77).>

Fig. 4-1. A cylinder seal showing two gods fighting a seven-headed monster. Four heads are dead and three are still fighting. Mesopotamia (c. 2000 B.C.).

Chapter Five

Adoni Has Risen

In the temperate and tropical zones, the decay of vegetation in summer and their subsequent revival in the spring presented to the early dwellers of these regions a manifestation of death and resurrection. A grain of wheat, corn, or barley, buried in the ground, sprouts and bears a couple of dozens similar grains. Imagine the power residing in the darkness of the earth that causes such a miracle. Only a god could have such power and the ability to repeat this great feat year after year. This god must also have the capability to undergo similar transformation; he should be able to die and subsequently get resurrected.

Mimicking what happens in nature to ensure its continuity was an accepted and a prevailing principle in ancient religions and mythologies. It was used as a sort of sympathetic magic. A god, king, or priest sprinkles water from the top of a hill to bring about rain, or lights a fire to make sunshine; planting seeds in pots or plates and watering them so that they sprout early in the Spring helps the god of vegetation to rise from the underworld and the vegetation to grow; and baking and eating enliven bread indicates haste and eagerness, and causes the crops to mature and ripen early.

Such a benevolent god should be worshipped and offered sacrifices. People should wail and lament his death and rejoice and celebrate his rebirth. Several primitive societies could have independently worshipped such a god and celebrated his yearly resurrection.

The Sumerian formed one such early society and they wove the threads of their legend around their eternally youthful god Damuzi, or Damuzi Apsu (1) (the son who gets resurrected, or the faithful son of Apsu). Damuzi falls in love with his sister Inana, the great goddess with ultimate power:

> The gods of the Land [Sumer] assemble before her.
> The great Anunna [major gods] do reverence to her.
> My Lady [Inana] pronounced the judgement of the Land
> in their presence (2).

Damuzi, the god of vegetation, dies in the heat of summer, but every spring, Inana comes down from Heaven, descends into the underworld and brings him back to life. Funeral services were held for him every summer and his return was joyously celebrated in the spring. To bring about his rebirth, the Sumerians planted seeds in shallow containers, watered them, and watched them grow. The old legend thus explained one of the great wonders of nature on the basis of the true love shared by a goddess and a god, Inana and Damuzi.

The Semite tribes that infiltrated the land of Sumer adopted the Sumerian Legend; Damuzi became Tammuz or Thammuz and Inana became Ishtar, the virgin goddess. The name Tammuz was bestowed on the month of July in which Tammuz dies, and Ishtar in time became so powerful that her name came to mean goddess. In the Sumerian legend, Inana is the sister of Damuzi, but in the Babylonian legend, Ishtar plays varied roles; to Tammuz she is a sister, a wife, an ever-verging wife, and in certain prayers, she plays the duel role of a mother and a wife.

But as in the Sumerian legend, Tammuz dies in the heat of summer and the Babylonians, and later, the people of the entire Near East lamented and wailed his death. When Ishtar tried to seduce Gilgamesh, he repudiated her saying,

46. For Tammuz, thy youthful husband
47. Thou hast decreed wailing year after year (3).

With the establishment of their empire, the Babylonians assimilated the functions of Tammuz into their national supreme god Marduk, and they celebrated his death in the month of July and his resurrection in April, just as the Sumerians had done for Damuzi before them.

The Legend moved west into the land of Canaan, and the Canaanites also celebrated the resurrection and mourned the death of Tammuz. When the Hebrews entered the land of Canaan, around 1200 B.C. they came in contact with the Canaanites and worshipped Canaanite gods, and like the Canaanites, they wailed the death of the youthful Tammuz;

Then he brought me to the door of the gate of the
Lord's house which was toward the north; and behold
there sat women weeping for Tammuz.
(Ezek. 8:14)

In other parts of Canaan, the legend acquired varied versions; In Ugarit the legends of the god of vegetation and that of the conflict between Good and Evil were blended together. In the heat of summer, Mot, the god of death, drought, and sterility kills valiant Baal, the god of vegetation. Each spring Baal's sister and consort Anath kills Mot, resurrects Baal and he causes rains to fall and vegetation to grow. The function of Baal is well described in Ugaritic texts;

Moreover Baal will send abundance of his rain,
Abundance of moisture and snow,

And he will send forth his voice in the clouds,.
His flashing to the earth in lightning.

In Canaan the ceremonies for the death and subsequent resurrection of the god of vegetation reached its culmination in the city of Jbayl (Byblos). Here the legend speaks of a king, named Qanur (4) (the Greek Cinyras), who, while intoxicated, impregnated his daughter Murrah (Myrrh). In another version, the goddess Asherah made Murrah fall in love with her father and he impregnated her. When the king realized that his daughter was with child, he threatened to kill her. Murrah ran away from her father's palace praying for Asherah or Astarte (the Babylonian Ishtar) and asking her for protection. The Mother Goddess, also known as Baalat Jbayl (Lady of Jbayl), moved by Murrah's lament and predicament, protected her by turning her into a myrrh-tree. The incense from this tree was and still is burned during religious ceremonies.

After a ten months' gestation period (not nine), the bark of the myrrh-tree split open, or exploded, allowing the lovely infant to be born. In another version a wild boar rent the bark of the myrrh-tree with its tusk assisting the adorable infant to come forth (5). Adoni (my lord) (6), the perfect, eternally youthful god, was born.

When the Mother Goddess Asherah saw the beautiful infant, she fell in love with him, hid him in a box, and descended with him to the underworld. Asherah gave the box to Allatu or Allat, the goddess of the underworld. When Allatu opened the box, and saw the beauty of Adoni, she fell in love with him also, and refused to give him back to Asherah. As the two goddesses were unable to reach an agreement as to the fate of Adoni, they resorted to the god of Heavens for advice, and asked him to decide the fate of the lovely infant. The supreme god declared that Adoni should live four months with Asherah in the upper-world, four months with Allatu in the underworld, and during the remaining four months of each year, he would be free to live wherever he pleases.

In another version, it was decreed that Adoni spends half the year in the underworld and the other half in the upper-world. In either case, Adoni represents vegetation (7) which lies buried in the darkness of the earth for about half the year-Autumn and Winter-and above ground the other half (8).

The legend of Adoni ends in a tragedy; while hunting on Mount Lebanon, the youthful god shot an arrow wounding a wild boar. The enraged animal attacked Adoni and killed him.

From Adoni's blood sprung the red anemone. The name of the flower is most probably derived from the word "Na'man" (darling) an epithet of Adoni. This flower, which blooms in Lebanon in the spring and more precisely around Easter (9), is known by its Arabic name "shaq 'iq al-Na'man" (wounds of the darling). Probably to add more romance to the legend, some scholars suggested that the anemone sprung from the blood of Asherah, who was running bare-footed in the wilderness of Mount Lebanon searching for her mortally wounded lover. The name of the flower certainly points to the wounds of Adoni and not Asherah.

According to a variety of sources, the death of Adoni was celebrated in Byblos in the spring. The iron rich reddish soil, washed down from the freshly plowed fertile fields on the banks of the sacred river, colors its water and the water of the sea crimson red. The blood of Adoni, annually wounded to death by the wild boar, runs down the river of Adoni-renamed Nahr Ibrahim.

Every year, the women of Byblos and surrounding areas prepared an effigy in the form of Adoni and carried it toward the sea. They also carried with them pots and dishes in which various kinds of vegetation have been grown. This was the annual mourning of the death of the beloved youthful god. They walked barefooted, weeping, wailing, chanting, sprinkling ashes on their head, and beating their heads and breasts until blood ran out (10). Their long march ended with the day at the sea shore, where after a solemn prayer, they committed the effigy and the planters to the sea and returned.

The next day those same women donning their best and most colorful garments, wearing heavy makeup, and laden with perfumes walked up the river. Young men, who hardly if ever participated in the funeral services held the previous day, joined the march that led to the cave of 'Ufqa (or Afqa) (spring in Aramaic), the source of the sacred river. From the sea shore to the sacred temple of Asherah and Adoni is some thirty kilometers, a good day's march for young men and women driven by the spirit of the rising god, and the reverie of the pleasure and joy awaiting them upon reaching the temple located in the pine forest that surrounds the source of the sacred the river.

Zosimus, a pagan author contemporary with Constantine the Great (A.D. 288–337), visited the temple and wrote;

> There is a site called Afka, between Byblos and Heliopolis (Baalbek)

where stands a temple of Aphrodite. Near the temple is a pool, which resembles a hand-made cistern. In the neighborhood of this temple and the surrounding place, a light shows itself in the air resembling a ball of fire when meetings are held on that place on prescribed times. It showed itself even in our time (11).

Thus, in the darkness of the night, the priests illuminated and opened the tomb of Adoni, and declared that the youthful god had risen from the dead. Then they touched the lips of the worshippers with balm and informed them that some day they, too, would rise form the grave (12). Thus without fail and in the presence of his worshippers, Adoni rose from the darkness of the grave and ascended the Heavens. This was the time for fun and jubilation; the beloved, youthful, and most beautiful of all the gods has risen from the dark confine of the earth. Adoni has risen, and this called for joyous celebrations, and they did celebrate; there was dancing, singing, drinking, shouting, screaming, and above all sacred prostitution. This last activity was not only an offering to please the god, but was also designed to encourage the productive process of nature, and to suggest to mother earth to give more abundant crops; it is a representation of sympathetic magic and an adaptation of the fertility cult.

Asherah, the Mother Goddess and the Tree of Life, was worshipped throughout the land of Canaan, and the festivities surrounding the death and subsequent resurrection of Adoni, although not with the same opulence as those at 'Ufqa, were celebrated in many communities across the land, and the legend of Adoni was immortalized in the verses of poets, from the local Phoenicians to the Greek Theocritus and Panyasis (5th century B.C.), the Latin poet Ovid (43 B.C–A.D.18), and the English Shelley, Milton, and Shakespeare.

Most Canaanite cities had a pantheon that includes a triad of deities, composed of a supreme god, a protective of the city; a mother goddess, his wife or consort; and a young god, related to the goddess as her son or lover, and whose yearly death and resurrection explains the annual cycle of vegetation.

In a broad sense and with some variations in details, the triad concept was adopted in Greek mythology; the supreme god was given the name Kronos or Zeus, the Mother Goddess became Aphrodite, and the young god, when not called Adonis, was given the name Dionysus, Heracles or Asklepios. When Greece became the dominant power in Phoenicia and the Middle East, ceremonies, similar to those held in Byblos for Adoni, were held for Asklepios on the 'Awwali River, near the Phoenician city of Sidon.

The river of Adoni, the shortest sacred river in the world, witnessed these annual festivities from the early part of the fifth century B.C. until Christianity became the religion of the Roman Empire. The Christians, abhorring such pagan activities, attacked them in their teachings as well as physically; the Bishop of Caesarea (c. 260–340) wrote;

A school of wickedness was this place for all such
profligate persons had ruined their bodies by excessive
luxury. The men there were soft and womanish-men no
longer. The dignity of their sex they rejected; with
impure lust they thought to honor the deity. Criminal
intercourse with women, secret pollution, disgraceful
and nameless deeds were practiced in the temple, where
there was no restraining law, and no guardian to preserve
decency (13).

And Constantine, the Christian Roman emperor, ordered the destruction of the temple of Asherah in A.D. 325. But the Phoenicians were
not ready to give up their faith in their old gods and accept the new
religion. By the end of the fourth century, the temple was rebuilt. The
Roman emperors kept up their attacks on the temple and the
Phoenicians faithfulls kept defending and rebuilding it until the middle of the sixth century, at which time nature provided the Christians
with a helping hand; a powerful earthquake hit the area in A.D. 555,
and delivered the coup de grace, that transformed the magnificent temple into piles of rubble.

The durability of the unyielding temple was described by the contemporary Lebanese poet, 'Umar Abu Rishah, whose Arabic verses
portray a beauty hard to preserve in translation;

The hand of destruction is exhausted,
Dreading the danger of touching it.
Here the ghosts of falsehood vanish,
And out of despondence, death commits suicide.

The remains of the sacred pool can be seen today, and a fig tree and
a walnut tree have grown in the foundation of the eastern wall of the
temple, and the local inhabitants still visit the sacred ground where the
temple once stood, tie colorful strips of fabric to the branches of the wal-

nut tree, make their offerings, not to Asherah, but to the Virgin Mary, and chant "al-majdu laha" (glory is her). Some Lebanese Christians refer to the Virgin Mary as the Lady of the Walnut Tree (14).

Greek traders or sailors, observing the women of Byblos mourn their Adoni, heard them chanting "ai lana" or "wai lana" (woe to us) (15). Not being familiar with the language, the Greeks thought the ladies of Byblos were calling on a god by that name, and adopted the lament using Ailinus or Linus as a chant at the death of a youth named Linus (16). This lament was used primarily by reapers over the death of the corn-spirit, and Linus was thus identified as a corn-deity. Homer mentions that the Phoenician Linus song was sung at the vintage, among other places, in West Asia Minor. The notion that the Linus song was also sung by Phoenician reapers (17) is highly improbable. It could have been sung on Phoenician soil by foreign settlers, for the Phoenicians, like other Canaanites, out of reverence, gave their gods titles of grandeur and Linus (woe to us) certainly does not qualify.

Whereas Adoni grew in stature and became a superior figure of mythology and legend, loved and lamented by numerous followers, far beyond the borders of Phoenicia, Linus remained a chant sung by reapers gathering their crops in various isolated farm communities in Greece, the Greek islands, and Western Anatolia.

From Phoenicia, the legend of Adoni spread into the Aegean, mainland Greece, Egypt, and later into parts of the Roman Empire. The celebrants introduced some variations but the body and the spirit of the eternal legend prevailed.

Early in the second millennium B.C. Cyprus became, to a certain degree, a Phoenician colony. Phoenician traders, attracted by its rich copper mines and the timber of its thick forests, built their settlements on its shores. They brought with them their gods, mythology, legends, customs, and celebrations. And they celebrated the death and resurrection of their youthful god and chanted their prayers for him and for the Mother Goddess whose love for him never waned.

As the Phoenicians and Greeks later fought over the dominance of the island so did their goddesses, Asherah and Aphrodite. But it is believed that Asherah had her own temples and retained her own followers well into the second century of the first millennium B.C.

A story, partly history partly myth, goes to say that Elisha (El's carpentress) the Phoenician princess of the city of Tyre fled her city after her brother murdered her husband. With her she took a group of Tyrian aristocrats and a large cache of gold. They sailed to Qart Hadasht (New City) (18), a Tyrian colony in Cyprus, which had a fine temple dedicated to the mother goddess, Asherah. From that temple they took 80 virgins destined to participate in the sacred prostitution rituals and sailed westward to build what became the great Qart Hadasht (Carthage) (19).

The Legend of Adonis (the "s" is a Greek addition) was transmitted to Greece and Europe via Cyprus, where it suffers only minor alterations. Here Cinyras was the king of Cyprus, not Byblos, and he impregnated his daughter Myrrha (the Phoenician Murrah), not while intoxicated, but to insure the continuity of his blood line on the throne. The Cyprus legend also states that sacred prostitution originated with the activities of King Cinyras and his daughters, and that Cinyras was also a lover of Aphrodite and the founder of her cult on the island (20).

The Greeks had their own mother goddess, Demeter, but they identified Asherah with Demeter's daughter Aphrodite (21), probably because of the overtly sexual role assigned to the mother goddess in the legend of Adonis. Here, Aphrodite, and not Demeter, saw the lovely new born infant and fell in love with him, and later shared his sexual favors with her sister Persephone, who reigned in the underworld. In Greece, women lamented the death of Adonis, not only because he was the god of fertility and vegetation, but also because to many his death meant the death of their fantasy lovers; thus they mourned what they were deprived of. Unlike the public rituals held in Byblos, here sexual activities were practiced in private by women of all classes.

A magnificent temple was built for Aphrodite in the southwest corner of Cyprus not far from where King Cinyras had his palace. Strange rituals were performed in and around the temple, most important among them was the ritual of sacred prostitution. The temple was permanently inhabited by young women who participated in these rituals. Time took its toll on the physical structure, but not on its spiritual and healing power; the farmers of the region still visit the ruins of the temple, wipe olive oil upon its crumbling rocks and pray, not to Aphrodite, whose divine power has long been forgotten, but to the Virgin Mary of Bethlehem.

From Cyprus the celebration of the love of Aphrodite for Adonis, and the death and resurrection of the ever-youthful god spread into the other Aegean islands and mainland Greece. There was hardly a town in Greece where these celebrations were not performed. But Adonis was hardly if ever worshipped independently from Aphrodite. The Greeks had their own gods of vegetation; Heracles, Dionysus, and Asklepios. In their function, these gods were closely associated with the Phoenician Adoni and the Egyptian Osiris.

In Athens the ceremonies for Adonis were held in midsummer. Here the women planted wheat, barley, fennel, lettuces, and a variety of flower seeds in baskets or pots filled with earth. They watered and tended their seeds, which fostered by the sun's heat, grew rapidly, but having little room for their roots to grow, withered away just as rapidly. The Athenian women carried their baskets and pots as well as coffins filled with corpse-like effigies and lined the main streets of their city. They filled the air with their chanting and wailing for the death of Adonis, then they marched carrying their baskets, pots, and the effigies of the dead Adonis and threw them all into the sea, or into rivers, or springs.

Similar ceremonies were later performed over most of Europe, and the small planters became known as the Gardens of Adonis. There is little doubt that they were intended to promote the growth of vegetation. As we have stated earlier, ancient people believed that mimicking certain phenomenon actually helped in producing it.

In Roman Catholic and Greek Orthodox churches in particular and in most other churches in general, the believers still sow various seeds in shallow containers, wait until the plants grow, tie ribbons around them and place them with effigies of Christ on sepulchers on Good Friday. Bouquets of flowers with effigies of various saints are still placed at the tombs of loved ones. Probably these activities are nothing more than a mere continuation of Adonis worship and rituals.

The legend of Adonis did not enter into Egypt until the middle of the third century B.C., after Ptolemy the second conquered Phoenicia. In an effort to befriend the people that he had subdued, Ptolemy II adopted their celebration of Adonis' death and resurrection and ordered the people of Alexandria to extend full honor to the Phoenician god.

Prior to that period, the ancient Egyptians were celebrating the death and resurrection of their great god Osiris. Many ancient Egyptian texts, the Book of the Dead among them, contain the phrase, maa-ne-hra (come thou back). This led historians to believe that maa-ne-hra (22) was a dirge sung by corn reapers over the death of the corn god, and a call for his return. Although Osiris and Isis were worshipped in ancient Egypt there are those who believe that the legend of the yearly death and subsequent resurrection of the Egyptian god of vegetation entered Egypt form the land of Canaan, and that the Egyptian priests simply adorned it with some of their magic (23). Late in the eighteenth century B.C. a conglomerate of people moved into Egypt from the land of Canaan, settled it and ruled it as kings during the seventeenth and sixteenth centuries. History books refer to these rulers as Hyksos (24), and it is speculated that they brought into Egypt their mythology, which include the legend of Osiris and his sister and wife Isis.

Osiris, like Adonis, was a personification of the death and resurrection of vegetation. Before becoming a god, he was the reigning king who reformed the Egyptians, reclaimed them from savagery, and taught them to worship the gods. His sister and wife, Isis discovered wild wheat and barley and informed him of their dietary value. (We know now that the cultivation of wheat and barley entered into Egypt from the Fertile Crescent around 6500 B.C.) Armed with this knowledge, Osiris taught cultivation to his people thus leading them to abandon cannibalism and embrace the blessings of civilization.

His brother Seth, maddened with envy, plotted against him and with the help of some of his men, measured the dimensions of Osiris and constructed a coffer to fit him perfectly. He put Osiris in the coffer, nailed it shut, and flung it in the Nile river. The coffer floated to sea, and all the way to Byblos, where a tree shot up and engulfed it in its trunk. At that time Osiris and Isis as well as the local gods, Adoni and Baalat Jbayl, were worshipped in Byblos. The king of Byblos, fascinated by the beauty of the tree, had it cut down and converted into a pillar for his palace.

By some magic Isis knew where the coffer was, visited the king of Byblos, became a nannie to his children and, in time, asked for his permission to look into the pillar. She opened it, took the coffer out and carried it back to Egypt. She left it in the Nile Delta aiming to retrieve it after visiting her son Horus. While hunting wild boar in the moonlight, Seth chanced upon the coffer, opened it, and upon recognizing the body of his brother Osiris, tore it into fourteen (twice seven) pieces and scattered them wide and far apart.

Isis learned of Seth's barbaric deed, and sailed in a papyrus boat up and down the marshes seeking the fragments of Osiris body. She found all fourteen and buried each one where she found it; thus building fourteen graves for Osiris in various parts of Egypt so that he may be worshipped by all the people of Egypt. In so doing, Isis had transformed Osiris from a local deity into a national god.

The legend goes to discuss family quarrels involving Isis, her son Horus, her brother-in-law Seth, and Hermes, and ends with the defeat of Seth, the beheading of Isis, and the dismemberment of Horus.

There were annual rites celebrating the death and burial of Osiris, but unfortunately their details have been lost. Probably they were performed during the month of November when the waters of the Nile were receding, and farmers began to plough the land. In part these ceremonies include the search for the torn body of Osiris, its discovery, and the solemn burial services that followed. What is well known are the lamentations that were recited during the burial services. Several copies of which were discovered and studied. Of these lamentations, Brugsch says, "In form and substance, they vividly recall the dirges chanted at the Adonis rites over the dead god." (25).

The burial services were followed by the joyous festival of Sokari, during which solemn processions of priests and dignitaries, carrying sacred emblems, banners, and images, circled the temples. This was one the most stately pageants that ancient Egypt had ever known. It was followed by the erection of the pillar which might have been a column with cross bars at the top. The Pharaoh himself, assisted by family members and priests, pulled at the ropes that raised the pillar at the Theban tomb.

The pillar could have been a representation of Osiris backbone, or of a tree stripped of its leaves as Osiris was a tree spirit, and the erection of the pillar represented the resurrection of Osiris. There could have been several other forms of festivities as the death and resurrection of Osiris were celebrated all over the land of Egypt.

During the reign of Ptolemy II, the yearly death and resurrection of Adonis began to be celebrated in Alexandria. They replaced the rituals of Osiris in that great city, which, thanks to the efforts of Ptolemy, son of Lagos, and his son Ptolemy the Second, became an impressive center of research and knowledge. In it, the most lavish of Adonis' rituals were conducted.

Pictures of Adonis and Aphrodite were displayed on two richly decorated beds set side by side in the midst of a large assortment of ripe fruits, cakes, and pots of flowers and plants. For reasons yet unknown, but maybe to insure an abundance of food supply, the cakes, usually made by young maidens, were in the shapes of various animals, birds, and fishes.

The marriage of the two lovers was celebrated one day, and the next day, women, in mourning attire, wailing, beating their heads and breasts, carried an image, or an effigy, of Adonis and walked to the sea shore where they committed it to the waves (26).

The rituals that were performed for Adonis in Alexandria differed slightly from those that were performed in Byblos; in Alexandria the rituals ended with Adonis' death, while in Byblos the last day was a celebration of his resurrection. There are indications that Byblos rituals were performed in the spring while the Greek poet Theocritus, in describing what took place in Alexandria, mentions the month of July, the same month, during which, the death of Tammuz was celebrated in Babylon. Although sacred prostitution was a dominant feature of these rituals in both Babylon and in Phoenicia, there is no mention of such activities in the Alexandrian celebrations.

Poets rival in their descriptions of the beauty of both Adonis and Aphrodite and of the great love they had for each other. One such poet is Theocritus, who wrote,

> "You, Adonis, have no equal among heroes,
> You are unique among those resembling the gods (27)
> You are the only one who can return to this world
> from the underworld."

Theocritus ends his poem, saying,

> Farewell, Adoni Farewell,
> Until another year—Peace.

You were benevolent in the past,
And benevolent you are forever (28).

After the destruction of Carthage, Rome became the world dominant power. Its armies conquered the land of Adoni, and became acquainted with the ceremonies and rituals surrounding the death and resurrection of the eternally youthful god. With some modifications, these rituals were adopted and subsequently celebrated in many parts of the Roman empire.

The best known of these celebrations are those that were held in Phrygia in Asia Minor. Here Attis played the role of the Phoenician Adoni. In many respects, the legends and the rites of the two gods were alike. Attis was born to a virgin mother, who conceived by putting an almond or a pomegranate in her bosom. Cybele, the great Phrygian goddess, saw the lovely infant and immediately fell in love with him. According to one account, Cybele was also his mother. To escape her intense and dominant love, the youth ran away, set under a pine tree, and mutilated his body. In another version, jealous Cybele killed the woman loved by Attis, and that made him rum away and commit that barbaric act. In yet another account, Attis, like Adoni, was killed by a wild boar. Nevertheless, all accounts agree that from his blood, violets (not anemone) grew under the pine tree, and that he himself, after death, changed into a pine tree.

The ceremonies for Attis were held late in March, probably after the spring equinox. A pine tree was cut and brought into the temple of Cybele where it was decorated with colorful woollen bands and wreaths of violets, and an effigy of a young man was attached to its middle. The decorated pine tree was then worshipped as if it were a divinity. On the second day, the picture of Cybele and all the sacred objects were taken to a brook and washed, while the effigy was kept for a year and then solemnly buried. The washing of the picture of Cybele was probably performed to bring about rain, just like the throwing of the effigy of Adoni into the water.

On the third day of the ceremonies, known as the Day of the Blood, the high priest of Cybele drew blood from his arms and presented it as an offering. Inscriptions, found in both Rome and in Phrygia, indicate that the high priest of Cybele was usually called Attis. Thus it is reasonable to infer that during these annual ceremonies the high priest played the role of the god Attis himself. This indicates that the high priests of Phrygia were also potentates, and could have formed a class of divine kings. A member of this class was annually sacrificed for the people of Phrygia and probably the world (29). This could have been a mimic killing followed by the effusion of blood from the priests arms.

The fourth day was the Festival of Joy or Hilaria, during which the resurrection of Attis was celebrated. Just as in at the Byblos ceremonies, the celebration of the resurrection of Attis followed closely that of his death. And just like the Phoenician Adoni, the Phrygian Attis was a god of vegetation. In essence the ceremonies performed at Phrygia were a mixture of the Babylonian and Phoenician rituals.

The Roman legend, probably the best known of Adonis legends, speaks of the boy Cupid, who, while playing with his mother, Venus the goddess of beauty and love, pierced her bosom with one of his arrows. Before her wound healed, Venus saw Adonis and was thoroughly captivated. She lost interest in her favorite resorts, absented herself even from heaven so as to follow Adonis and bear him company, for Adonis became dearer to her than heaven.

With him, dressed like the huntress Diana, she rambled through the woods and chased the games that is safe to hunt, but kept clear from those that nature has armed with deadly weapons. She charged Adonis to do the same, "Courage against the courageous is not safe. Beware, do not expose yourself to danger and put my happiness to risk." (30).

Having counselled the youthful god, Venus mounted her chariot, drawn by swans, and took off through the air. But Adonis was too noble to heed such warnings, and when his dogs roused a wild boar from its lair, he cast his spear at the animal, but merely wounded it. As in the Byblos accounts, the boar charged Adonis, plunged its tusks in his side, and left him dying.

The groans of the dying god reached the ears of the lovely goddess before her swan-drawn chariot reached over Cyprus. The goddess turned back to earth. She stopped her chariot next to the lifeless body of Adonis. She approached the blood-bathed body, and bent over it, and, crying as only a goddess could cry, she beat her breast and tore her hair. Through tears and sorrows, Venus declared, "My grief shall endure, and the spectacle of your death, my Adonis, and my lamentations shall annually be renewed. Your blood shall be changed into a flower."

As she spoke, she scattered nectar on the blood of the dead god. Bubbles rose from the mixture, and a red flower, the color of blood, sprung up. As it opened its petals, the wind blew them away; and so it was called Anemone or Wind Flower (31).

As the goddess ordered, the death of Adonis was lamented in Rome year after year. The old Sumerian legend thus endured. Some names and rituals have changed, but the legend itself did not. Tammuz, Adoni, Osiris, and Attis are descendent of the Sumerian Damuzi; and Venus, Aphrodite, Isis, Cybele, Asherah, and Ishtar are descendent of the Sumerian Inana. The legends of them all spoke of love and suffering, of a mother goddess, and a savior young god, of blood offering, death, resurrection, and eternal life. To a certain extent, these are the foundations of Christianity (32).

---

(1). Apsu is the underground sweet water abode of the Sumerian god Enki. The word Apsu is probably the origin of the English word "abyss".

(2). Gilgamesh Epic, Tablet VI, Column I.

(3). Gilgamesh Epic, Tablet VI, Column II.

(4). There were several kings by that name who reigned in both Canaan and Cyprus. The Phoenician word "qanur" is the origin of the Greek word "ginyra", meaning harp.

(5). Freyha, Anis, (1991:29).

(6). Out of reverence, the Canaanites bestowed titles on their gods and referred to them by their titles rather then by their proper names. Thus Adoni could be the title of either the Babylonian god Tammuz or the Canaanite god Baal.

(7). Several scholars, who studied the legend of Adoni, believe that he is a corn god or a god of vegetation, while others believe that he is the god of boars because of their involvement in his birth and death. To the Canaanites, the boar was a sacred animal.

(8). Frazer, James G. (1981:i.282).

(9). Many believe that the word "Easter" has its origin in the name of the goddess ishtar.

(10). This kind of lamentation and mourning rituals are also described in the Ugaritic texts; when Baal died, the supreme god El, his father,

...scrapes his skin with a stone,
With a chipped flint [sharp] as a razor,
He cuts off side-whiskers and beard;
He rends his shoulders with his finger-nails;
He scratches his chest as a garden plot.

But the laws of the Old Testament forbade such practices:

Ye shall not cut yourselves,
Nor make any baldness between your eyes for the dead.
(Deut. 14:1)

(11). Jidejian, Nina. (1968:127).

(12). Durant, Will. (1935:197).

(13). Jidejian, Nina. (1968:127).

(14). Today, in lebanon there are those attempting to revive the name and the legend of Adoni if not the celebrations. As a result of their activities, there are Adoni coffee shops, Adoni T-shirts, and a small town named Adoni; they hope to reverse the wheel of time and bestow the name of the youthful god on his sacred river.

(15). At funeral services, the women in present day Lebanon still use the same chant.

(16). Frazer, James G. (1981:i.365).

(17). Ibid. (1981:i.399).

(18). In time the name of this city became Citium or Kitium, the birth place of the great Phoenician scholar/philosopher Zeno of Citium.

(19). Wernick, Robert. Smithsonian; Vol. 25, No. 1. April 1994. p. 125.

(20). Sacred prostitution originated some two thousand years earlier in Mesopotamia and was then a part of the spring celebrations.

(21). In another legend, Aphrodite was born from the genital parts of Ouranos, whose son Kronos had cut with a sickle and had "thrown out into the boisterous sea." [Poems of Hesiod. 175 and the following verses.]

(22). The Greeks misunderstood "maa-ne-hra", as they did the Byblos chant "wai lana", and changed it to Maneros. explaining it as the name of the only son of the first king of Egypt. According to the Greek story, Maneros invented agriculture and met an untimely death, hence the Egyptian lament.

(23). AL-Rihani, Ameen. (1986:328).

(24). The Egyptians named these kings Hika Khasut (Foreign Rulers), and the Greeks later garbled it into Hyksos, and erroneously translated it as Pastors Kings. In general theGreeks had little aptitude for accurate transliteration or translation.

(25). Frazer, James G. (1981:i.34).

(26). In one of his versus, Theocritus states, "We carry his body to the sea of eternal sorrow."

(27). Ptolemy, in honoring Adonis, described him as resembling the gods, and not a god. In so doing he avoided adding the Phoenician god to the Greek pantheon and alienating some of his (Ptolemy's) Greek followers.

(28). These verses were translated from the Arabic. [Al-Rihani, Ameen. (1986:336,337)].

(29). The Encyclopedia Britannica, Ninth Ed. XVIII. 853, states that the high priest, "the representative of the god was probably slain each year by a cruel death, just as the god himself died."

(30). Bulfinch, Thomas. (1979: 66).

(31). Ibid. (1979:65–67). Anemone are also called wind flowers.

(32). Al-Rihani, Ameen. (1986:331).

Fig. 5-1. An artistic sketch of 'Afka and the Roman Bridge over Adoni River.

Chapter Six

The Bull Cult

The word 'bull' is thor in Ugaritic, thawr in Arabic, tor in Aramaic, shor in Akkadian and Hebrew and taur in Greek, Latin, and many of the Romance languages. Knowing that the word is common to all ancient Semitic languages, and that it has the sound and characteristics of a Semitic word leaves little doubt as to its Semitic origin (1). Its presence in Greek, Latin, and many Indo-European languages suggests that it entered the Indo-European world from the Near East through the Aegean or Anatolia and spread westward with the bull cult.

In addition to the verbal similarity between the Semitic and the Indo-European word, the role that the bull played in mythology, religion, and sport was essentially the same in the North Semitic region (2), in Egypt, and in the European countries bordering the Mediterranean.

The excavations of the royal tombs of Ur yielded several exquisitely carved bull's heads. This is the earliest known association between bulls and royalty, an assocation that goes back to about 5000 B.C.

According to Frazer (3), the worship of wild animals, or totemism, is the religion of a society in the hunting stage, and the worship of cattle is the religion of a society in the pastoral stage. The development of religion in Sumer serves as a proof of Frazer's general statement;

Anu, the supreme god of Sumer, the father of all the heavenly gods, and the head of the Sumerian triad: Anu, Enlil, and Enki, was always represented by a large bull. As an expression of reverence, the great bull Anu was also assinged the sacred number sixty. And Ninsson, the ancient Sumerian goddess, is also the Good Wild Cow who gave birth to the Good Calf. She is also the mother of Gilgamesh, the God-King. This is the earliest known association of divinity and bovine. In the second stage of the development of the Mesopotamian society, the pastoral stage, the bull became closely associated with both gods and kings. The line separating ancient kings from gods was unusually soft and usually crossed.

From early recorded history through the late Assyrian Period, figures and sculptures of bulls have equally decorated royal palaces and religious shrines. During the Early Babylonian Period, the bull became associated with the storm god Adad (Haddad or Ishkur), and thunder clouds were referred to as "bull calves". Artists of that period must have observed the similarity between a bull's horns and the crescent moon as many of their seals portray an association of a bull's head and the moon god, Sin or Nanna (4).

Composite figures, partly human and partly bovine, were introduced into Mesopotamian art as early as the third millennium B.C. and winged and wingless bulls with human heads became common motifs from the early Sumerian Period through Neo-Babylonian times. The sculptures of man-headed bulls were also very dominant during the Assyrian Period. They adorned the palaces of the great Assyrian kings; among them Assurnasirpal II (r. 833–859 B.C.), Sargon II (r. 721–705 B.C.), and Esarhaddon (r. 689–669 B.C.).

The bull also played a significant role in ancient Mesopotamian literature. The Gilgamesh Epic contains the earliest known records of a bull-fight, and ushers the bull as a symbol of strength. It describes gods and heroes as having the strength of bulls. The Gilgamesh-Enkidu fight is described in the following words: "Gilgamesh and Enkidu wrestled with each other, locked like bulls." And the hero of the Epic is said to be "completely powerful...like a wild bull."

Goddess Ishtar (Sumerian Inana) felt insulted when Gilgamesh repudiated her amorous advances. She ascended to heaven seeking the help of her father, the great god Anu.

> 93. Ishtar spoke to Anu her father;
> 94. "Father, make the Bull of Heaven. Let him kill
>   Gilgamesh in the very place he lives.
>   (Gilgamesh Epic, Tablet IV).

After some questioning, Anu acquiesced to his daughter's demand and created the Bull of Heaven. Ishtar then led the Bull of Heaven down to earth, and to Uruk, the capital city of the God-King, Gilgamesh. Upon entering the walled city, the bull snorted twice and each time he killed hundreds of men.

> 130. At the third snort a hole opened before Enkidu.
>   Enkidu fell into it.
> 131. But leaped out and seized the Bull of Heaven by his
>   horns (6).
> 132. The Bull of Heaven threw spittle into Enkidu's face.
> 133. With its thick tail he whipped up its dung.
>   Half-blinded, Enkidu calls on Gilgamesh for help;
> 134. Enkidu shaped his mouth, and said,
> 135. Speaking to Gilgamesh:
> 137. "How shall we overthrow him?"
> 147. Enkidu circled him, chasing the Bull of Heaven.
> 148. He seized him by the thick of his tail.
> 152. And between the nape and the horns, he (Gilgamesh)
>   stuck his sword (7).
> 153. When they killed the Bull of Heaven, they tore out
>   his heart,

154. and placed it before Shamash (8).

And Gilgamesh dedicated the horns to his personal god Lugalbanda. Ishtar, observing the killing of the Bull of Heaven, cursed his killers:

159. "Woe unto Gilgamesh, who has besmirched me and has killed the Bull of Heaven!"
160. When Enkidu heard this Speech of Ishtar,
161. He tore out the right thigh of the Bull of Heaven and tossed it at her saying:
162. "If only I could get hold of thee,
163. I would do unto thee as unto him;" (Tablet IV).

The killing of the Bull of Heaven by Gilgamesh and Enkidu must have either been a very popular story in Sumero-Akkadian time, or wrestling with wild beast was a very popular sport; several cylinder seals, belonging to this period and showing young men wrestling with beasts, were uncovered in Mesopotamia. And the sportive side of bull-wrestling is made abundantly clear by a seal showing a wrestling bull with a rope-like belt tied around its midsection, probably to provide the human wrestler with secure hold.

The Babylonians were also strong adherents to the bull cult; their national god, Marduk, whose name means Calf of the Sun, was always depicted as a bull, and thunder was his voice. And by about 1000 B.C. they bestowed the name "tor" (taurus) on one of the constellations.

The importance of the role played by the bull in the ancient mythology of Mesopotamia is further demonstrated by the close association of the bull with the gods. Ancient Mesopotamian art depicts most gods as having the body of a human being with two bull's horns sprouting from its head. The horns are the only distinctive markings that differentiate a god from a mere mortal. Furthermore, to associate themselves with the gods, and as a symbol of their unlimited power, most of the kings of the Akkad Dynasty had the sign of divinity placed before their names and are always depicted wearing bull-horned crowns.

The Bull Cult In Canaan

The artists of Ugarit followed in the footsteps their neighbors to the east and depicted their gods (El, Baal, Yamm, Mot, etc.) as having the horns of a bull. El, the head of the pantheon, was usually called "Thor-El" or simply "Thor" (Bull), and on occasions, a young god was called 'igil (calf) or 'igil El (calf of El), but never a Bull. The title of grandeur was reserved to the head of the pantheon.

Those same artists further demonstrated the affiliation of the bull with Ugaritic culture and mythology by frequently representing the storm god Haddad or Haddad-Rimon riding on a bull, and by molding weights in the shape of a bull (9).

El is often quoted as referring to himself as Thor. In an effort to console his weeping son, Kret, El inquires,

> "Who is Kret that he would weep?
> Or shed tears, the Good One, Lad of El?
> Does he desire the kingdom of Thor, his father,
> Or sovereignty like the Father of Man?"

In response, Kret informs El that all he wants is a model son to carry his line. El then instructs his son to acquire a bride and adds:

> "Lift your hands heavenward,
> Sacrifice to Thor, your father, El (10)."

These verses as well as several other passages of the Ugaritic texts give El this designation probably in reference to his immense strength. And for the same reason, when Baal wants to allude to the power of his sister Anath, he addresses her saying,

> "The horns of thy strength, O Virgin Anath
> Let Baal anoint the horns of thy strength."

The Old Testament also refers to El, the God of Israel, as hash-Shor (the Bull) (Judges 6:25). It also calls on the ladies of Bashan, "Ye kine of Bashan" (Amos 4:1,3). Such designations were common in the Old Testament prior to the Exile, but were edited out during the purification period that followed.

Contrary to Mesopotamian traditions, there is no indication of any sport involving bulls in the land of Canaan; there is no sign of bull-wrestling, bull-fighting, or bull-jumping. This could be a result of the reverence the Canaanites had for the bovine animals, as it might be considered degrading for the head of the pantheon to wrestle with a mere human in an act of sportful recreation.

But in the fertility cult, mating is the primary function of the gods of fertility, and bovine creature are often mentioned as gods mating partners, insuring the continuity of the cult. The Ugaritic Texts state that Baal, the most active male deity in the cult, mate with a "bakkirah" (heifer):

> He lies with her seven times and seventy times,
> He lies with her eight times and eighty times:
> And she conceives and bears Mt (11).

In all probability, these verses were intended to provide a vivid description of the potency of the valiant god in the performance of his function as the vigorous god of fertility. Although the word, "bakkirah" could be a title bestowed on a maiden-and many believe it is the title of the Virgin Anath-nevertheless, referring to the mating partner of the Aliyan Baal as a "bakkirah" is a clear indication of the close association of the fertility cult and the bovine animal.

This intimate relation is further demonstrated in a passage in Text 76 of the Ugaritic Texts. Here the Virgin Anath, the goddess of love and war, while searching for her brother, Baal, chances a cow which have been impregnated by him. She returns to Baal's mountain palace and informs him:

> She gives forth her voice to Baal:
> "With glorious news, be informed O Baal,
> Yea be informed O scion of Dagon (12),
> for a "Bull" (a calf) is born unto Baal,
> Yea a buffalo unto the Rider of the Clouds!"

These excerpts present a clear picture as of the important role played by the bovines in the fertility cult of Ugarit; the god of fertility has chosen a cow and a heifer to assist him in the performance of his function, probably insuring the continuity of the cult. Some believe this choice was made so that Baal, as a result of mating with a heifer, gains strength and that prepares him for his up coming fights with the forces of Evil represented by Yamm and Mot.

Furthermore, out of reverence to the bovine animal, the Canaanites used the word bull as a title of grandeur, or as a sign of respect. Kret, the son of El, asking his wife to prepare food for his guest, says:

> "Hear O Lady Hurrai!
> Cook the sleekest of the fatling;
> Open the flagon of wine;
> Invite the seventy bulls,
> Even the bulls of Great Hubur and Little Hubur" (13).

Ugaritic literature, like ancient Mesopotamian, Greek, and Hebrew literature, is characterized by a repetitive unhurried style. So these verses are repeated to indicate that Hurrai, as commanded by her husband, welcomes his guests, offering them food and libation,

> She brings into his presence;
> His stags, she brings into his presence,
> The bulls of Great Hubur and Little Hubur.
> They came into the house of Kret.

The fact that these passages were found only in Ugarit does not mean that their content was not widely known; El, Baal, Anath, and Asherah were worshipped in all of Canaan, and the association of the fertility cult with the bull was widely known and accepted. This is attested to in the ancient names of many Canaanite towns and geographical localities; a most descriptive name is Qarna-El (the Two Horns of El), the name of a hamlet in north Lebanon. There is also Brumana (House of Rimon or Haddad-Rimon), a famous Lebanese summer resort, and Terbaal (the Mountain of Baal), a hill overlooking Tripoli, and probably Tripoli itself. Also the name of the Greek god, Pan, the guardian of the shepherds, who was always depicted as having two horns, still survives in the name of the Syrian coastal city of Banias, and another town by the same name on the Syrian-Israeli borders.

The popularity of the Canaanites bull cult is further manifested in its acceptance by Israelites who settled southern Canaan. Among the devotees to the cult was the family of Moses whose brother, Aaron, presided over the setting of the Golden Calf. And the Golden Calves in Bethel and in Dan were worshipped as the gods who delivered the Israelites out of Egypt (1 King 12:28,29).

In addition to the previously discussed association of the gods of the fertility cult and the bovine animals, the Ugaritic texts describe heavenly creatures that are partly bovine and partly divine, resembling to a certain degree, the Sumero-Akkadian Bull of Heaven;

> Born are the Devourers!
> The gods proclaim their names (14),
> On them are horns like bulls,
> And humps like buffaloes,
> And on them is the face of Baal.

These creatures, created by gods with the body of a bull and the face of a god, are culturally the offsprings of the Mesopotamian Bull of Heaven and the ancestors of the Minotaur (Bull of Minos) of Crete.

Although the rest of the Ugaritic Tablet, like most Ugaritic tablets, is partly mutilated, it contains a few legible words that indicate that Baal followed the monsters, seized, and destroyed them.

As we shall see, there is an apparent similarity between the legend of the Bull of Heaven, the Ugaritic creatures, and the Minotaur of Crete. Furthermore, the Greek legend comprises elements from both the Ugaritic and the Babylonian legends.

According to the Greek legend, Pasiphae, the wife of the legendary King Minos of Crete, became infatuated with a bull of extraordinary beauty, and developed a burning desire to mate with that bull. She ordered the court inventor, Daedalus (literally, the cunning worker), to build for her a model of a cow, in which she hid and presented herself to the beautiful bull. The bull obliged. The parallel between this legend and that of Baal mating with a heifer is obvious.

As a result of her encounter with the beautiful bull, Pasiphae was impregnated and gave birth to bull-headed monster that became known as the Minotaur. The monster was kept in a labyrinth so artfully designed and constructed by Daedalus that, once in it, no one unassisted could find his way out of it. Each year seven youths and seven maidens, a tribute that the Athenians were forced to pay to the king of Crete, were offered to the Minotaur to devour. Year after year, the Minotaur roamed in the labyrinth and was fed with human victims until he was finally killed by Theseus, the son of Aegeus, the king of Athens. For this exploit, Theseus was assisted by King Minos' daughter, Ariadne, who had fallen in love with him, and who provided him with a ball of thread that he could use to leave a trail through the maze of the labyrinth and armed him with a sword to kill the Minotaur. Once inside the labyrinth, Theseus used Ariadne's sword to kill the Minotaur and got out by retracing his steps along the thread. He met with Ariadne, and triumphantly sailed back to Athens (15).

The Sumerian Bull of Heaven, the Ugaritc Monsters, and the Minotaur of Crete were all mystical creatures designed to kill and devour human beings. Both the Bull of Heaven and the Minotaur were killed by human heroes, and in all probability, Baal the valiant god of Canaan, did slay the monsters of the Ugaritc texts. In short, all three renditions are slightly varied reverberations of the same legend.

Mesopotamia and the land of Canaan proved to be fertile ground for legends involving composite monsters, and the Minotaur is but one of the monsters that drifted west into Greece to be killed by the various heroes of Greek mythology. In all probability, all the Greek legends portraying the slaying of monsters have their roots in Near Eastern mythology. Hydra, Chimaera, Sphinx, Echidna, and Typhoneus of Hesiod's Theogony are closely related to Near Eastern composite monsters who were similarly vanquished (16). True, the Sphinx is of Egyptian origin, but in all probability it reached Greece by way of Phoenicia where its form was altered. The original Egyptian Sphinx has the body of a lion and the head of a Pharoah (17), while the Greek Sphinx, like the Phoenician Sphinx, has a winged lion body and the head of a woman.

The Bull Cult In Egypt

The bull cult appeared in Egypt about the same time it did in Mesopotamia, and like the Mesopotamians, the Egyptians associated the bull with their gods and their pharaohs. Pharaoh Narmar, who unified Upper and Lower Egypt around 3000 B.C. was usually represented either as "Horous," the Conquering Falcon, or as the "Mighty Bull" who demolishes the walls of his enemies with his horns (18).

Egyptian mythology depicts many Egyptian gods in the form of a calf or a bull. The great god, Ra-Atom, who was a manifestation of the first Egyptian god, Nu or Nun, appeared in the morning, as a young calf named Khepri; by noon-time he became the brilliant sun, Ra; and by sun-set, he depicted himself as the old man, Atom. Thus, the association of the bovine animals with Egyptian gods goes back to the roots of Egyptian mythology.

The widely worshipped Egyptian god, Osiris, was usually identified with the bull Apis of Memphis and the bull Mnevis of Heliopolis. While other sacred animals were worshipped in certain parts of Egypt, these two bulls were worshipped in all of Egypt and also in the Phoenician city of Jbayl (Byblos). The popularity of the worship of these two bull-gods lead to the speculation that they might be descendants of the sacred cattle worshipped by the Egyptians during the pastoral stage of their social development to become considerably later the embodiments of the corn-god, Osiris.

The Egyptian goddess Isis, like Ninsoon, the ancient Sumerian goddess, was identified with a cow. Statues of Isis show a female figure with cows horn. Thus bulls and cows played an important religious role in ancient Egyptian society. Cows were esteemed holy and never sacrificed, and bulls were sacrificed only if they bore certain natural identifying markings. A priest examined every bull and put his seal on the animal having the proper identifying marks so that it might be sacrificed. Before the sacrifice, the ancient Egyptian priests invoked upon the head of the bull all the evils that might otherwise befall the land of Egypt, then killed the bull and cast its head in the Nile to be washed away (19).

After conquering Egypt in 525 B.C. the Persian Emperor Cambyses plunged his dagger into the bull revered by the Egyptians as their god Apis. He further profaned Egyptian temples and ordered the burning of their idols. Soon after, Cambyses was stricken with a sever illness, lost his thrown, and was probably driven to kill himself. All this proved to the Egyptians the correctness of their belief and the power of Apis to avenge and to punish his enemies.

In contrast, to the Hebrews the bull was the preferred animal of sacrifice. The large animal was sacrificed on very special occasion, after an abominable sin was committed. A bull without a blemish was sacrificed to lift a sin committed by the high priest or the entire nation.

The Bull Cult Moves West

The Gilgamesh epic, first in oral form, was circulating in Mesopotamia as early as 2700 B.C. and must have reached the shores of the Aegean no later than the middle of the second millennium B.C. About this time, the epic was translated into Hurrian and Hittite. Several tablets, containing large segments of the epic, were uncovered in Asia Minor, attesting to its popularity in this region during that period. Later on, and through these channels, the Greeks were exposed to the epic and this provides the most plausible explanation to the intimate relationship between the epic and the works of early Greeks embodied in Homer's and Hesiod's traditions (20).

The Greeks were exposed to the advanced Mesopotamian culture and Egyptian mythology and literature through Anatolia and via Phoenicia, whose merchants transported the goods of these countries across the Eastern Mediterranean into the Aegean and Greece. Through these channels, the Greeks became familiar, not only with the cults, but also with the mythology, law, science, and literature of these ancient societies. These early contacts led to the greatness that was Greece.

One of the many examples that demonstrates the dependence of early Greek literature on Near Eastern traditions is the reiteration of the onerous insult caused by a mortal heaving the leg of a bull at a deity. Enkidu, upon hearing Ishtar cursing his friend, Gilgamesh, heaved at her the leg of the Bull of Heaven that he and Gilgamesh had just killed. This grievous insult, with most of the details scarcely altered, is echoed in the Odyssey: Ctesippus addressed the guests of Telemachus, the son of Odysseus saying:

"Come now let me offer him a cordial gift,
Which he in turn can offer to the woman who washes his
feet,
Or any other servant in the house of the divine Odysseus."
That was said, and with a sturdy hand, he snatched up an ox
hoof,
That lay in the basket and threw it.
Odysseus avoided it by an easy shift of the head."
(Book XX: 295-300)

Telemachus rebuked Ctesippus and went on to say, "…Our guest was able to avoid the hit. Otherwise, I would have sent my sharp spear through your midriff." A mention of the heinous insult is also made in Book XXII: 290–292.

Enkidu's action sealed his fate, the gods decided that he should die, and Ctesippus would have fallen to Telemachus's spear if he had not missed his mark. In both cases, a mortal man insulted a deity with the hoof of a bull, leaving no doubt that the author or authors of the Odyssey had prior knowledge of the contents of the Gilgamesh epic.

In Greek mythology, the association of bulls and deities is common; Zeus found it necessary to change into a white bull to gain the affection of Europa so that she swims with him or ride his back from the Tyrian shore to Crete. In the same myth, a cow was designated to lead Cadmus to the plane of Panope and point out to him where to build the city of Thebes. The author of the myth must have known that to the two Phoenicians, the princess Europa and her brother Cadmus, the bovine creatures were the embodiment of a god. It is also possible that the Greek legend is based on an older Canaanite legend and preserves some of its Canaanite elements.

Many of the Greek gods were represented in the shape of a bull or having the face or the horns of a bull. Pan, the Greek god, guardian of the shepherds, was always depicted as having two horns. The Greek god Dionysus is closely associated with the Egyptian god Osiris and the Phoenician god Adoni. All three are gods of vegetation and spend a portion of each year in the underground. Although Adoni was always represented as a handsome youth, Osiris was always represented in the shape of a bull, and Dionysus was also believed to appear, at least occasionally, in the shape of a bull, and Greek mythology refers to him as "Bull," "Bull-shaped," "Bull-faced," "Bull-horned," "Horned," and "Cow-born."

In their prayers to Dinoysus, the women of Elis hailed him as a bull,

> "Come here, Dionysus, to the holy temple by the sea:
> Come with the graces of thy temple, rushing with thy
> bull's foot, O goodly bull, O goodly bull!" (21).

Furthermore, the Greek goddess Io was always represented by statues showing female figures with cows horns, just like the Egyptian representations of their goddess Isis.

The Cretans killed and devoured live bulls as a regular feature of Dionysian rites. In so doing, they represented the death and the suffering of Dionysus at the hands of Titans, and at the same time, by eating the flesh and drinking the blood of the bulls initiated communion with their god.

A similar but more elaborate bull's sacrifice took place in Athens, where "bouphonia" (the killing of the bull) was held in late June-early July, right at the end of the threshing period (22).

The association of the bull with corn spread into Europe, and the corn-spirit often assumes the form of a bull or a cow. In east Prussia, for example, to describe a spot where the corn is thick and strong, they say, "The bull is lying in the corn." In west Prussia, when a wind sweeps over a corn field, they describe it saying, "The steer is running in the corn," and if a harvester strained himself, "The bull pushed him." The farmers of Thurgau, Switzerland call the last sheaf of corn, "the cow," and similarly, to the farmers of Swabia, Southwest Germany, the last bundle of corn in the field is "the cow," and he who cuts the last ear of corn "has the cow" (23).

Other features of the bull cult, the association of the bull with deities and the sportive side of the cult must have entered into Europe via the same channels. By the end of the second millennium B.C. the east Mediterranean became an accessible and a safe passage way, making Crete, and the Phoenician cities, a center of the cult. On the walls of the Minoan palaces uncovered at Knossos in the early part of the twentieth century, one finds paintings of bull-fights, bull-heads, and bull-jumping very similar to what was uncovered in Mesopotamian palaces. Some of the Cretan paintings depict acrobats engaged in what seem to be impossible and very dangerous feats. This led some authorities to voice the possibility that the Cretan bull-jumping was not solely a sporting activity but had some rituals associated with it, making the risk an essential element.

From Crete, bull-fighting moved into Greece, and classical Greek authors left descriptions of bull-fights conducted in Thessaly, in northern Greece, where at the conclusion of the fight, the bull was killed in a religious ceremony.

The bull-fighting tradition then entered the arenas of imperial Rome where it continues until the barbarian invasions in the fifth century. With the decline of Rome, bull-fighting declined as an organized sport, but was kept alive in many localities in the countryside.

By the eleventh century, the sport was re-created by Spanish nobility, and was used as a form of entertainment during major events. The tradition still survives, not only in Spanish bull-fighting, but also in the many rodeos, steer wrestling, and bulldogging in the United States.

It is possible that various societies in similar stages of their development worshipped various animals and vegetation and later associated them with their kings and gods. It is also possible for a society to learn or adopt the rituals and the mythologies of its neighbors. The association of the bull with the gods started in Mesopotamia, spread throughout the Near East, and into Europe, where it took hold for over two millennia.

Alexander of Macedon, after conquering Egypt, declared himself a Pharaoh, and the Egyptian High Priest called him "Son of Amun". Thus Alexander became a god, at least to the Egyptians, and acquired the title, "the Two-Horned." The meaning of this designation is long lost, but the title survives. Arab historians refer to the great conqueror as Alexander "Dhu al-Qarnayn" (having two horns), and erroneously explain it to mean that he was the conqueror of two continents (24). The two horns, whether they adorn the head of Alexander or any ancient personality, are a symbol of divine power.

To distance Judaism from the bull-horned gods, the Hebrew prophets planted such horns on the heads of monsters (Rev. 13:1). And for the same reason, early Christian artists, transferred the horns from the heads of gods to the heads of devils. Whether the bull's horns adorn the heads of gods, kings, or devils, the mystic of the bull cult and the association of divine strength with the bull are clear and enduring.

Did the Bull Cult Move North?

The Phoenician traders sailed through the Pillars of Hercules and on their third expedition, c. 1110 B.C. founded the city of Cadiz. Greek sources refer to these Phoenicians as Tyrians (from Tyre) and state that those same Tyrians founded Utica in c. 1101 B.C.

The island city of Cadiz became a thriving sea port and gained prominence first, from a commercial point of view, as it guarded the rich silver mines of Tartessus (Tarshish), and second because of its location on the Atlantic eastern shores, it became a spring board for further explorations. From this center, the Tyrians explored the west coast of Africa to the South and the west coast of Europe to the North. Himilco, c. 450 B.C., sailed north along the Atlantic coast of Spain and

France, and ventured as far as the British Isles. "It is certain that Himilco wanted to follow the tin route to its remotest sources and that he visited Ireland after coasting the whole of Western Europe" (25). The Phoenicians must have had an extended contact with the native inhabitants, long enough to introduce some Phoenician words into the English language. Aside from the almost universal word "sabi'" (seven), one finds the common words: "yayn" (wine), "sipinatu" (ship), "'arz" (earth) and Old English (eorthe), and many others (26).

Looking into the mythology and legends of the people that inhabited Northwestern Europe, one finds somewhat modified elements of Near Eastern origin. There is Be'al, the supreme Celtic god, whose affinity with the Phoenician Baal is striking; the two gods have the same name and practically the same function. The Druids, the priests of the Celtic tribes, identified Be'al with the Sun, and thus, like the Phoenician Baal, he is a weather god.

There is also Tyr, the fearless god of battles, whose name can be easily identified with the name of the Phoenician city. Tyr was the only god who had the courage to put his hand in the mouth of Fenris, the troublesome wolf. A condition set by Fenris to allow the other gods to bind him-a kind of a precaution that the band was to be later removed. The band was never removed and Tyr lost his hand to Fenris' jaws and became a one-handed god. In addition to the name, the legend itself is a rehashing of Near Eastern legends describing the conflicts between Good and Evil.

The names of the old Anglo-Saxon days of the week seem to have direct link to the old Babylonian-Canaanite names, and seem to have reached the Norse people directly from the Phoenician Semites and not through the Roman Empire, whose invasion came a few hundred years later. Here the Anglo-Saxon name for the day of the Sun is Sunday and not Dominica, the day of the Lord; and Freya, the Norse goddess of love, and not Venus, replaced Ishtar and acquired the sixth day of the week. And the fifth day of the week is not Dies Jovis (Day of Jove or

Jupiter) but Thursday, the Day of Thor. Is this Thor, the Norse god, or the head of the Canaanite pantheon? Or are the two gods one and the same? We have established earlier that "thor" is a Semitic word. Did the Phoenician seafarers settle in Northwestern Europe long enough to teach its inhabitants some Near Eastern mythology? This we can not be sure of, as it has not been historically established, but the possibility should not be completely ignored nor ruled out. The Norse legend of Thor has many Near Eastern features. The Norse Thor, like the Canaanite Thor, is known for his strength and nobility, and like many Near Eastern gods, he had to perform supernatural feats to prove his supernatural power. This could be all coincidental, and the prehistoric Thor of the Norse could have been in existence prior to the Phoenician's venture into northwestern Europe. It could also be a remnant of their visits.

---

(1). It should be noted that the Semitic word for a young heifer is "'ejla" and it is "agelaien" in old Greek (Odyssey 20:351).

(2). Although there were sculptures of lions and sphinx in Mesopotamia, the bull sculptures were dominant. On the other hand, to the South Semites (the Arabs), the lion was exclusively the symbol of courage and strength, and the stallion, not the bull, was and still is the admired noble animal.

(3). Frazer, James G. (1981:ii. 61).

(4). Black, Jeremy and Green, Anthony (1992:47).

(5). Black, Jeremy and Green, Anthony (1992:51).

(6). Enkidu is most probably the first man on record to "seize the bull by the horns."

(7). This is still the way the bull is killed at the end of a successful bull-fight.

(8). Placing the heart of the Bull of Heaven in front of Shamas is a sacrificial offering to the Sun God.

(9). Curtis, Adrian (1985:62).

(10). The myth of Kret is rehashed in the Iliad with hardly any change in details. At the order of El, Kret invaded Udum to capture his future wife, the fair Hurrai; thus Kret corresponds to the Greek Menelaus, Hurrai to Helen, Udum to Troy, and Pebel to Priam.

(11). As we have stated in Chapter Four "seven" is a scared number in all Semitic cults. the seventy and the eighty are included for added emphasis. Many biblical scholars believe that the name Mt, pronounced Mosh, is the origin of the name of the Hebrew lawgiver. Mosh or Mosheh means 'one born' in Canaanite and Hebrew languages.

(12). Invariably, the Ugaritic texts refer to Baal as the son of Dagon. He is also Valiant Baal, Aliyan Baal, and the Rider of the Clouds.

(13). Lady Hurrai is Kret's wife and Hubur is their home town. So Kret is honoring his countrymen by referring to them as bulls, or he is inviting only the bulls of the city-its nobility.

(14). To be given names means to be created and identified.

(15). Bulfinch, Thomas (1979:152,927).

(16). Frazer, R. M. (1966:44-47).

(17). The world famous Sphinx of Egypt has the body of a wingless lion and the head of a pharaoh, probably Khafre, the builder of the second pyramid of Giza. The body of the world famous monument is 57 meters long and its head is 20 meters high.

(18). Gordon, C. H. (1965:100).

(19). Frazer, James G. (1965:ii.200).

(20). Gordon, C. H. (1965:51).

(21). Frazer, James G. (1981:i. 325,326).

(22). Frazer, James G. (1981:ii. 38).

(23). Frazer, James G. (1981:ii. 19).

(24). al-Andalusi Saʾd (1991:20).

(25). Moscati, Sabatino (Eng. Trans.) (1968:181).

(26). Some phonologists believe that the word Britain (House of Tin) is of a Phoenician origin. There are also those who profess that the Britons, Scots, and Anglo-Saxons are all of a Phoenician origin. [Waddell. L. A. 1924].

Fig. 6-1. A bull from the temple of Nine Hur Saj, near Ur, Mesopotamia.(c. 2450 B.C.). Copper, 62 cm high - British Museum, London.

Fig. 6-2. Gilgamesh fighting the Bull of Heaven. Notice the rope around the bull mid section.

Fig. 6-4. Bull-vaulting in Crete: A Minoan bronze figurin

Chapter Seven

The Snake,
the Symbol of Healing

Representations of snakes are frequent in prehistoric Mesopotamia, but the religious value of these early symbols is not clear. Motifs of two snakes entwined together were very common during the Sumerian period and continued to be used as a seal markings and as amulets until the end of the second millennium B.C. This is probably a depiction of a pair of snakes in the mating position. Later snake portraits are found in both religious and secular arts. During the Neo-Assyrian and Neo-Babylonian periods, the snake became a divine symbol, identified in ritual texts as the god Nirah, who is often depicted with snakes as his lower extremities.

Although the ancient Mesopotamians worshipped several snake gods, Nirah, a fully animalian deity, was the most renown. Like most ancient gods, he was a local god and, early on, was worshipped in the city of Der, located in the northern territory between Elam and Mesopotamia. During the third dynasty of Ur, the cult of Nirah was combined with that of Irhan, a deity representing the river Euphrates and therefore fertility and life itself. But in time, Nirah gained in stature, and was elevated to the rank of the great gods; during the middle Babylonian period, he was worshipped in the temple of the great god Enlil in the city of Nippur where he soon became the protective deity of the temple.

Other gods of healing, Ninurta (chief of physicians), who was usually represented in the company of his wife, Gula; Ninazu (lord of physicians), and his son Ningischzinda; all had the rod and the serpent as attribute. And Sanchan, the venerated serpent, was a symbol and a god of healing (1).

The reason for the veneration of the snake in ancient civilizations and for its association with the gods of healing is not clearly understood, but its ability to twist its body into a complete circle, with no apparent end, makes it a suitable symbol of eternity. The fact that snakes inhabit holes in the ground where the venerated dead are buried might have provided the reptile itself with a certain degree of veneration as it may have been regarded as the bearer of the will of the dead.

Moreover, The representation of several snake gods in the accompaniment of scorpions may indicate that an element of fear is also involved in the veneration of these creatures.

Another important feature which may have led to the veneration of the snake lies in its ability to cast its old skin and appear to rejuvenate. This is a unique attribute that inspires awe and wonder, and the people of Canaan, observing the sake miraculously casting its skin, expressed their astonishment by giving it the descriptive name "hayiat" (alive). Legends about the "alive" entered into the social, mythical, and religious life of the various Semitic groups from Babylon into the Nile delta and Egypt.

The reason for the ability of the sake to cast its old skin and rejuvenate is well detailed in the Gilgamesh epic: the hero of the epic, searching for eternal life, came upon Utnapishtum, the hero of the Babylonian Flood, who after the Flood, became a god and was granted eternal life. At Gilgamesh's insistence, Utnapishtum informed him about a wondrous plant found at the bottom of the sea, and directed him to its location. The thorny plant was given the Babylonian name, "'Amalu Al-Zahir Shaybu" (Hope of the One With Gray Hair). In English literature, the name of this plant usually appears as, "Old Man Becomes Young".

Gilgamesh, with the help of a boatman, retrieved the plant, but instead of eating it then and there, he tried to take it back to his capital city of Uruk, planning to save it until he reached old age. Then upon eating it, he would regain his youth.

On his way to Uruk,

> Gilgamesh saw a pool whose waters were cool.
> He went down into the midst and washed in the waters.
> A serpent sniffed the scent of the plant .
> And came up (out of the water) and carried off the plant.
> When he returned, he had sloughed its skin.
> Then Gilgamesh sat weeping
> The tears flowed upon his cheeks.

Thus, the serpent, after eating Gilgamesh miraculous plant, was able to cast its old skin and regain its youth. This is but one of many fables about the venerated snake sloughing its skin and rejuvenating.

Instead of cursing the snake for robbing him of his precious plant, Gilgamesh, through his tears, pours his heart out saying:

> I have accomplished no good for myself,
> But I have benefitted the lion of the Ground.

Here the epic refers to the serpent as the "Lion of the Ground", a title of grandeur and extravagance, arising from the esteem and reverence, the author had for the creature. The serpent is still venerated even after it robed the god-king of his miraculous plant and the ability to rejuvenate and the hope of eternal life.

The snake is also respected for its mobility and agility; in describing the struggle between Good and Evil, the Ugaritic texts refer to the Canaanite gods as being strong as bulls and agile as serpents;

> Mot is strong, Baal is strong.
> They gore like buffaloes.
> Mot is strong, Baal is strong.
> They bite (strike) like serpents.
> Mot is strong, Baal is strong.
> They kick like racing beasts.

In these verses, the bull and the serpent are used as descriptive terms to demonstrate the superior powers of the two gods and the severity of the battle between Good and Evil. In Ugaritic poetry, the words bull and buffalo are used interchangeably.

The Indo-Europeans Hittites, upon establishing contacts with the Semites across the Fertile Crescent, became acquainted with the snake cult and adopted some of its features into their mythology. There are two Hittites snake stories structured around Illuyanka. In one of these stories, Illuyanka is a giant sea serpent, and in the other it is a giant land creature which comes out of a hole in the ground. These two legends, which glorify Illuyanka, the serpent, were featured in the Hittites literature and formed a part of the Hittites spring festival.

In a variety of ways, the Egyptians also associated the snake with many of their gods. The glorious sun in the Egyptian clear sky was the Egyptians' supreme god Ra or Re, whose symbol is a winged sun-disk. Two serpents (cobras) protect the sun-disk, and the two wings of a falcon make it fly across the sky. This charming symbol gained popularity in the entire Near East, and was subsequently adopted by many Near Eastern countries.

Also the Egyptian goddess of motherhood, Isis, is often featured as a having a serpent's tail, or sitting between two serpents. This association is exceedingly significant because Isis brought her husband, Osiris, back to life after he was killed by his jealous brother, the evil monster Seth. In the legend of Osiris, Isis is thus associated with Good as she brought the bull Osiris back to life and helped him become the "Ruler of Eternity." Her word "brings to life him who was no longer living." And in the Ebers Papyrus, she is referred to as the "Great Enchantress."

Isis is also the mother of Horus, the falcon-god who roams the heavens and symbolizes the power of Good against Evil. While Horus was still an infant nestling in his nest, his mother, Isis, frantically guarded him from the killer-monster Seth. Approving of the mother concern for her infant, Edjo (the cobra), Dejebat (the heron), and Sckhet-Hor (the cow) offered what little help they could provide (2). Thus, in Egyptian mythology, both the snake and the cow were allied with Good against Evil.

The young god Horus, always depicted with a falcon on his side, or having the wings of a falcon, is sometimes featured with a pair of snakes in each hand. Thus, ancient Egyptian mythology, by associating the serpent with the supreme god Ra, the god of eternity Osiris, the mother goddess Isis, and her son Horus, provides, although at times in a roundabout way, a relation between the reptile, eternal life, and the power of Good.

The snake also played a role in early Judaism. While in the wilderness, Moses made a snake out of brass (known in Hebrew as Nes) and put it upon a pole "that if a serpent had bitten any man, when he held the serpent of brass he lived." (Num. 21:19). This snake was later put in the Temple of God and worshipped probably as an embodiment of a snake-god. The Israelites continued to venerate the snake until King Hezekiah of Judah removed all the symbols pertaining to the Canaanite fertility cult from the Temple, and "broke in pieces the brazen serpent that Moses had made: for unto those days the children of Israel did burn incense to it." (2 Kings 18:4). The destruction of Moses' serpent by King Hesekiah did not prevent Jesus from using Moses earlier action as a symbol of his ascension, "And as Moses lifted up the serpent in the wilderness, even so must the son of man be lifted up." (St. John 3:14).

But, as part of their religious reform, the Israelites reacted to the Canaanite's snake cult, as they did to many of the features and customs of the Canaanite fertility cult, by vilifying the serpent for beguiling Eve: "Thou art cursed...Upon thy belly shalt thou go, and dust shalt thou eat all the days of thy life." (Gen. 3:14). In the Old Testament, the serpent is also used figuratively to represent the enemies of Israel, the hated Assyrians (Isa. 14:29), and it is called both "devil" and "satan" (Rev. 12:9 and 20:2). The vilification of the snake as the symbol of evil carried into Christianity, where Jesus disciples are given power to tread on serpents (Luke 10:19). These strong condemnations of the snake by the Hebrew reformists and the early Christians attest to the popularity of the snake cult in the Canaanite civilization, and the reverence the snake enjoyed in Near Eastern cultures.

Even in ancient mythology, vilification and condemnations were directed, not at all snakes, but at the evil and crooked snakes. In Sumerian mythology, in Ugaritic texts, as well as in the Old Testament, god kills the "Crooked Serpent." Egyptian mythology also speaks of the Evil Snake whose aim is to stop the Sun, but was killed by a tom-cat before achieving its goal. Much later, Hesiod speaks of "the terrible serpent who lives in a lair of dark earth out at the world's farthest limits and guards the apples of gold."

(Theogony: 334,335).

These condemnations of the crooked, evil, and terrible serpent had very little effect if any on the snake cult, and proved to be nothing more than gentle perturbations in the continuum of the veneration of the serpent. In many communities of the Middle East, the snake is still called "mubarakat" (blessed one). In those places, it is still customary to treat the snake with respect and address it accordingly. A lady, upon observing the reptile, usually waves her hand saying, "Go away O mubarakat, do not harm me and I will not harm you." To describe the gentle nature of the snake, people in the Middle Eastern villages, where snakes abound, often repeat the adage: "Do not get close to a scorpion, and next to a snake spread your blanket and sleep."

The Phoenician seafarers performed their function, spreading the snake cult across the Mediterranean, while their cousins, the regional land merchant, the Arameans, spread it eastward as far as the Indian subcontinent. As a result, to this day the snake cult is very much alive and the snake is still venerated in the Middle East, India, Greece, and much of Europe.

According to an Indian creation story, the benevolent god Vishnu rested between the various stages of creation on the wide body of the snake Ananta-Sesha, the one with seven heads. The legend represents Ananta-Sesha floating over the cosmic waters with Vishnu sleeping under its protective heads for millions of years. During which time, Vishnu ripens and unfolds again into another universe. This is the same presentation expressed panoramically during the birth of Brahma, the transformation of a lily into Brahma. Here the mother is depicted lying down over the wide-bodied serpent, Ananta-Sesha. For the new mother's added comfort, the serpent has twisted its body into seven loops and is floating on its back over a body of water, carrying the mother, the new born infant, and the mid-wife. The reptile has seven heads curling in a protective fan-like arrangement over the mother's head. In a single representation, the Indian legend puts the new born infant and his mother in the presence of the symbols of healing and of life, the serpent and the sacred number seven.

The serpent also played a role in the Indian flood story. When the earth was completely covered with water, the benevolent god Vishnu appeared at the surface of the water in the form of a huge fish having one gigantic horn protruding from its head. Manu, the Noah of the Indian Flood story, anchored his boat to the fish's horn using the enormous body of the serpent Vasuki as a rope. By securing the boat to the safety of Vishnu's horn, Vasuki saved all living things from drawing.

A Snake Goddess
Is a Mother Goddess

In Ugaritic texts, Asherah (Astarte) is the mother goddess. She is the consort of El, the head of the pantheon, and the mother of the "seventy gods." She is the symbol of life and of fertility, and is depicted either with snakes coiled around her to symbolize her healing power, or as the "Tree of Life" offering ears of corn to animals. As the "Tree of Life", the Mother Goddess is shown with her bare breasts full of milk to demonstrate her motherhood and her ability to suckle the royal new-born babies.

In her capacity as the "Tree of Life", the popular Mother Goddess is providing food to human beings and to animals. in Near Eastern mythology, life was associated with food and eating certain type of food may bring eternal life.

In the myth of Kret, El, the father of mankind, visits Kret in a dream. Kret is crying, and El questions him,

> "What ails Kret that he cries?
> And Kret replies:
> "Grant that I may beget sons.
> Grant that I may multiply kindred."

El blesses Kret, instructs him, and informs him that,

> The woman you take into your house
> …
> will bear seven children, yea eight.
> …
> To you she will bear the lad Yassib,

who will suck the milk of Asherah,
Yea suckle the milk of the virgin (Anath),
the wet nurses [of the gracious gods].

Kret is the son of El and Asherah, and therefore an immortal god, but he is to be married to Hurrai, the daughter of King Pebel, the king of Udum. Thus their son will be half-god half-man, and should suckle the milk of the Mother goddess and the Virgin Anath if he is to become a god and gain immortality.

Figures of bare breasted goddesses with flounced skirts and tight laced bodices were uncovered at Knossos in Crete. These goddesses have snakes coiling around their bodies and in their hands, and were collectively called Snake Goddesses by the archaeologists who uncovered them (3). Now it has been recognized that all the figurines do not belong to the same goddess, and the association of these with snakes is a designation of their relation to various aspects of life. Among the Minoan snake goddesses, there is the Household Goddess, who protects human dwellings, the Goddess of wild animals, who reigns over the wild beasts and who, in addition to snakes, carries a miniature animal on her head, there is also the Mother Snake Goddess (4). A 3rd-2nd century relief depicts Demeter holding grain and poppy pods between two serpents, thus combining the two features of Asherah as a mother-goddess and a goddess of healing.

The Mother Snake Goddess was as popular in Crete during the Minoan civilization as was Asherah in Canaan during the same period. The large bare breasts, full of milk, shown on the figurines of both Asherah and the Snake Goddesses indicate that the mother goddesses are properly equipped to suckle the young gracious gods. The association of snakes with Asherah, Demeter, and the Snake Goddesses is an indication of their power to rejuvenate and to perpetuate youth. The same role has thus been assigned to Asherah of Canaan, Demeter of Greece, and to the Snake Goddesses of Knossos.

Figures of bronze and stone serpents have been discovered in Canaan, palestine, Gezer, and Transjordan, and figurines of snake goddesses, similar to those uncovered in Knossos, were unearthed in Ugarit and in Tel Beit Mirsim in Palestine indicating that the snake goddess was worshipped in many parts of the ancient Near East (5).

The Tree of Life was a common fixture in Near Eastern mythology and religion. It appears frequently in Babylonian and Canaanite mythology, and it was planted in the midst of the garden of Eden (Gen. 2:9). It was also widely believed that the serpent was a symbol of rejuvenation and eternal youth, thus one may view Asherah of Canaan, Demeter of Greece, and the Snake Mother Goddess of Knossos as symbols of eternal life, or at least of rejuvenation.

Most of these figures were carved during the Bronze Age, about the middle of the second millennium B. C. with that of Ugaritic Asherah being perhaps couple of centuries older. As a result of the similarity between the figurine of Asherah and these of the Snake Goddesses, several archaeologists are of the opinion that Asherah's figurine is of Minoan origin. The resemblance in the form and function of these figurines indicate, to a large extent, that during the late Bronze Age, Crete and northern Phoenicia belonged to the same cultural sphere.

The veneration of the snake in the fertility cult of Canaan must have entered Europe through Minoan Crete, where the snake was regarded as the guardian of the house and a Snake Goddess was a Household Goddess. This same snake cult has survived to this day in many parts of Europe as it has survived in the Middle East. In certain regions of Greece, Italy, Albania, and Sweden, peasants still sprinkle bread crumbs or pour milk into a hole in the floor of their house attempting to provide nourishment to the household snake.

The well established and solidly entrenched snake cult led to many legends about the reptile, both in Europe and the Middle East. Legends about the snake were told in ancient times and are still told today.

One such legend, of historic significance, is the Greek legend associating Cadmus the son of Agenor, king of the city-state of Tyre, with the snake. It points to Phoenicia as the origin of the Greek Snake cult, and serves as an example of the love the Greek gods had for the reptile. Recalling that Cadmus (East) is Canaanite name leads one to believe that the author of the Greek legend had some knowledge of the language and customs of the land of Canaan and that he could have based his legend, at least in part, on an older Canaanite fable whose central theme is a Phoenician princess being raped by the sea.

Cadmus, at the command of his father, went searching for his sister Europa (6), Who had been carried away by Zeus. The Greek god, to gain Europa's confidence and affection, disguised himself in the form of a bull, the epithet of her supreme god, El. Cadmus sailed to Greece, but unable to locate his sister and not daring to return home without her, consulted the oracle of Apollo (7) as to where he should settle. He was directed to find a cow in the field and follow her until she stopped. There he should build a city and name it Thebes. Cadmus' cow wandered for sometime until she reached the plain of Panope. There she stood, raised her head to the sky, and filled the air with her lowing.

Cadmus stooped down, kissed the soil, and gave thanks. Then he ordered his servants to seek pure water, intending to offer a sacrifice for Zeus. Nearby, in the middle of a verging grove, the servants found a cave from which bursts forth the purest of water. As they dipped their pitchers in the cool water, a horrid serpent raised its head and sent forth a fearful hiss. Stricken with terror, the Tyrians could not run away nor fight, and the serpent, heavy with venom, slew them all.

Cadmus, after a long wait, went searching for his men. He carried a javelin and a lance in his hands, and a bold heart in his chest. As he entered the woods, he saw the bodies of his men, and the monster, with bloody fangs, still watching over them. Stricken with rage, he exclaimed, " O! faithful friends. I will avenge you or share your fate!" True to his words, Cadmus lifted a huge rock and hurled it at the monster. The impact, that would have shaken the wall of a fortress, made no impression at the reptile. Then he threw his javelin, and it penetrated the serpent entrails. Crazed with rage, the monster broke the weapon off and moved toward Cadmus, who retreated pointing his spear at the monster's open mouth. Attempting to attack, the serpent threw its head back, and it landed against the trunk of a huge tree. Cadmus saw his chance, and with his spear he pinned the monster to the trunk to the tree. The monster, as it struggled in the agony of death, bent the thick trunk of the tree.

As he stood alone, contemplating the corpses of his faithful men and the enormous size of his dead foe, Cadmus heard a voice commanding him to take the monster's teeth and plant them in the ground. He did as ordered and immediately, as soon as he completed his task, spears began to appear from the ground, then helmets, next came the shoulders and the breasts of men. In time an army of armed warriors stood in front of the frightened Cadmus. As he prepared himself to encounter his new enemies, one of the heavily armed men said, "Meddle not with our civil war." As he spoke he slew the man next to him with his sword, and he himself fell to the arrow of another.

The melee lasted but a few minutes. All were slain except five. Then one threw his weapons and shouted, "Brothers, let us live in peace!" The fighting stopped, and these five survivors, grown from the teeth of the serpent, helped Cadmus build the city of Thebes, which historically had an old fortress known as the castle of Cadmus. Probably the name of the ancient city was also Cadmus, and was subsequently changed to Thebes.

With the construction of Thebes completed, the gods punished Cadmus for killing the serpent, sacred to Ares, by making him serve the god of war and his consort Aphrodite. While serving the divine couple, he fell in love and subsequently married their daughter Harmonia (harmony), the healer. To honor the occasion with their presence, the gods came down from Mount Olympus. Marvelous gifts they bestowed on the bride. But as a consequence of Cadmus' killing the serpent, viewed in Greek mythology as a symbol of wisdom and caution, a doom hung over the family of Cadmus and Harmonia. Their daughters, Semele and Ino, and their grandchildren Actaeon and Penteus perished.

Cadmus and Harmonia left Thebes for the country of the Enchelians, where they were received with great honor and Cadmus was made king. But the death of their children still weighed heavy on their minds. One day, while in a state o melancholy, Cadmus exclaimed, "If a serpent's life is so dear to the gods, I wish I were myself a serpent." As soon as these words were uttered, Cadmus began to change form. Harmonia observed what was happening and prayed to share in her husband's fate. Her prayers were answered, and Cadmus and Harmonia became serpents.

They lived in the woods, and mindful of their origin, they neither avoided the presence of human beings nor did they hurt any one (8).

Strange as it may sound, to this day in Amioun, a town in North Lebanon, there is a large family, named Hawi (9), whose members do not kill snakes and they claim that snake bites do them no harm. At times, they are called upon to catch a house snake and release it in the wild. They never claimed to be descendants of Cadmus and Harmonia, and I do not believe they are familiar with the Greek legend.

Remnants of the ancient snake cult may still be detected in the eastern Mediterranean regions, where legends about the reptile, its courage, nobility, and affection still abound. one of the earliest legends, dates back to about 2000 B.C. It was uncovered in a cliff along the Nile River, written on a papyrus roll and packed in an earthen jar. It describes a shipwreck in which all aboard, except one, perished. The surviving sailor was cast on a strange island by a great wave. After a long rest, the hungry sailor started searching for something to eat. While filling his mouth with fruits and vegetables, he was seized by an enormous, long-bearded, serpent, who was ruling the island as its king. The serpent treated its captive with kindness for three whole months then, loading him with much treasure, returned him back to Egypt.

The distant island in the Red Sea, at the entrance of the Indian Ocean, seems to have sunk and vanished forever (10).

A not so old snake legend gained prominence during World War I. It relates to the gallant snake of Kalenovo, a small village in Macedonia. When all the inhabitants of Kalenovo were forced to flee their village, the brave snake simply refused to leave and stayed behind. The British Unit that occupied the area provided the household Kalenovo's snake with regular army rations for the duration of the occupation (11).

A more recent legend took place in the early 1970's in Raqqa, a Syrian town on the bank of the Euphrates River. This is where the renown 'Abbasid Khalif, Harun al-Rashid, built Haraqlah to commemorate his victory over the Byzantine army. One of the local inhabitants, guarding al-Rashid's monuments, killed a snake while on duty. That same day a uniformed driver in an official-looking car came to his home and ordered him to town for questioning. But instead of going to town as he claimed, the driver drove him to Haraqlah, where he was escorted into an underground chamber. As he entered a crowd gathered around him, and he heard a woman scream, "This is the man who killed my son." When the horrified guard looked up, he saw that all the people around him had snake-like faces.

He was tried for murder, but was acquitted on the ground that he killed in self-defense. The trial took the best part of three hours, after which he was driven back to his house by the same uniformed driver and in the same official-looking car.

The experience left the guard unconscious for three days. After which he described his experience only once, before his untimely death. As a result, al-Rashid's monument was left unguarded ever since; no one dares to guard it.

The reader is free to call the following story a fable or accept it as a true story. My mother was fond of telling it repeatedly. While a toddler, and my family was in an olive grove picking olive, I was left with a spoon and a bowl of rice pudding. When my mother returned to check on her son, she found me sharing my dessert with a large black snake, one spoon-full for me and one for my companion. Mother repeated the customary statement "Go away O! mubarakat, do not harm me and I will not harm you." And the snake simply went away.

In the Middle East there could be hundreds such stories, and there is the popular adage, "Snake stories have no end."

Feeding and worshipping serpents are manifestations of the awe human beings have for the reptile and for its ability to do harm. These behavioral acts transcend all cultural boundaries and thrive in primitive settings shared by human beings and snakes. Thus, the veneration and the respect that many native American tribes had for the rattlesnake, and the flourishing snake worshipping in West Africa and the Punjab bare no relation to the snake cult the Near East and Europe (12).

The Snake as the Symbol of the Gods.

We have already discussed the worship of the snake gods in ancient Mesopotamia, how the snake god Nirah became the god of fertility and life. We have also mentioned the association of the Sumerian god of healing, and the Egyptian gods of eternity with the snake, and talked about the veneration the Canaanites had for the reptile. In time the reptile, the epithet of the gods, became a symbol that represents these feature.

In the land of Canaan, Phoenicia, Syria, and Palestine, the snake, the symbol of life, became the epithet of Eshmun (13), who in his capacity as the god of healing was often represented holding a caduceus, a rod about which two serpents were twined (14). He is also depicted with a serpent biting its tail. In this configuration, the snake forms a circle, with no apparent end; an excellent representation for the god of infinity.

This god did not enter into the Phoenician pantheon until the seventh century B.C. and probably at first, as his name indicates, only as a designation of a previously established god. At first, Eshmun shared character and functions with the popular canaanite god Adoni (15). Before becoming a god in his own right, his name, Eshmun, could have been used as a designation of Adoni. While Adoni (my Lord) was used originally as a designation of either the Canaanite god Baal or the Mesopotamian god Tammuz.

Subsequently, Eshmun grew in popularity and stature and was continually referred to, in the Sidonian inscriptions, along side Baal and Asherah. And as it is customary in the Near East, many of the later kings of Sidon bore the name of their god: King Eshmunazar II (Eshmun helps), the middle of the fifth century B.C. left inscription that reads in part "…We built a temple for Eshmun, the Holy Prince, near the spring of Jadjal in the mountain…" (16).

In the outskirts of the city of Sidon, near the foothills, on the south side of the 'Awwali River, stand the ruins of the large temple of Eshmun. The temple was built near a spring whose water was thought to have healing property and therefore was sacred. By the entrance of the temple, the spring of Jadjal forms a large pool, where people used to bathe and wash away their illnesses.

Rocks from the old structure have fallen down into the sacred pool, but the glory of yesteryears is still there and may be felt in the ruins of the majestic structure, the wilderness of its surroundings, and its well-preserved and artistically designed foreground.

A gold plaque, found near the temple, depicts the god Eshmun, the Greek goddess Hygeia (health), and a child. Eshmun holds in his right hand a staff around which two serpents are entwined, and Hygeia holds a serpent, allowing it to drink from a cup. Between them sits a young boy looking at Eshmun. The fact that most of the votive pieces found in and near the sight depict children suggests that Eshmun, the god of health and eternity, was also the pediatrician of his time.

The most significant finds of Eshmun's temple, dug by nineteenth century excavators, were pillaged. Only a collection of sarcophagi is housed in the National Museum of Beirut, most of the rich art works, uncovered at the temple and around Sidon, are now in the Louvre and the Topkapi Archeological Museum in Istanbul. The Louvre also houses inscriptions detailing the life of King Eshmunazar and stating that he and his mother built the temple of Eshmun.

As if to bring their gods close to the Phoenician Eshmun, the Greeks, during their occupation of Phoenicia, added a structure to the north side of Eshmun's temple. This addition, some 11 by 10 meters, contains inscriptions honoring Asklepios (the Latin Aesculapius), the Greek god of the medical art, or "the blameless physician" as Homer calls him. The Greeks usually represented Asklepios with one and on rare occasions with two snakes entwined around a column. Mercury, the Greek god of commerce and of thieves was usually represented with Eshmun's symbol of two snakes entwined on his staff.

According to a Greek legend, the goddess Iris transported the caduceus and the healing power to earth on a rainbow. The legend adds that Hermes took the caduceus from Iris, and gave it with the healing power to Asklepios, who in turn taught the art of medicine to his daughter Hygeia.

Two snakes entwined around a staff was used as a symbol of health and wellness by the Sumerians two millennia before it passed into Phoenicia to be later adopted by the Greeks.

During the Greek occupation of Phoenicia, the 'Awwali River became known as the Asklepios River, and it is quite possible Asklepios became the name of the entire temple of Eshmun, and rituals, similar to those performed for Adoni on the Adoni river, were performed for Asklepios on the Asklepios river.

This lack of respect for the history and religion of subjugated countries was common among ancient conquerors and the Greeks were no exception. Here, they went too far; they appropriated river, temple, legend, and symbol and claimed the knowledge and the culture of the people of Phoenicia.

One of the walls of the temple of Eshmun displays a relief of a man attempting to capture a plumed cock. It was common among Phoenician worshippers to sacrifice cocks to Eshmun, a practice that the Greeks adopted in sacrificing to their god Asklepios.

Temples were built for Eshmun along the shores of the Mediterranean wherever Phoenicians built their settlements and everywhere his divine name was mentioned, it was followed by the designation "Holy Prince" and the form of a snake biting its tale. In this circular configuration, the snake did not only stand as a symbol of rejuvenation but also for the concept of infinity, a very appropriate and designative epithet for the god of healing and of eternity.

In Carthage, across the waters of the Mediterranean from Sidon, during the waning hours of the last of the Punic wars, the few remaining Carthagenian fighters, with their city in flame, retreated to the Byrsa Hill, on top of which stood the majestic temple of Eshmun. In the holy temple, the desperate few fighters, their leader, and his family made their last stand, resolving to die defending their holy shrine rather than surrender to the hated Romans. As the battle approached its disastrous end, Sophonisbe, the wife of Hasdrubaal, the leader of the Carthagenians, stood with her two little sons on the wall of the burning temple. From that position, she saw her husband leave the temple to grovel before Scipio Aemilianus, the Roman general, maybe to beg for his life and the lives of the remaining few. She howled a curse upon him for his cowardice, grabbed her two sons and jumped with them into the purifying fire. In so doing, Saphonisbe and her two children did not only escape the cruelty of the Roman attackers, they also joined with Eshmun in an eternal embrace.

The snake cult and the association of the snake with the gods of healing spread across the Mediterranean and appeared on many of its islands and coastal communities. They invaded Greece where Eshmun was identified with Asklepios, whose symbol was that of Eshmun: one or two snakes, coiling around a rod in the standing up position.

In 293 B.C., when the plague raged in Rome, the Romans thought the only cure they knew, the sacred serpent, and sent messengers to Epidaurus to bring one back. They also built a temple for Aesculapius (the Roman Asklepios) on one of the scenic islands of the river Tiber (17). The Roman god of healing, like his Phoenician counterpart, prefers a dwelling by the water.

The symbols of Eshmun and Asklepios are not different from the early Sumerian Motifs representing two entwined snakes and used as a designation of their god of healing, and as decoration for their vases. the ancient gods of healing, Nirah, Eshmun, and Asklepios were associated with snake symbols, and the two entwined snakes is the symbol of present-day medical profession.

Although Eshmun was the most prominent Phoenician god of healing, he certainly was not the only one. Motifs of gods of healing and sacred snakes were uncovered in many areas of Phoenicia and neighboring regions. Of these gods, the one known to have entered into Greek mythology is Shadrapa (Spirit of Healing). A stele, uncovered in 'Amrit and dates to the fifth or sixth century B.C. reads , "To his Lord, to Shadrapa, because he heard the voice of his words." This is the earliest known mention of Shadrapa, who was subsequently mentioned in inscriptions found in Carthage, Palmyra, and Greece. In the Greek inscriptions his name appears as Satrapas, and in the Palmyrene representations, he is accompanied not only by serpents, but also by scorpions (18).

The association of the snake with healing started in Sumer, passed through the land of Canaan into Greece, and possibly Egypt, then spread throughout the western world. This is the channel through which most concepts, myth, and knowledge passed.

---

(1). Krumbhaar, E. B. (1958:38).

(2). Redford, Donald B. (1992:47).

(3). The Greek goddess, who embodied most of the features of the snake goddess of Knossos, is Athena, the calm, gracious patron of the city, and not Olympus, the fierce goddess of war as represented by Homer. Perhaps this, and the superficial resemblance of the names, led to the association of Athena with the Virgin Anath, the Canaanite's goddess of love and war.

(4). di Neuhoff, Sonia. (1970:209).

(5). Hutchinson, E. W. (1968:209), and Graham, Lanier. (1997:150,151).

(6). The name Europa has its origin in the Canaanite word 'arb meaning west. In Greek mythology, the Phoenician princess, Europa, usually appears as a woman sitting in a willow tree. This perhaps points to the association of Europa with tree-worship.

(7). Although Cadmus was a Canaanite, he consulted the oracle of the Greek god Apollo and not a canaanite god, because he was in Greece and all ancient gods were worshipped as local gods.

(8). Bulfinch, Thomas. (1979:94).

(9). The name Hawi is very descriptive; it means snake-sorcerer, and it is related to the Hebrew name Hawwa (Eve), which has a similar meaning. The phrase, "the mother of all living", appended after the name Hawwa in the Old Testament is a recent and incorrect addition.

(10). This old Egyptian legend, like many other Oriental stories, found its way into Greek epic. In its details and as a whole, it is the story of Odysseus in the land of Phaeacians. The details of the Egyptian legend are scattered in Odyssey 5, 6, 8, and 9. Both the Egyptian Isle and the Greek city of the Phaeacians disappeared and both the Egyptian sailor and Odysseus returned home laden with riches.

(11). Hutchinson, R. W. (1968:209).

(12). Frazer, James G. (1981:ii. 93–95).

(13). The etymology of the name is uncertain, but may be related to the word "eshm" (name). The "un" ending may indicate the affectionate diminutive form of the name. The words "eshm" and "esm" have their origin in the word "sama" (to rise) and (sama') (heaven). Thus "eshm" could also mean high and powerful. In Northern Lebanon, in the small village of Bterram, my birth place, there is a small shrine that bears the name Eshmuneit, probably the only shrine, in existence, for the consort of the god Eshmun. This shrine, dug in solid rock, goes back to probably the first half of the first millennium B.C. Hardly any body in the district remembers who Eshmun or Eshmuneit were, but a cross has recently been erected of the roof of the shrine, and many of the inhabitants, most of them Orthodox Christians, often visit the shrine of Eshmuneit touch its walls, light candles, and bless themselves.I thoroughly studied the inside walls of this shrine, it has no outside walls as it is mostly under ground, but found no legible inscription or any depiction of a snake. On our way to visit the temple of Eshmun in the outskirts of Sidon, some eighty kilometers south of Bterram, my sister declared, "we are on our way to visit the in-laws."

(14). Krumbhaar, E. B. (1958:121).

(15). Adon is the Canaanite word for lord or master and the "i" ending is the first person possessive pronoun; thus Adoni means "my lord". The word was used earlier by the Canaanites not as a proper name, but as a reference to their valiant god, Baal. Later the Hebrews used it to refer to their god, Yahweh, without uttering his name. Out of reverence, when a Hebrew saw the name Yahweh, he said, "Adoni". Later the Greeks change it to Adonis, and the river, just north of Beirut, became known as Nahr Adonis and not Nahr Adoni.

(16). 'Abbudi, Henry H. (1991:87).

(17). Krumbhaar, E. B, (1958:123)

(18). Moscati, Sabatino. [Eng. Trans.]. (1968;37). The scorpion is the totem of the Egyptian goddess Selket, the guardian of the dead and of marriage.

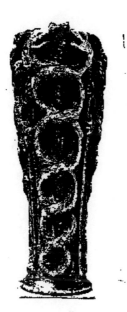

Fig. 7-1. Two snakes entwined around a libation cub dedicated to Gudea, lord of Lagash, Sumer. (c. 2000 B.C.) Soapstone, 23 cm. Musee de Louvre, Paris.

Fig. 7-2. The Mother Goddess Ashera (Astarte) with a serpent coiling around her upper body. Ugarit, (18th century B.C.) Ivory. Musee de Louvre, Paris.

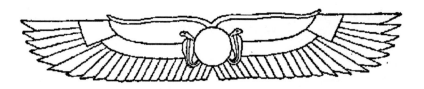

Fig. 7-3. Winged Sun-Disk, Symbol of the Sun-God, guarded by two cobras.

Fig. 7-4. Horus, son of Isis and Osiris, holding two snakes in each hand.

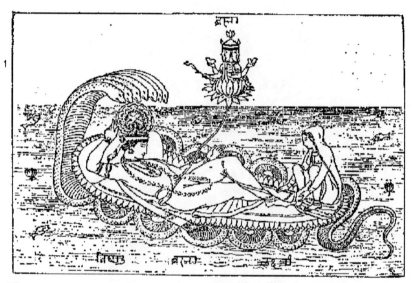

Fig. 7-5. The birth of Brahma. Mother and child are protected by a seven-headed serpent.

Fig. 7-6. The snake goddess of Knossos, Crete, with two serpents. (c. 1500). Archaeological Museum, Heraklion, Greece.

Chapter Eight

Medicine

As diseases must have existed as soon as life was formed, and that early human beings tried to rid themselves, in one form or the other, of the pain and discomfort caused by illnesses, it is safe to say that the art of medicine is as old as humanity itself.

This art is not restricted to human beings, many animals and even some plants have ways of combating sicknesses. Many trees are known to excrete certain chemicals to combat fungi and other parasites that attack them. Many animals have uncovered the medical properties of certain vegetation, and eat them to cure what ails them. Other animals get together and pick away the parasites from one another.

The wily fox is said to rid itself of fleas by biting a piece of wood, or the like, and lowering its body gently, tail first, into a pool of water or a creek. When it is completely submerged and all the fleas are on the wood, the fox opens its mouth, the piece of wood floats away and the fox emerges flea free. Similarly, rabbits in the wild rub their bodies against savory bushes to get rid of fleas and other parasites.

The ibis, a bird common in the Nile basin and sacred to the ancient Egyptians, counteracts constipation, with which it is often inflicted, using its long bill as a rectal syringe (1).

Primitive peoples probably practiced two completely different methods of medication: a practical method originating from the obvious, and another resulting from combating the unknown and the mysterious. When a thorn or a similar object penetrates the flesh, removing it relieves some pain and discomfort and therefore is a cure. Pressing one's hand or finger on a wound stops the bleeding and thus is a form of medication. On the other hand, a cure for a mysterious or supernatural illness, such as a high fever or epilepsy, is not as obvious and therefore requires some supernatural approach. Early humans, Not knowing the nature of such mysterious illnesses or how they entered into the body of the victim, accused demons and evil spirits. In such cases, a magician or a exorciser, using various means, rid the patient of the demons, or a good benevolent god was called upon to take away the evil spirits and cure the inflicted; hence the ancient conflict between the good gods and the evil demons, between Good and Evil.

An epidemic was usually attributed to a god, an animal, or an insect, but rarely if ever to contagious individuals. When the angel of the Lord "smote in the camp of the Assyrians an hundred fourscore and five thousand" (II King, 19:35), Egyptian records attribute the outbreak to Ptah, who was represented in the temple of Thebes with a rat in his hand. Also the plague that was inflicted on the Greeks at Troy, was attributed to Apollo Smyntheus, the god of rats. The manner by which plague is spread by contagion was not recognized until the work of Ibn al-Khatib (A.D. 1313–1374).

Flies played an important role in the spread of diseases, and ancient peoples assigned gods to protect them from flies. The Babylonians had their Nergal, the Hebrews had their Baal-Zebub (the lord of the flies), and the Greeks had their fly god, Zeus Apomuios.

To combat diseases, the help of supernatural benevolent powers was invoked directly with prayers and sacrifices, or through a medium, an expert in the art of communicating with such super beings. This magic medicine survived practically unchanged into the twentieth century; it is still practiced in certain remote areas inhabited by people removed from present-day medical advances, as is the case on a few Polynesian islands, and in small isolated pockets in central Africa and Australia.

As they did in most other endeavors, the Near Eastern centers of civilizations cooperated in their long fight against diseases. Over the years, Egyptian physicians visited Mesopotamia and Canaan and treated royalties and rulers, and Mesopotamian physicians reciprocated. Egyptian medical papyri often attribute some of their prescriptions to the Kefti (the people of Crete), and Odyssey, IV, 220 states that, Hellas owes to the Egyptians his knowledge of many remedies. The Greeks also modeled their blameless physician, Asklepios, after the Phoenician god of healing, Eshmun.

Mesopotamian Medicine.

Most of the almost one thousand medical tablets uncovered in Mesopotamia treat most diseases as invasions of the body by evil spirits or harmful demons and describe cures based on the various methods used to rid the inflicted of these demons. An evil spirit may be forced to leave a patient if scared or disgusted or forced out by a healing god, who was usually associated with a snake, the symbol of healing.

On one of the oldest of these tablets, the Sumerians attribute numerous diseases to harmful demons and evil spirits and call upon their goddess, the great physician of the Black Headed People (the Sumerians), for medical help. In their incantations, she is addressed by various names, such as Bau, Ninisinna, and Gula (2).

In a similar manner and on several tablets, the disease that overwhelmed Tabi-utul-Enlil, the ruler of Nippur, is describes in these terms, and his prayers to the various gods and goddesses, bagging them to rid him of the evil demons was the only cure mentioned.

An evil demon has come out of its (lair);

It struck my neck and crushed my back,
It bent my high stature like a poplar;
...
Food became bitter and putrid,
The malady dragged its course,
...
My flesh was wasted, my hands were wan.
All day the pursuer pursues me;
At night he granted me no respite whatever
My limbs were shattered and rendered helpless,
In my stall I pass the night like an ox.
I was saturated like a sheep in my excrement;

Then he mentions how his diviner has failed him and his gods have deserted him.

The disease of my joints baffled the chief exorciser,
And my omens were obscure to the diviner,
The exorciser could not interpret the character of my disease,
And the limit of my malady, the diviner could not fix.
No god came to my aid, taking me by the hand,
No goddess had compassion for me, coming to my side.

He is baffled by his punishment as he was always a pious ruler, who performed his duties towards gods and men.

As though I had not set aside the portion for the god,
And had not invoked the goddess at the meal,
Had not bowed my face and brought my tribute;
...
And had not taught my people fear and reverence
...
Prayer was my practice, sacrificing my law,

The day of worship of the gods (was) the joy of my heart,

...

I thought that such things were pleasing to a god.

Here Tabi-utul-Enlil is stating that for being such a pious man, he should not have gone through all the suffering. He did not merit the punishment that befell him. The good god should have prevented the evil spirits from entering his body. But he never lost faith in his benevolent god. Finally the good spirit appears, and cures all his ailments; a mighty storm drives all the demons out of his body.

He sent a mighty storm to the foundation of heaven,
To the depth of the earth he drove it.
He drove the evil demon into the abyss.

...

He tore out the root of my disease like a plant.

Cured, he praises his god, offers sacrifices, and calls upon all his subjects to have faith, and never to despair (3). This piece of Babylonian literature provides a clear insight into the Mesopotamian view of diseases and their cures. There was no differentiation between demon and disease; the two words were used as synonyms. And so were the words god and cure.

Although magical cures were prevalent in the Mesopotamian society, the oldest society for which we have clear medical records, there are indications, that even in the early stages of the Mesopotamian development, plants and other substances were consumed for medical purposes and some specialized medicine was in existence.

A clay tablet, written toward the end of the third millennium B. C. was uncovered in Nippur and brought to the Museum of the University of Pennsylvania, where it was translated by Samuel Kramer and Martin Levey. This clay tablet, the oldest medical document on record, contains over a dozen remedies extracted from plants such as myrtle and thyme, and from trees such as willow, pear, fir, fig, and date. It also mentions extractions from milk, snake skin, and turtle shell as well as table salt and potassium nitrate.

This tablet has two drawbacks; it fails to mentions the diseases for which these remedies were intended, or the quantities to be used in their treatment (4).

Another clay tablet that dates back to the middle of the eighteenth century B.C. was uncovered in Mesopotamia; it mentions aloe vera as a cure for "anything that ails you." An Egyptian papyrus, written around 1500 B.C., confirms some of the Mesopotamian claims; it states that aloe vera reliefs skin afflictions, infections, and constipation.

Recent scientific studies proved the correctness of what Mesopotamians and Egyptians had determined over 3500 years ago. Growing scientific evidence proved that Aloe vera has enormous therapeutic powers; it heals burns, skin lesions, and frostbite; it reduces inflammation and enhances immune response. If taken internally, certain components of aloe reduce stomach acids, relieve the pain of arthritis, and reduce blood sugar in diabetic patients.

The therapeutic effect of plants is also mentioned in one of the Sumerian creation stories; Uttu, the goddess of plantations, after being impregnated by her great-grandfather Enki (Lord-Earth), fulfilled her duties and created a variety of plants. Enki visited Uttu's plantations and, in an effort to determine their medical power, he ate some of them. The goddess Ninhursag (Queen-mountain), enraged by what had happened, cursed Enki, who, as a result, fell grievously ill (5).

The great gods, the Anunnaki, seriously troubled by Enki's illness, brought Ninhursag to Enlil (Air-god), their leader, who persuaded her to heal Enki. To perform that function, she placed the sick god close to her vulva and began to create a god (a specialist) for each one of the diseases that inflicted him;

Ninhursag placed Enki at her vulva...

'My brother what hurts you?'—'My tooth hurts me.'
'I have caused Ninsutu to be born for you.'
'My brother, what hurts you?'—'My mouth hurts me.'
'I have caused Ninkasi to be born for you.'
'My brother, what hurts you?'—'My rib hurts me.'
'I have caused Ninti to be born for you.'(6).

...

But undoubtedly the general population believed that harmful demons and evil spirits were the cause of all diseases and magical cures were predominant. This led to prescribing and adopting various protective methods, such as hiding from the sight of evil demons, which in turn led to the use of masks and symbolic chains that protect loved ones from harmful contacts. Another way of hiding from an evil spirit was by painting the patient in a variety of colors, which led to present-day tatoos. Changing the name of the patient was another way of fooling the evil spirits, preventing them from finding him.

Other forms of protection against harmful demons include the administering of seven drops of a liquid, the assistance of a special person (a child, a virgin, or a firstborn), and a variety of amulets such as odd shaped stones, and threads spun from virgin kids. Such charms were attached to the head, neck, or limbs of the patient, or even tied about his bed or at the entrance of his dwelling. These ancient protective devices may be viewed as the precursors of the ornaments or signs used today, such as the statues of Buddha, crosses, and small boxes containing Koranic verses, usually worn around the neck, and also of the signs of the cross painted above the doors of certain homes and statements such as "God, bless our home," hung on the wall.

In a society governed by magic, demons, and fetishes, individuals arose who had the power to pacify angry spirits and triumph over powerful evil forces. They were the priest-magician-physicians, who rose to prominence in most primitive societies. They called for the help of a benevolent god to frighten away evil spirits. In many instances, they foretold the future by observing the stars and other phenomena, such as the liver of an animal or a fellow human being, and taught the people how to avoid forthcoming calamities. In modern religion, their function is taken by prophets and saints, who could intercede with God on behalf of others and their intercession could have positive results (7).

Ancient Mesopotamian society was host to such practices from the early Sumerian period until the end of the eighteenth century B.C. the time of Hammurabi's legislation. Its medical practices were mostly dominated by magician-priests. Ancient Mesopotamians were ardent astronomers-astrologers, and astrology played an important role in their every day life, especially in their medical practice. The conjunction of the stars at the birth of a child was thought to determine his lot all through life and the time and manner of his death. This belief is still held by many, and prominent newspapers still publish a daily astrological column, one of many ancient Mesopotamian myths still flourishing in our own time.

Another form of magical concept came about from the belief that the blood is responsible for all vital functions, and that for the continuation of life, blood must be provided with the proper nourishment. The organ that receives the blood, the liver, was assumed by the Mesopotamians to be the seat of all life processes. Accordingly, when an animal was sacrificed, its liver was thoroughly examined for signs of destiny; divinations were derived from its position, its form, and any irregularities it possessed. This concept passed unaltered from the Sumerian into Assyrio-Babylonian medicine, and then west into Canaanite, Hittite, and Etruscan medicine (8). The Etruscans in turn passed it to the Romans. The Latin word for liver, "haruspex", has its origin in the old Babylonian word for liver, "har". Divination using livers of animals or slain enemies, survived in Greece for several centuries after the advent of Christianity (9).

The Canaanites considered both the heart and the liver as the seats of emotions. This is clearly stated in Ugaritic literature:

> El laughs in his heart,
> And is convulsed with mirth in his kbd [liver].

This concept entered the Hebrew literature, and is still alive in French and Italian cultures (10).

In Mesopotamia, magic in medicine took various forms; if a demon inflicts a patient by entering his body, several methods may be used to get rid of the invading evil spirit. A magician-physician, may scare off the demon by wearing a terrifying mask, covering himself with animal skin, making wild noises, shaking rattles, clapping his hands, dancing, jumping, and raving until the patient laughs and the invading demon is frightened away. Ancient Babylonians probably discovered the healing power of laughter. Such shaman may also suck the demon out of the patient through a hollow tube, and while performing his act, often recited incantations ordering the demon to leave the patient:

> Away, away, far away, far away,
> Be ashamed, be ashamed! Fly, fly away!
> Turn about, go away, far away,
> May your evil, like the smoke, mount to heaven (11).

The last line may indicate that the exorciser burned an image or an effigy of the demon while chanting. This was a common ritual, known as the Nusku ritual, one of the many forms of the then widely accepted sympathetic magic. By setting the image of the demon on fire, the exorciser as well as the patient expected the demon to burn also. The Nusku ritual was usually accompanied by a chant:

> I raise the torch, their images I burn,
> The images of the Utukku, Shedu, Rabisu, Etimmu,
> Of Labartu, Labasu, Akhkhszu,

Of Lilu, Lilit, and maid of Lilu,
And all the evil that seizes men.
Tremble melt and dissolve,
Your smoke rise to heaven.
Your limbs may the sun-god destroy.
Your strength may Marduk, the chief exorciser, the son
of Ea, restrain! (12).

Often the images of the demon was bound, hand and foot, depriving them from movement or escape, their eyes were pierced, their tongues were pulled out. The mutilated images were then thrown into the fire.

In a culture where the word disease and demon became synonyms, the variety of illnesses called for a large number of different demons, and every demon became a specialist, assigned a specific function or disease. Thus, the demon Labartu had his specialty, threatening the life of mothers at childbirth, and Ashakku caused devastating diseases resulting in the consumption of the body such as tuberculosis, while Ti'u was associated with headaches accompanied by high fever, and jaundice was attributed to Axaxazu, who turned the body yellow and the tongue black. In short, every disease had its demon and the list is almost endless. The large number of demons indicates that the people believed that a single demon could not cause all the various diseases. This is a manifestation of a complex and advanced society.

The severity of the illness is in proportion to the strength of the invading demon, and the cure is affected by exorcising these demons. If the magician could not scare off the demons with his ravings and dancing, he resorted to drugs usually made up of disgusting filth administered to the patient and intended to force the invading evil spirits to leave. This approach was based upon the then prevailing notion that the stomach of the patient is stronger than that of the demon, and the patient could tolerate the filth better than the demon.

Another method of extracting the demon from the body of the patient was to find a substitute, a lamb, a pig, or a bird. The chosen substitute was placed near the sick person and killed by tearing out its inside, enticing the demon to leave the patient and enter the body of the substitute. The animal was then offered to the gods in sacrifice, and its meat was not consumed by humans. The notion that evil spirits and demons may pass from a man with an unclean spirit to a substitute survived and spread west with Christianity as Jesus ordered the unclean spirit, Legion, to leave a mad man and enter a herd of swine (Mark, 5). Based on the notion that an evil spirit could enter a person and drive him insane, many people so inflicted were chained and put into dark caves, dungeons, or locked in a cellar, barn, or attic to force the evil spirits to leave them. This procedure continued to be practiced in parts of Europe and the Middle East well into the nineteenth century.

Nevertheless, some specialized lunatic asylums were established as early as the fifteenth century first in Spain, probably under the influence of Islamic models. Under religious auspices, in London, the priory of St. Mary of Bethlehem was converted in the fifteenth century into housing lunatics, where, many patients were kept in brutal restraining conditions. In time St. Mary of Bethlehem became known as the notorious 'Bedlam'.

If a treatment cured a patient, it did so because it was bad for the demon and forced him to leave. If an administered concoction acted favorably on a patient, it was because the demon did not like its smell or its taste. In the case of the most common of diseases, stomach troubles, the proper remedy caused vomiting or loosening of the bowels, forcing the demon out of the body with the vomit or the excretion. Thus a drug that cures an upset stomach works because it forces the evil spirits and the harmful demons to leave the inflected.

The manipulation of certain parts of the body to cause some relief from cramps was naturally thought to have forced the demons to leave as they did not enjoy such manipulation and did not want to submit to it again.

In time this approach, based on scaring or disgusting the invading evil spirits, gave way to pleasing and appeasing them by providing the patient with delicious drugs: honey, milk, and sweet-smelling herbs.

If everything failed, the patient was taken to the market place, where passersby were required to stop and talk to him, or his companions to determine if anyone had experienced the same disease or knew someone who had. Based on their past experience, the passersby prescribed a cure. Thus, when someone suffered from a long-lasting illness, every experienced adult in the community became a doctor.

In addition to magic and exorcism, ancient Mesopotamians practiced a completely different form of medicine. Their past and common subjective experience with irrigation and the effect of water on the growth of vegetation had given them the idea that water held a healing power. As this phenomenon is common and readily observable, many ancient civilizations reached similar conclusion, and sweet water was universally the medicine of choice.

The Sumerian god Enki, whose abode was Apsu the underground sweet water, was also the god of healing, and so was the Babylonian god of underground sweet water, Ea, the wisest of all the gods. To wash away ailments, the patient either drank the water, sprinkled it over his head, or bathed in it, and many rivers and pools became sacred, and revered for their healing power.

Ea, also known as the god of humanity, who warned Utnapishtim, the hero of the Babylonian flood, of the forthcoming deluge, gained prominence as a healing god because of his association with the rites where water was used to drive away evil spirits and demons. An elaborate exorcising water ritual was developed by the priests of the city of Eridu, and continued to be practiced through the period of the Assyrian empire. In the name of Ea, the sick person was sprinkled with holy water to provide him with relief from the clutches of the demons. An incantation associated with the Ea-ritual reads:

> With pure, clear water,
> With bright, shining water,
> Seven times and again seven times,
> Sprinkle, purify, Cleanse!
> May the evil Rabisyu depart!
> May he step to one side! (13).

The belief in the healing power of sweet water moved west from Mesopotamia, into the land of Canaan, where the Phoenician god of healing Eshmun and many other lesser gods were associated with clear water. As we have indicated in our discussion of "The Snake, the Symbol of Healing," the Greeks and the Romans also associated their god of the medical art, Asklepios, with the Phoenician Eshmun and therefore with the healing powers of water.

The Babylonian further associated Ea, their god of healing, with other rituals among them rubbing the patient with butter, milk, or oil while chanting the proper incantation;

> Pure oil, shining oil, brilliant oil.
> Oil which makes the gods shine,
> Oil which mollifies the muscles of man.
> The oil of Ea's incantation, with the oil of Marduk's incantation,
> I pour over thee; with the healing oil;
> Granted by Ea for easing (the pain) I rub thee;
> Oil of life I give thee;
> Through the incantation of Ea, the Lord of Eridu,
> I will drive the sickness, with which thou are afflicted, out of thee (14).

The general belief that diseases were caused by invading evil spirits or harmful demons and that the cure was to scare, disgust, appease, or wash them away with clear water, oil, butter, or milk was so well ingrained in the Mesopotamian society that even with the establishment of a professional class of physicians, the popular demand for supernatural diagnosis and magical cures persisted. Sorcerers and exorcisers retained their popularity even during the reign of Hammurabi, who established laws regulating the medical profession.

During the golden age of Babylon, King Hammurabi put forth his time honored code of law in which he details rewards for various successful operations and describes penalties for failures.

> If a physician performed a major operation on a
> nobleman with a bronze lancet and has saved the
> nobleman's life, or he opened up the eye of a
> nobleman with a bronze lancet and has saved the
> nobleman's eye, he shall receive ten shekels of silver.

The Babylonian society was composed of three classes, nobility, commoners, and slaves, and the eye of a commoner was worth half that of the nobleman; and if a practitioner saved the eye of a slave, his reward was two shekels only. To discourage impostors, Hammurabi put stiff penalties on failure. "If a surgeon shall make a severe wound with an operating knife and kill the patient, or shall open an abscess with an operating knife and destroy the eye, his hands shall be cut off." Probably this was intended to prevent imposter from practicing medicine.

The penalties were of course less severe if the patient was a commoner or a slave. "If a physician shall make a severe wound with a bronze operating knife on the slave of a free man and kill him, he shall replace the slave with another slave. If he shall open an abscess with a bronze operating knife and destroy the eye, he shall pay half the value of the slave."

The fact that such legislation was required in the eighteenth century B.C. proves that such operations were fairly common, and that the people of Babylon enjoyed the services of a class of able physicians, and that empirical medicine began to displace magic and exorcistic medicine.

It is safe to state that from this period on, Mesopotamian medicine acquired two distinct approaches to the treatment of diseases: the use of magic and the application of medication. These two methods of treatment were not kept apart; medical measures kept some minor use of magic (probably to satisfy the patient), while magic treatment incorporated the use of most available pharmacopoeia (15).

Clay cuneiform tablets written during this period show that Mesopotamian physicians were often called for consultations in various countries of the Near East including Egypt, the leading country in the medical art, and they were handsomely paid for their services.

Among these physicians, the most renowned was the Mesopotamian court physician, Arad Nanai, who lived in the second half of the seventh century B.C. and left writings that include prescriptions and letters reporting to the king and advising him on matters of health (16).

In one such letter, Arad Nanai informs the king about the progress in the treatment of an injury to the eye of a prince.

> Arad Nanai to the king my lord, thy servant Arad Nanai.
> Hearty greetings to the king my lord. May Ninib and Gula
> grant happiness and health to the king my lord!
> Hearty greetings to the little chap whose eye causes him
> trouble. I put a bandage (cover) on his eye. Yesterday,
> towards evening, I took off the bandage that had been
> applied,
> removing also the dressing below, and their was blood on
> the dressing as much as the point of the little finger.
> To which ever one of thy gods this is due, his command has
> surely been heeded.

Hearty greetings. Let the king my lord rest assured; in
seven or eight days he will be well (17).

Mesopotamian medicine had a remarkable influence on the development of medicine in Greece and the West. Many of the names of
plants used in medicine and in cosmetic ointments entered western
languages from Mesopotamia, usually through Greece, either by translation or mere transliteration. In the English language, such words
include rose, cherry, sesame, hyssop, balsam, myrrh, hemp, jasmine, and
saffron (18).

Also, the mesopotamian view of diseases and cures spread over the
entire Near East, and was adopted by most Near Eastern nations
including pre-Yahwist Judea. With the advent of monotheism, the sole
God became the dispenser of good and evil, of health and disease. Thus
diseases were ordered by the divinity as means of punishment and education. "By His will God makes leprosy come and go" (Exodus, 4:6,7).
This belief delayed the evolution of medicine in Israel and, with the
advent of Christianity, in Europe. Drugs and physicians were not
needed since clerics, the representatives of God, took over their functions. This practice dominated most of Europe, gaining impetus with
the collapse of the western Roman Empire in the fifth century. The
church's dominance over Europe, during that period, influenced all
aspects of intellectual activities and certainly medical practices.

Out of compassion for the sick, "hospitals" were built by monastic
orders, where gravely ill patients were brought to either recover or die,
as was the will of God. Monks offered comfort, prayers, and sacraments,
but there were no physicians or medicine. Diseases were caused by
supernatural forces and were beyond the power of feeble human beings.

As it was in Mesopotamia several thousand years earlier, where every
disease was caused by a special demon, in Europe every illness was
cured by its patron saint. Saint Blaise cured upper respiratory infections, Saint Roch became the patron of plague victims, to cure small-

pox, prayers were directed to Saint Nicaise, rabies sufferers directed their prayers to Saint Hubert, and Saint Dymphna cured insanity. On account of its strange manifestations, epilepsy was known as the "sacred disease" and had three patron saints: Saint Valentine, Saint Sebastian, and Saint Vitus (19). The royal touch of divinely appointed kings was thought to cure practically all illnesses. This was the state of the medical profession in most of Europe all through the Dark Ages (20).

Egyptians Medicine.

The contribution of ancient Egyptians to the field of medicine inspires as much owe and wonder as their contribution to the field of architecture. In the medical and pharmacopoeial arts, they were far superior to all their contemporaries. The ancient Egyptians worked on the development of the art of medicine for the best part of six thousand years, and the oldest papyri uncovered in Egypt certainly represent the achievement of several previous millennia. The early Greeks and Romans correctly referred to Egypt as the cradle of medicine. As the Mesopotamians were the astronomers of antiquity, the Egyptians were its unchallenged physicians and pharmacists.

Although there was some beliefs in evil spirits and magic in early Egyptian medicine, where priests and magicians relied on spells and incantations to cure their patients. The Egyptians soon replaced their priestly and magical medicine with the proper use of drugs usually administered by competent lay physicians called "swnw" (probably pronounced sounou).

Early on in their history, the Egyptians adopted what they thought of as public health practices, such as the circumcision of males and probably of females children-usually done by priests-, the frequent use of enemas, the collection of clean rain-water, and the construction of sewage systems for the disposal of wastes.

The frequent use of enemas and laxative drugs in ancient Egypt, (some believe that the Egyptians learned the procedures from the sacred ibis), was the result of their recognition that much of the food taken into the body is superfluous, and that this excess food is the cause of diseases.

They had a common name "ukhedu" for all foul substances. As a result, remedies used to promote bowel movement and extract the intestinal "ukhedu" were often used to rid the patient from other ailments. For instance mild cathartic drugs were used to treat eye diseases as well as respiratory ailments. The pus in an infected wound was viewed as an "ukhedu" and a laxative applied to the wound would force the pus out and cure the patient.

The ancient Egyptians left a number of medical papyri, of which eight have been uncovered. The three most important are: the Ebers Papyrus (now at the Museum of the University of Leipzig), the Brugsch Papyrus (now at the Berlin Museum), and the Edwin Smith Papyrus (given to the New York Historical Society in 1906 by Smith's daughter). There is also the Kahun Medical Papyrus, uncovered in Faiyum in 1889 by F. Petrie, and dated c. 2000-1800 B.C. Its legible fragments indicate that it dealt primarily with gynecology. Numerous other prescriptions and incantations were uncovered in various parts of the land of the Nile.

The significance of the art of medicine to the ancient Egyptians may be deduced from the fact that most of their medical papyri states that their ancient pharaohs were closely connected with the practice of medicine, and from the Egyptian tradition which relates that the son of King Menes, the founder of the first dynasty, was the author of several books on anatomy.

The pharaoh Zoser, of the third dynasty, referred with pride to his knowledge of the art of medicine; he bore the title Sa (Healer), and left inscriptions on his temple walls designating him as "Divine Physician" (21).

The importance of the medical art to the Egyptians may also be inferred from their mythology, in which all their gods possessed the power of healing, with Thoth being the ablest and the most ancient. He was credited for healing Horus from the sting of a scorpion. Thus, the goddess Selket-Scorpion became the symbol of all unknown diseases. In one version of the Egyptian legend of the struggle between Good and Evil, Thoth treated the wounds of both Horus and Seth. With the rise of Alexandrian science, Thoth became identified with Hermes, the master of all ancient sciences. The Egyptian Hermes was later taken over by the Greeks, who revered him as Hermes Trismegistus.

Isis, the great enchantress who cured Ra, is mentioned as often as Thoth in Egyptian incantations and invocations, and her word "brings to life him who was no longer living" (22).

The father of Egyptian medicine, and most probably the Father of Medicine, is Imhotep "He Who Comes In Peace". According to his biography, written by J. B. Henry (Oxford University Press, 2nd Ed. 1928), Imhotep, the son of Ptah, lived in the thirtieth century B. C. He was a grand vizier, a high priest, a physician, a sage, a scribe, an astronomer, a superior architect, and was later revered as the god of medicine. He designed and built the tomb of his king, Zoser; the world's oldest surviving building of stone masonry. He is also credited with the design of the pyramids (23), but above all, he is the greatest of ancient physicians, and one of the few truly great physicians of all time. As we shall see later, he is probably the author of the magnificent Smith Papyrus.

In the preparation of their prescriptions, the Egyptian physicians used practically every thing they could lay a hand on. They used honey, various kinds of beer, yeast, oil, dates, figs, garlic, onion, fennel, myrrh, lettuce, crocus, opium, cardamom, and juniper, and a variety of metals and minerals, such as table salt, antimony, copper, ocher, sodium carbonate, and others. They also included parts of various animals, birds, and fish. Honey was the most popular of all drug ingredients used in ancient Egypt with djaret being the second most popular. Djaret, whose nature is not clearly known is probably a plant extract (24).

The medical papyri, mentioned above, contain detailed descriptions of all then known illnesses and a large number of prescriptions. The Ebers Papyrus alone contains about one thousand and states that the heart, not the liver as thought by the Mesopotamian physicians, is the center of the blood circulation; "there are vessels attached to it (the heart) for every member of the body." The heart was recognized as the body most important organ and the seat of intelligence and emotion.

The Ebers papyrus begins as follows: "Here begins the book of the preparation of medicine for all parts of the body of a person…" Then it goes on to describe prescriptions for various ailments. "If you examine a person who suffers in the region of the stomach and vomits frequently, and you find a protuberance in the anterior parts, and his eyes are tired and his nose is stopped, then you say to him: 'It is putrefaction of the excrement, the excrements are not passing through the intestines'; prepare for him: wheat bread, absinthe in large amount, add garlic steeped in beer, give the patient to eat of the meat of a fat beef and a beer to drink composed of various ingredients, in order to open both eyes and his nose and to create an exit for his excrement."

The bacteria infested water of the Nile, the frequent sand storms that swept over Egypt, and the fact that many ancient Egyptians were stone cutters made eye diseases a common and a perpetual epidemic and many eye remedies became common knowledge. The Ebers Papyrus contains various treatments for the eyes. "To drive away inflammation of the eyes have ground the stems of the juniper of Byblos, have them steeped in water, and apply to the eyes of the sick person and he will quickly be cured. And "To cure granulations of the eye you will prepare a remedy of collyrium verdigris, onion, blue vitriol, powdered wood; you will mix it all and apply it to the eyes of the sick person" (25).

The Ebers Papyrus mentions that a physician named Hwy was the author of a remedy for the disease of the eye. This physician, who had the title "The Greatest of the Seers" and whose tomb is one of the most ancient of the medical school of Osiris at Heliopolis, must have died several centuries before the Ebers Papyrus was written, proving beyond any doubt that the Egyptian medical papyri contain the knowledge and the experience of earlier physicians.

Archaeologists, excavating in and around Deir el-Medina, near the modern city of Luxor, uncovered during the first half of this century tens of thousands of documents written between 1275 and 1075 B.C. Although some survived on sheets of papyrus, most were written on shards of pottery or flakes of limestone. One of the most interesting was written by a draftsman named Pay or Poi to his son Pe-Rahotep, telling him, "Do not turn your back on me; I am not well...May you bring me some honey for my eyes, and also some ocher which is made into bricks again, and real black eye paint...I am searching for my sight and it not there" (26).

This treatment, which appears in older, specialized medical papyri, may have become common knowledge by the end of the second millennium B. C. allowing a common draftsman to order it for himself. Indeed honey has antiseptic properties; the bees, to protect their honey, treat it with enzymes that generate highly reactive chemicals known as free radicals which kill bacteria on contact. And ocher, an ingredient in many ancient Egyptian prescriptions, feels cool to the eyelids and reduces swelling.

By far the most important of all the medical papyri uncovered in Egypt is the Edwin Smith Papyrus. It is one of the oldest and most complete medical treatises of all antiquity. The fifteen-foot-long roll was uncovered at Luxor in 1862. In 1920, the known Egyptologist, James Henry Breasted, in collaboration with Dr. A. B. Luckhardt, began a careful study and translation of the famed document, a labor that required most of a decade to complete.

The Edwin Smith Surgical Papyrus is historically the first medical treaty to contain written descriptions of surgical procedures, to mention the brain as a vital organ, and to provide the earliest examples of inductive scientific reasoning. This led Breasted to compare the studies and discoveries mentioned in this papyrus to Sir Isaac Newton observing the falling apple and discovering the law of gravitation.

This Papyrus was written about 1700 B.C. but there is some agreement among archaeologists that it is a recent copy of an ancient manuscript written probably during the Old Kingdom (3000–2500 B. C.). Although it contains no mention as to who is its author, Breasted suggested that it may have been written by Imhotep himself, and that it may be the Secret Book of the Physician quoted in the Ebers Papyrus.

The Edwin Smith Papyrus is a unique and a most complete treatise in the history of surgery, and in spite of the early period during which the original text was written, the sophistication and completeness of its accounts indicate that the medical art was practiced for centuries, perhaps millennia, before reaching such deep and thorough understanding.

This papyrus is an account of forty-eight traumatic lesions and some diseases of the thorax. It teaches the physician that the edges of the wound should be brought close together and the wound should be bandaged while the edges are held in this position. All cases are described accurately, beginning with examination, then diagnosis, prognosis, and treatment. It teaches the physician to be frank and open with his patients as it lists the prognoses in three different groups: injuries that are treatable, where it reads "the physician (swnw) will cure this disease", those of uncertain outcome, but the swnw will try to treat the patient any way, and incase of compound fractures or depressed skull fractures, it states "nothing can be done in this case", it recommends that nature be allowed to take its course, "the patient will die."

In this ancient and valuable surgical text, where the employment of magic in medicine is reported only once, the brain is mentioned for the first time in history, and is recognized as the site of mental functions and the center that controls the lower limbs. Injuries to that vital and sensitive organ receive special consideration. It states that in the case of fracture to the skull, the bony fragments should be removed by means of an elevator (probably an implement designed for this purpose).

To apprehend the magnitude of the medical work performed prior to the writing of this papyrus, one has to imagine the number of experimentations carried out to determine that moldy bread, when applied as a poultice, heals the wounds. Of course Egyptian physicians did not know that moldy bread contains antibiotics. It was a matter of trying a variety of substances until finding what works.

The importance of the Smith Papyrus is not only in its accurate description of surgical cases and the detailed anatomical knowledge it contains, but also in the fact that it gives clear indication that some five millennia ago, Egypt had well organized schools of medicine run by able surgeons and physicians free from the interference of priests and magicians.

We have already mentioned the school of Osiris at Heliopolis, whose director bore the title "The Great Seer". Another important medical school was the School of Sais, which was probably founded during the period of the third dynasty (about 4000 B. C.). Its director bore the title "The Greatest of Physicians".

Egyptian physicians formed a highly respected and well organized class of professionals with autonomous positions in well run and well equipped medical schools. Here the Hermetic writings containing the canons and ethical codes of medical art were preserved and were later passed down into the time-honored Hippocratic oath. These physicians were just as respected as high priests and bore titles comparable in rank and importance to those of priests. In tombs near the great Pyramids, titles such as "Superintendent of the Secrets of Health in the House of the God Thoth" and "The Superintendent of the Palace for Sanitary Fumigation in the House of the God Thoth" were found. Similarly during the period of the fourth and fifth dynasties, one finds titles such as

"The Chief of Physicians," and "The Consulting Physicians of the Palace," and there were medical specialists, like the physician Ypy, who bore the title "Consultant to the Place to Heal the Sight."

To regulate the use of medical prescriptions and drugs, it was necessary to have a government office to supervise such activities. This office was established and was run by a government official known as the "Superintendent of the Office for Measuring Drugs" (27).

Egyptian medicine, which flourished for five millennia, began to deteriorate after the Persian occupation in 525 B.C. when a crazed Cambyses led his forces down the Nile, profaned Egyptian temples and schools, and took as prisoners many Egyptian priests, physicians, and scholars. The wise Darius sent back to Egypt the famed Egyptian physician, Udjohorresne, to restore the "house of life". But his effort to rebuild and restore some of the Egyptian medical schools to their former prominence was short lived, and sorcerers and magicians occupied the positions once held by the great physicians of antiquity.

Egyptian medical knowledge was not confined to the land of the Nile, and Egyptian medical drugs found their way to many Near Eastern countries and later into Greece where they acquired great reputation. As early as the thirteen century B.C. the king of the Hittites asked Ramses II for a physician and an incantation-priest to come to central Turkey and attend to his sick sister. Also the kings of Persia in the fifth and sixth centuries B.C. had Egyptian court Physicians.

The Phoenicians, in the first half of the first millennium B.C. equipped their ships with chests, that contained first aid medications, most probably acquired in Egypt. During the first naval engagement of the Greco-Persian war, the Persian allies, the Phoenicians, captured a wounded Greek sailor named Pytheos, who earned their admiration for his courage and valor. He was brought, with other captives, on board ship where the Phoenician physician pulled out the medical chest and treated him while the other captives looked on with amazement. To them a medical chest aboard ship was a novelty (28).

But the novelty caught on, and both Greek and later Roman ships where equipped with medicine chests. In a Roman shipwreck found off the coast of Tuscany in 1989, and dating back to c. 100 B.C. a medical chest, containing 136 compartments filled with various ointments and herbs and a small wooden statue of Asclepios, was uncovered (29).

Greek Medicine

Influenced by Mesopotamian medicine, ancient Greek associated diseases with demons and sought remedies with incantations and prayers. As in most ancient societies, mystic superstitions appear with high frequency in early Greek culture, explaining diseases as the work of harmful demons and evil spirits. Falling ill is thus a curse or a magic spell inflicted by a sorcerer, a ghost, a demon, or a witch.

All Greek gods, like their Egyptian counterparts, were associated with the power of healing: Apollo, "who chases away all ills", was the inventor of the art of healing. Asclepios, "the blameless physician," treated the gods. Hygeia, who was often represented with her father Asclepios and, at times, with the Phoenician Eshmun, was the goddess of health. Artemis, who was identified with the Egyptian Istasp, was the protectress of women and children. Aphrodite, usually identified with the Canaanite Asherah, was the protectress of sexual life. The mysterious epidemic that befell Athens and other Greek cities in 430-427 B.C. increased the popularity of the Asclepios cult, and magnificent shrines were built for him in Greece, Crete, Kos, and later in Turkey.

As each Greek city had its own pantheon and cults across the country were varied and constantly changing, the Greeks possessed an overwhelming number of gods, who were all venerated as healers, but Asclepios, like the Egyptian Thoth, retained his supremacy.

About a millennium after it lost ground in Mesopotamia, priestly medicine spread throughout Greece and dominated the medical art from about the fifth century B.C. up to the early parts of the fifth century A. D. At that time, a strange mixture of the cult of Asclepios and of the cult of the Christian saints came into being.

The Greeks thought of the human body as being composed of four fluids, or humors; blood, phlegm, black bile, and yellow bile, a view attributed to Hippocrates. The correct proportions of the four humors translated into good health "good humor," and illnesses were the results of an imbalance of the four humors. Physicians prescribed drugs, diet, and exercise to restore that balance, and in many instances they drew blood from patients for that same purpose (30).

The practice of bleeding patients endured until the middle of the nineteenth century and probably killed more people than any disease except for the great plague and smoking. This and other medical practices led the fervid Roman politician Cato the Elder to declare that Hellenistic physicians were part of an international conspiracy designed to murder the people of Rome (31).

The best known physicians of the ancient western world is Hippocrates (c. 460–380 B. C.). He was born, lived, and worked on the Aegean Island of Kos (Cos). This is a period known as the Hellenistic golden era, and medicine, thanks to Hippocrates and others, shared in the progress. The increased contacts between Greeks and the people of the Near East during that period made the medical knowledge of Egypt and Mesopotamia better known in Greece and the West, and the Greeks gratefully acknowledged that they owed much of their medical knowledge to the Egyptians.

The immense surge in medical knowledge brought about during that period, mostly by Greek physicians, rests upon the great accomplishment of Egyptian physicians and of the Egyptian empirical work that lasted over five millennia. Hippocrates, Prasagoras of Kos, Herophilus of Chalcedon, and other Greek physicians played an important role in the development of western medicine, but they had at their disposal the knowledge accumulated during several millennia of Egyptian practices.

Hippocrates, often called the father of western medicine, like most other Greek physicians of his period, claimed to be a descendant of Asclepios. The historical Hippocrates was a famous physician and an able teacher. He established a medical school that in essence rejected the notion of supernatural causes for illnesses and cures and taught physicians to base their practices on empirically sound clinical experience, but he is probably best known for the oath bearing his name (32)

Hippocratic medicine, as given in the Corpus, is characterized by three principles: close observations of symptoms, an openness to all ideas, and a willingness to explain the causes of disease (33). The Hippocratic Corpus is a collection of some sixty tracts, written by a variety of authors, but ascribed to Hippocrates. Not one of those tracts can be securely identified as his, and many of the details of his life and work were later additions.

It has been reported that Isaac Newton once said: "I saw far because I stood at the shoulders of giants." This statement is definitely more appropriate of Hippocrates.

---

(1). Durant, Will. (1935:183).

(2). Kramer, Samuel Noah. (1981:64).

(3). Jastrow, Morris, Jr. (1915:477–481). This is one of several similar compositions found in Mesopotamia, and may have influenced the author of the Book of Job.

(4). Kramer, Samuel Noah. (1981:60–64).

(5). Saggs, H. W. F. (1962:418).

(6). Several scholars have pointed out the similarity between the creation of Ninti (Lady of Life) or (Lady of the Rib) and the creation of Eve from the rib of Adam.

(7). In Islam, they are the "wali" and their "wilaya" (sainthood) is based on the verse, "Lord! Thou hast bestowed on me some power, and taught me something of the interpretation of events." Qur'an, 12:101.

(8). Krumbhaar, E. B. (1958:36).

(9). Ibid, (1958:119).

(10). In the English version of the Old Testament, the old Hebrew word "kbd" has been translated as "spirit", "soul", "honor", and "glory". Thus, Psalm 16:9, in its original form reads:

therefore my heart is glad,

And my kbd [liver and not glory] rejoices

(11). Krumbhaar, E. B. (1958:50).

(12). Jastrow, Morris, Jr. (1915:245). The names mentioned in this chant are those of various sickness causing demons.

(13). Ibid. (1915:247)>

(14). Jastrow, Morris, Jr. (1915:246).

(15). Oppenheim, A. Leo. (1964:295).

(16). Krumbhaar, E. B. (1958:39).

(17). Jastrow, Morris, Jr. (1915:494)

(18). Durant, Will. (1935: 276).

(19). Porter Roy, Editor. (1996:90).

(20). When priests' prayers were the only medicine available to the christians of Europe, the people of Muslim Spain were enjoying the services of professional physicians in well equipped hospitals. [Sa'id al-Andalusi. (1991:58–78)].

(21). Krumbhaar. E. B. (1958:47).

(22). Ibid, (1985:46).

(23). Breasted, James Henry. (1935:71,72).

(24). Selin, Helaine. (1997:692).

(25). Krumbhaar, E. B. (1958:53,54).

(26). McDowell, Andrea G. "Scientific American" Dec. 1996; Vol. 275, No. 6. PP. 100–105.

(27). Krumbhaar, E. B. (1958:60,61).

(28). Green, Peter. (1996:118).

(29). James, Peter and Thorpe, Nick. (1994:5).

(30). Martin, Thomas R. (1996:145,217).

(31). James, Peter and Thorpe, Nick. (1994:5).

(32). In its original form, the Hippocratic Oath begins as follows: "I swear by Apollo the healer, by Asclepios, by Hegeia, and all the power of healing, and call to witness all the gods and goddesses that I may keep this Oath and Promise to the best of my ability and judgement."

(33). Porter Roy, Editor. (1996:58).

Fig. 8-1. A self-portrait of Amenhotep adoring Thoth, the Egyptian god of healing.

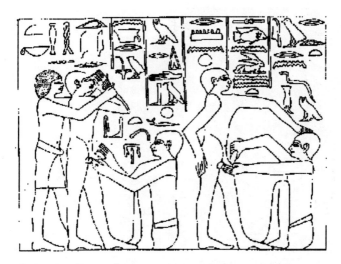

Fig. 8-2. An Egyptian relief showing youths being
circumcised. The hieroglyphic inscription of the left
has the surgeon saying to his assistant "Hold on to him;
don't let him faint"

Fig. 8-3. A Babylonian baked clay tablet(c. 650 B.C.) gives a good description of the symptoms of epilepsy. The horizontal lines separate the various sections of the text which reads,

"If at the time of possession, while he is sitting down, his left eye moves to the side, a lip puckers, saliva flows from his mouth, and his hands, leg, and trunk of the left side jerk like a slaughtered sheep, it is migcu (epilepsy). If at the time of possession his mind is awake, the demon can be driven out. If at the time of possession his mind is not awake, the demon can't be driven away. [Wilson, Kennier, and Reynolds; 'A Babylonian Treatise of Epilepsy' Medical History, Vol. 34. (1990) p. 192.

Chapter Nine

Ancient Astronomy

In the development of astronomy and mathematics and in a broad sense, Greece, Iran, and India are indebted to Mesopotamia, Islam to Greece, Iran, and India, and Western Europe to Islam. Along this tortuous route, it took over three millennia for the work of the early Sumerians to reach Western Europe.

Astronomy is the oldest and one of the most popular of the physical sciences; all the ancient civilizations of the world left records of their astronomical observations. That includes, in addition to the peoples of the Near East, India, and China, the peoples of Africa, of North and South America, and the Aboriginal people of Australia.

Fascinated with what they observed in the heavens and not knowing the nature of what they saw, the early dwellers of the Near East, and probably the world over, perceived the stars, the planets, the sun, and the moon as miraculous objects having supernatural power, and viewed them divine. Like most ancient civilizations, the peoples of the Fertile Crescent saw the heavens as a realm of power, and imagined that a knowledge of that power might be acquired by the careful observation of the movements celestial objects. They strived to acquire this knowledge in the hope of using it to establish order and stability in their daily lives, such as avoiding calamities, averting disasters, protecting their kings and loved ones, and managing their crops and herds.

Mesopotamian Astronomy

The Mesopotamians believed that they, as human beings, were created for the sole purpose of serving the gods who reside in the heavens, and that events on earth were reflections of what takes place in the heavens. To properly perform the function for which they were created, they became ardent star readers. Their faith led them to study those luminous objects in order to serve them and interpret their wishes. As a consequence of this faith, the roots of astrology and astronomy were planted in Southern Mesopotamia during the early Sumerian period and there they grew and prospered.

The early star-gazers, on account of their ability to read the wishes of the gods and predict future events, formed a highly respected and privileged class. Working in the privacy of their elevated ziggurats, those astrologers-priests wielded enough power in the courts of their rulers to influence government policies and actions as well as the education, agriculture, art, and literature in their societies.

Astrologers gleaned information from reading the heavens and conveyed it to their kings, warning them of and protecting them from calamities that might otherwise befall them, destroy their thrones and their kingdoms.

These were the Mesopotamian priests who became astrologers and astronomers, and barred the common man from practicing these vocations. Under their tutelage, astronomy and astrology became highly important, secretive, and respected disciplines. As a result of their diligent and sustained effort, these early priests left thousands of cuneiform tablets detailing the results of their observations and predictions.

Kings and rulers depended upon their court astrologers to provide them with the divine wishes gleaned from the motion of the stars. Astrologers were thus consulted by kings and high officials on all important matters, and in many instances their opinions were not challenged. They were the rulers all-important advisors. The success of a military campaign depended upon the approval and support of the god, and the court astrologers had to provide the methods and the means to guarantee such approval and support.

The important responsibilities of the Mesopotamian astrologers and the high degree of respectability they commanded guaranteed the growth and prosperity of both astrology and astronomy. With each generation of star observers, the astronomical records and the calculations required for their comprehension became more complex and more demanding, presenting more challenges that exacted more dexterity and more advanced skill. All these efforts were required to interpret the various omens that the gods interweaved into their motions on the celestial sphere.

The astrology, astronomy, and divination made by Mesopotamian scribes, and their observation, and calculation of the positions of heavenly bodies must be viewed as parts of a single descriptive science of the heavens.

In time this science grew in complexity and stature. During the days of the kings of Sumer and Akkad, in the twenty-third century B.C., Mesopotamian astronomers recorded an observation of the eclipse of the moon, the first such observation ever recorded. Modern astronomers have calculated that this eclipse of the moon did actually occur in 2283 B.C.

A record of another eclipse belonging to the same period was uncovered in the city of Ur and was translated as follows;

"In the month of Simanu an eclipse occurs on day 14, the [Moon-] god in his eclipse is obscured on the east side

and clears on the west side below, the north wind blows,
[the eclipse] commences in the first watch of the night
and it touches the middle watch...The king of Ur will be
wronged by his son, the sun-god will catch him and he will
die at the death of his father..."

Professor P. J. Huber of the University of Bayreuth provided the
above translation and calculated the date of the eclipse as April 2 in
2094 B.C. He believes the stated historic details describe the murder of
King Shulgi of the third dynasty of Ur by his son.

The fact that most of the Babylonian names for the stars and the
constellations are Sumerian indicates that Mesopotamian astronomy
and astrology goes back to the early days of Sumer, when the idea of
zodiacal constellations was established. The Sumerians names of the
three important constellations are:

mul
   gu.an.na (bull of the sky)= Taurus
mul
   ur.gu.la (lion or lioness)= Leo
mul
   gir.tab (scorpion)= Scorpio

For the geographical latitude of Sumer and for the year 4000
B.C., W. Harper calculated the dates of the helical rise of the
Pleiades (in Taurus), of Regulus (the main star in Leo), and of
Antares (the giant red star in Scorpio), and determined that the ris-
ing dates of these easily recognizable stars coincided with the spring
equinox, the summer solstice, and the autumn equinox, respectively.
Thus explaining why the Sumerians regarded Taurus, Leo, and
Scorpio as important constellations (1).

The contribution of the Mesopotamians to astrology and astronomy is better understood if one divides the four millennia of its development into four periods:

1. The first period begins with the early Sumerians and continues until the end of the Hammurabi dynasty, c. 1530 B.C.

2. The second period corresponds to the Kassite and Assyrian domination of Mesopotamia (1530–612 B.C.). It ends with the destruction of Nineveh and its rich library.

3. The third or Chaldean period, often referred to as the Neo-Babylonian period, coincides with the reign of the Chaldeans (611–540 B.C.), and ends with the Persian invasion of Babylon.

4. The fourth period, during which both observational and mathematical astronomy were at the peak of their development, extends from 540 B.C. to A.D. 75.

During the first period, the Babylonian Creation Story, Enuma Elish (When Above) was written. Its fifth tablet sheds light on Babylonian knowledge of astronomy as it describes how the Babylonian supreme god, Marduk, establishes the new world order, and cites his creation of heavenly bodies:

> He established the stations for the great gods.
> The stars, like unto them, and the constellations he fixed;
> He ordained the year and marked its section.
> Twelve months he divided by three constellations.
> And the days of the year he fixed according to the stars,
> He established the station of Nibir (Jupiter) to mark their bounds,
> That none of the days may deviate, nor be found lacking.

Marduk, after assigning the various stations to the other great gods, took Nibir as his own. According to Enuma Elish, the Babylonians associated their supreme god Marduk with Jupiter. Later Marduk became known as Jupiter. It would have been impossible for the Babylonians, early in the second millennium B.C., to know that Jupiter is the largest of the planets. The association of the supreme god with Jupiter, and not with the brightest of the planets, Venus, must therefore involve some other characteristics. The motion of Jupiter on the celestial sphere often provides it with the commending position of being high in the firmament. It is the brightest of the planets while in opposition. Venus, the third brightest object in the sky after the sun and the moon, was not assigned to Marduk probably because of its proximity to the sun; it always appears low on the horizon and never high in the sky. greatness and eminence were always associated with height.

Mars was not the choice either as it takes it approximately 1.88 earth years to complete its journey across the celestial sphere, while Jupiter requires 11.9 earth years. Based on this readily available information, Babylonian astronomers could have easily concluded that Jupiter must be farther away than Mars and therefore higher up in the heavens. The highest and the brightest of the planets was assigned to the supreme god.

The fifth tablet continues;

> In the midst of the heaven, he places the zenith.
> Nanar (the Moon), he brought forth and entrusted the
> night to him;
> Placed him there, as the luminary of night, to mark of
> the days;
>
> Thou shalt shine with horns to make known six days;
> On the seventh day with half a tiara (2).
> On Shaputu (3) thou shalt stand in opposition [to the sun] in
> middle of the month.
> When the sun has overtaken thee on the foundation of heaven
> [the horizon],
> Decrease [the tiara of] light and form it backward.

This indicates that during that early date, Babylonians astronomers had full knowledge of the periods, the positions, and the phases of the moon.

During the first period, astrology also played an important role, and astrologers gained in stature. They dealt mainly with predictions based primarily of the state of the sky on the night the crescent moon becomes visible. One such prediction reads: "If the north wind blows across the face of the sky before the new moon, the crop will grow abundantly."

Towards the end of this period, Babylonian astronomers began carefully mapping the sky, fixed the positions of various stars and made accurate records of the rising and setting of the planet Venus.

Astrologers, realizing that Venus is both an evening and a morning star, began to focus their predictions on its appearance and disappearance; "If on the tenth of Arahsamna, Venus disappeared in the East, remained absence for two months and six days, and was seen on the sixteenth of Tebitu in the West, the harvest of the land will be successful."

In the belief that the position of Venus controls the crops, a record of its appearance and disappearance was kept for twenty-one years. This helps in dating events that took place toward the latter part of this period. Based on this record, recent calculations indicate that the Hammurabi dynasty ruled Mesopotamia from 1830 to 1531 B.C. and the great king himself ruled from 1728 to 1686 B.C. (4).

During the second period, a collection of omens known as "Enuma Anu Enlil" was written. It consists of some seventy clay tablets that contain over 7000 omens, which were consulted by astrologers after viewing the sky to help them make their predictions. The omen astrology which prevailed in Mesopotamia until the end to the seventh century B.C. that is until the end of the second astronomical period, differs from horoscope astrology, which gained prominence during the fourth period. Omen astrology, in its predictions, depends on features visible in the sky without any reference to zodiacal signs and is concerned mainly with matters of general interest, such as war and peace, wet or dry periods, good or bad harvest, and the health of the rulers.

On the other hand, horoscope astrology deals with the fate of individuals based on star configurations at the moment of their birth and/or conception, and depends primarily on the twelve zodiacal signs.

To this period belongs one of the earliest surviving report of a solar eclipse. It was found in the Assyrian Eponym Canon under a year which is equivalent to 763–762 B.C. It simply reads; "In (the month) of Sivan the Sun was eclipsed." The month of Sivan corresponds to May-June, and according to recent calculations, a large solar eclipse visible in Mesopotamia occurred on June 13 in 763 B.C.

Also during the second period, it became customary to make more frequent observations and keep better astronomical records. Beginning with the reign of the Babylonian king Nabunassar (747–734 B.C.), astronomical observations became continuous and records of these observations were carefully kept (5). Also, detailed records of lunar eclipses began to be kept during the reign of Nabunassar and continued until 317 B. C. These records became available to Ptolemy, in the second century A.D., as he indicates in his famous book, Almagest. Keeping astronomical records became a Babylonian practice and continued during most of the third and fourth periods.

Each of the twelve months of the Babylonian calendar, which was already in use, was assigned three stars. The Babylonian astronomers made a list of these stars and called it "the three star each". The 36 stars that formed this list were further divided into three sets of twelve; the "stars of Ea" or northern stars; the "stars of Anu", being the god of heavens, near the stellar equator; and the "stars of Enlil" or southern stars (6). The planets Venus, Mars, and Jupiter were included in this list.

To help in record keeping, star maps were constructed in both circular and rectangular forms, usually with three sets of numbers in each one of its sections. These numbers increase in equal increments until they reach a maximum during the summer then decrease in the same equal increments to reach their minimum in winter. The numbers on the outer ring of each section of the star map are twice as large as those in the middle of the section and four times as large as those on the inner ring.

The three numbers in each section indicate that the Babylonians divided the day and the night into three "watches" each. The duration of these "watches" were measured by means of a water clock. The number on the outside ring of the star map determines the weight of the water poured in the water clock. If this is the case, the numbers in the middle ring refer to "half-watches" and those in the inner ring to "quarter-watches" or hours. This interpretation of Babylonian star maps is supported by Herodotus' statement "...and the twelve parts of the day did the Greeks learn from the Babylonians" (7).

Also belonging to this period is the compendium known as MUL.APIN, of which several copies have been preserved. The first tablet of this compendium begins with a list of thirty-three stars of Enlil, twenty-three stars of Anu, and fifteen stars of Ea and their relative positions. All the stars of Anu lie in a zone between +17 and -17 degrees declination. The path of Enlil is northof Anu's zone and the path of Ea is south of it.

Furthermore, MUL.APIN gives the dates of rise and culmination of fixed stars and constellations as well as thorough descriptions of their motion. This precise knowledge was used to calculate the exact times of lunar eclipses (8). One such prediction reads: "On the fourteenth an eclipse of the moon will take place; woe for Elam and Amurru, good for my Lord the King. Let the heart of my Lord the King rejoice...an eclipse will take place..." The prediction must have come true, as the author later adds, "...it (the eclipse) has taken place. In the occurrence of this eclipse lies happiness to my Lord the King." A more important and truly dramatic clay tablet, written in 568 B.C. (about the middle of the third period) during the reign of Nebuchadnessar, states that a lunar eclipse predicted to take place on the fourth of July, 568 B.C.

"failed to occur." Modern astronomers have verified that a lunar eclipse did take place on that date, but during the day, when the moon was not visible in Mesopotamia.

During the Neo-Babylonian or Chaldean period (9), astronomers paid more and more attention to the course of the moon and the five naked-eye planets. They carefully and regularly recorded the conjunctions of the moon and the planets with fixed stars. Furthermore, they dated the first and last visibility of each planet and noted that the sun, the moon, and the five planets are always in the same zone, which coincides with the zodiacal belt. Babylonian astronomers named this zone "the path of the moon."

To many of the peoples of the Near East, the seven celestial bodies-the sun, the moon, and the five classical, or naked-eye, planets-became seven gods. On a given day, prayers were offered to one of these gods, resulting in a seven-day cycle of worship and giving rise to the seven-day week (Chapter Four, The Sanctity of Seven).

Babylonian astronomers of this period also carried out the work discussed in MUL.APIN a step further. They divided each of the four zodiacal segments cited in MUL.APIN into three parts, corresponding to three months of the year. This resulted in a zodiacal circle divided into twelve segments corresponding to the twelve zodiacal signs. As each month of the schematic year has thirty days, the zodiacal circle was thus divided into 360 degrees, and each degree corresponds to one day. This led to the horoscope astrology, which became fully developed by 410 B.C.

Regardless of whether one considers horoscope astrology a priceless or a worthless field, the Babylonians, in developing it, provided humanity with a window to the future that countless peoples have been looking through for over two and one half millennia. This is a clear indication that the Babylonians knew not only astronomy but also human nature, and the interest of human beings in predicting the future.

Also during the third period, knowledge of Babylonian astronomy transcended the boundaries of Babylonia, and most of the peoples of the Orient became cognizant of some of its aspects. The people of Canaan, in addition to adopting the five naked-eye planets and the sun and the moon in their prayers and calendar, showed great interest in the practical side of that knowledge, and made use of it in charting their voyages and finding their destinations. The Phoenician seafarers, the first to sail by day as well as night, saved precious time sailing the high seas guided by the North Star. Their commonly known dependence on this star led the classical Greeks to refer to it as the Phoenician Star. However, the Greeks did not gain this knowledge until after their victory over the Persians in 480 B.C. During the early stages of the Greco-Persian war, the Phoenicians, the allies of the Persians, sailed their war fleet through the treacherous waters of the Aegean in the darkness of the night to take the Greek fleet completely by surprise. The Greeks were simply unaware that such a feat was possible.

During that period, the Ionian cities, the commercial leaders of the Aegean, were in constant contact with Phoenician and Egyptian port cities. Through these contacts, they were introduced to the astronomy and mathematics of the Near East. In this fashion, Babylonian knowledge of astronomy-the movement of stars, planets, sun, moon, and the periodicity of eclipses-was transferred into the Ionian culture, providing the Ionians with the foundations upon which they built their understanding of the physical world.

The first known Ionian astronomer, Thales (c. 625–545 B.C.) was an able statesman who traveled widely. While in Babylon, he obtained lists of observations of the heavenly bodies. From such lists, Babylonian astronomers had already learned the periodicity of eclipses, and had accurately predicted several solar and lunar eclipses. With these lists in his possession, Thales presumably could predict when the next eclipse would occur. It has been reported that, upon returning to his home town of Miletus, the most influential of Ionion cities, he did predict a solar eclipse that took place in 585 B.C. But "Modern astronomers doubt that Thales could actually have predicted an eclipse." (10).

Thales set an example that was followed by aspiring young Ionian and Greek scholars; many of them made their pilgrimage to Babylon seeking the knowledge of its scribes. In so doing, the Greeks, over a relatively short period, acquired the knowledge of mathematics and astronomy that the Babylonians had accumulated over thousands of years.

Thales and Anaximander (c. 610–540 B.C.), also from the city-state of Miletus, made their contribution when they theorized that the physical world was regulated by a set of natural laws rather than by the arbitrary action of deities-a very significant and a revolutionary deviation from ancient Babylonian thoughts.

Pythagoras of Samos also belongs to this period. His knowledge of Babylonian mathematics led to the famous Pythagorean Theorem, which states that in a right triangle the square of the hypotenuse equals the sum of the squares of the other two sides. Pythagoras left his home town for Italy around 530 B.C. and, probably influenced by the thoughts of Thales and Anaximander, taught that the physical world might be better understood through numerical methods.

These Ionians thinkers, by abandoning the Near Eastern mythology with which astronomy was tightly interwoven, wrested the natural world from the power of the gods and placed it in the hands of natural scientists, who began to discern its laws.

During the fourth period (539 B.C.–A.D. 75), in spite of the fact that Mesopotamia was consecutively under Persian, Seleucid, and Arsacid rules, Chaldean astronomers maintained their diligent work and Babylonian astronomy continued to flourish reaching its culminating point. The great series of Babylonian astronomical observations was continued uninterrupted. A clay tablet-now at the University Museum of Philadelphia-belongs to this series and reports an eclipse of the moon followed by an eclipse of the sun.

Another solar eclipse was reported on two separate clay tablets-both in the British Museum. The details provided on these tablets attest to the ability and diligence of the Chaldean astronomers of this period. Professor H. Hunger of the University of Vienna translated the two tablets as follows:

> "Year 175 (Seleucid), intercalary 12th month, day 28. At 24 degrees after sunrise, solar eclipse. When it began on the south-west side, in 18 degrees of day in the morning it became entirely total. Venus, Mercury, and the Normal Stars were visible. Jupiter Mars, which were in their period of disappearance, became visible in its eclipse [...] It threw off (a shadow) from south-east to north-west. (Time-interval of) 35 degrees for onset, maximal phase and clearing".

This solar eclipse occurred on April 15 in 136 B.C. when Jupiter and Mars were too close to the sun to be visible under normal conditions. The "Normal Stars" were reference stars in the zodiac belt (11).

During this period, the motions of the sun, the moon, and the five classical planets were correctly calculated, and their positions on the celestial sphere were mathematically defined. Thus towards the beginning of the fourth century B.C. the application of mathematical methods to planetary motions gained prominence. It is possible that mathematical methods originally supplemented observation, and was used when observation was not possible-"when it is clear, observe, when it is cloudy, compute" (wrote Swerdlow) (12).

To reduce the complexity of their calculations to a manageable level, Babylonian astronomers set forth certain assumptions in the form of principles:

1. The periods, and thus the mean motions, of the sun and planets are invariable.

2. The (mean) sun moves uniformly with its mean motion of one zodiacal rotation in one year.

3. The phenomena of the planets takes place at fixed characteristic elongations from the (mean) sun.

4. The mean motion of the sun in the synodic time measures the synodic arc between phenomena. The first principle is correct, the other three are simple representations of complex and irregular phenomena, and the Chaldaeans scribes knew that (13).

Among other Babylonian observations written during this period are those known as the "goal-year", which contain the following relations:

> Saturn in 59 years makes 57 revolutions in anomaly and two in the ecliptic.
> Jupiter in 71 years makes 65 revolutions in anomaly and six in the ecliptic.
> Mars in 79 years makes 37 revolutions in anomaly and 42 in the ecliptic.
> Venus in eight years makes five revolutions in anomaly and eight in the ecliptic.
> Mercury in 46 years makes 145 revolutions in anomaly and 46 in the ecliptic (14).

Based on these relations, Hipparchus concluded that in 126,007 days and 1.0 hour there are 4,267 synodic months, 4573 returns in anomaly, and 4612 sidereal revolutions less 7.5 degrees.

The four best known Chaldean astronomers of this period are Nabu-rimannu, Kidinnu, Sudines, and Seleuceus. Nabu-rimannu carefully studied the astronomical records that were available to him and which contained the results of previous continuous observations made over a period of more than two hundred and fifty years. On the basis of these records, he calculated the time required for the sun and the moon to complete their revolutions, and recorded the exact dates for the eclipses of the sun and the moon, as well as other celestial events. His calculations of the length of the year gave a value of 365 days, 6 hours, 15 minutes, and 41 seconds. This is less than 27 minutes longer than value calculated by modern astronomers (15).

The Greeks were still using the inconvenient and inaccurate moon-month calendar, approximating the solar calendar by inserting an extra month every third, fifth, and eighth year. A Greek engineer and builder named Meton became aware of the length of the year as measured by Nabu-rimannu and adopted it in formulating a new Greek calendar.

About a century after Nabu-rimannu performed his work, and with the more accurate astronomical tables available to him, Kidinnu was able to show that the tropical year-the length of the year as measured from equinox to equinox-is shorter than the sidereal year-the time it takes the sun to complete one circle relative to the fixed stars. At present, we know that the sidereal year is about 20 minutes longer than the tropical year. Without realizing it, Kidinnu discovered what became known as the precession of the equinoxes, where ever so slowly the projection of the earth's axis traces an imaginary cone; it takes some 26 millennia for the earth's axis to complete this imaginary cone (16). Kidinnu's discovery was later hailed as Hipparchus' greatest achievement.

Taking the unit of time as the synodic month of about 29.5 days, Nabu-rimannu assumed that the motion of the sun in certain parts of the zodiacal belt was 30 degrees per month, and in the remaining part it was 28 7' 30". On the other hand, Kidinnu assumed that the motion of the sun was a function of time, increasing linearly up to a maximum value and then decreasing in the same fashion until it reached a minimum value. This type of variation is mathematically described by a function known as a zigzag function.

Both Kidinnu and Nabu-rimannu took the velocity of the moon to be a zigzag function of time, but for the lunar latitude and the duration of daylight they assume a more complicated function that resembles an uneven, rough sine function.

Also during this period various methods were developed to calculate the longitude and latitude of the moon at all times. Astronomical quantities such as the time of the new moon and the time of the full moon, the times of the setting and rising of the moon and of the sun, and the times and magnitudes of eclipses were calculated regularly and sometimes daily.

Similar calculations were extended to cover the motion of the five naked-eye planets, and tables were generated to provide the longitudes and the cardinal points of these planets. These points include:

(a). the points of first and last visibility of the planets, known as morning-first and evening-last,

(b). the stationary points, where the retrograde motion of a planet begins or ends, and

(c). for the outer planets, the points of their opposition to the sun. Babylonian astronomers further calculated the synodic arc, which is the increase in the longitude of a planet between two similar cardinal points, such as from one evening-last to the next evening-last. According to Nabu-rimannu, the synodic arc has different values in different parts of the zodiacal circle. For example, the zodiacal circle of Jupiter was divided into two or four parts and that of Mars into six parts. This types of division was used in Egyptian planetary tables of the first two centuries A.D. and in the Hindu tables of the six century A.D. (17).

To compute the dates of the cardinal points, Babylonian astronomers assumed that each planet, when at its cardinal points, has a fixed elongation from the sun.

Nabu-rimannu and Kidinnu should be reverently remembered as the true founders of astronomical science. Their calculations are the foundations of mathematical astronomy and their achievements have earned them a place among the great astronomers of all times.

Greek astronomers studied the work of these two giants, took it for their own, and then hellenized their names, calling them Naburianos and Kidenas.

The genius of Babylonian astronomers and the magnitude of their contribution to the field of astronomy are attested to by the large number of books and scientific articles written about the subject during the present century.

> "It was with good reason that the
> wisdom of the Chaldaeans inspired wonders and admiration
> throughout the ancient world, and their legacy of the omen
> series, diaries, and ephemerides is still worthy of our own
> wonder and admiration. In addition, Neugebauer always insisted
> that the scribes developed a strictly mathematical interest in
> lunar and planetary theory comparable to Hipparchus and Ptolemy,
> and I have no doubt that he too was correct." (18).

Around the last quarter of the fourth period, serious approaches to the study of astronomy appeared among the inhabitants of Anatolia, the Aegean, and Greece. A well accomplished astronomer named Hipparachus was born in northwestern Asia Minor towards the beginning of the second century B.C. but spent most of his career working in Rhodes. Available to Hipparchus were many of the astronomical tables compiled by Chaldeans astronomers and that included a complete or nearly complete list of lunar eclipses observed in Babylon since the reign of Nabunassar (c. 747 B.C.). Hipparchus thoroughly studied these tables and adopted the calculations of Nabu-rimannu and Kidinnu. In so doing, he transformed Greek astronomy from a purely theoretical into a practical predictive science.

Both Hipparachus and later Ptolemy (19) used the Babylonian approach of dividing the celestial circle into 360 degrees and based their calculations on the Babylonian sexagesimal system.

In Almagest, Ptolemy exhibits heavy dependence on information garnered by Hipparchus, who, in turn, shows great dependence on Chaldean (Babylonian) sources. The general nature of the dependence of Greek astronomy on Babylonian mathematical methods was recognized as early as A.D. 1900. Excavations and research carried out during the twentieth century provided additional proof of the great magnitude of this dependence.

Early in the third century B.C., another Greek astronomer, Aristarchus of Samos, theorized that the earth revolves around the sun, which he described as being much larger and considerably farther away than it appears. Aristarchus made a slight mistake in stating that the earth revolves around the sun in a perfectly circular instead of an elliptical orbit. Later astronomers, among them, Hipparchus and Ptolemy, rejected Aristarchus' heliocentric model in favor of the traditional geocentric one because their calculations of the positions of celestial objects based on the proposed circular orbit failed to agree with observations.

As an indication of the decline of astronomy after Ptolemy, who included the geocentric model in his time-honored book Almagest (20), the correctness of the heliocentric model was not recognized until it was proposed again, some eighteen hundred years later, by the Polish astronomer Copernicus (A.D. 1473–1543).

Egyptian Astronomy

In Egypt, where careful, detailed, and complete records of most aspects of life were found, no astronomical or astrological records dating prior to the fifth century B.C. have been uncovered. Although Egyptian literature written before the middle of the first millennium

B.C. contains references to the sun, moon, stars, and planets, no astronomical treatise approaching those uncovered in Babylon in detail and
completeness have been found in Egypt. Even the texts of the
Cosmology of Seti I and Ramses II deal mostly with time-reckoning.

Many orientalists believe that ancient Egyptian astronomers must
have documented their observations, but those papyri, for reasons yet
unknown, did not survive, or were carefully hidden where they could
not be found. The Egyptian priests-astronomers regarded their profession as an esoteric science, not to be disclosed to the common people,
whose superstitions should not be destroyed by factual information. It
should be stated that Egyptian papyri that were stored in large cities in
the damp valley of the Nile deteriorated, and only those placed in the
relatively dry fringes of the desert survived.

The pharaohs may also have prevented their astrologers from
spreading their knowledge, as it could conceivably have had restrictive
effects on their divine authority, which should know no bound.

The absence of astronomical treatises does not mean that ancient
Egyptians lacked the knowledge or were uninterested in the subject;
there are more than eighty astronomical monuments, found mostly on
the ceilings of private and royal tombs and on temples; there are also
numerous star clocks found on the inside of coffin lids.

The most significant and the oldest of these monuments are the
recently uncovered megalith alignments and stone circle of Nabta in
the southern desert just west of the Nile River. The circle is slightly less
than four meters in diameter and contains slabs which may have been
used for sighting along the horizon. The megaliths, some of which are
about three meters high and two meters wide, are arranged to mark the
east-west and the north-south directions.

These structures, in addition to their astronomical and cosmologi-
cal values, may have been used to provide directions for nomadic
groups navigating across the Sahara and as a ceremonial complex for
religious rituals.

Radiocarbon dating of various artifacts found in the area indicates that religious rituals were conducted in the complex prior to 4000 B.C. which makes the Egyptian monument about a 1000 years older than the megaliths of England and Europe (21).

Along the Nile Valley, the five naked-eye planets are depicted on the tomb ceilings of Seti I and Ramses II (c. 1300–B. C.) as well as other sites, usually in the following order, Jupiter, Saturn, Mars, Mercury, Venus. Jupiter, Saturn, and Mars were considered manifestations of Horus, the falcon of the sky, while Mercury was associated with Seth (the evil monster). In early times, Venus was pictured as a heron, but later became known as the "Crosser" indicating that it was recognized by Egyptian Astronomers as being both a morning and an evening star (22).

In addition to their interest in the classical planets, the ancient Egyptians worshipped Sirius, the brightest star in the heavens, which they called Sothis. The appearance of this bright star in the pre-dawn glare of the sun signaled the life-giving annual flooding of the Nile River. Sirius, whose helical rise thus became a very important date played an important role in the development of the Egyptian calendar (23).

The Egyptians constructed the entrances of most of their pyramids facing very closely to the easterly direction of the rising of Sirius. This astronomical alignment is either for calendrical purposes or out of reverence to the god of the flooding of the Nile. Similar alignment appears in the Kushite pyramids of central Sudan, which must have been adopted by the people of Kush after their conquest of the land of the Nile around 800 B.C. (24).

One is led to believe that Egyptian astronomers must have known enough to enable them to produce the magnificent Egyptian calendar, which required a great deal of work, observation, and correction before it reached its final and quite accurate form. It is known that the

Egyptians had an acceptably accurate solar calendar as early as 4236 B.C. (25).

Furthermore, the ingenuity of Egyptian architects and their knowledge of astronomy enabled them to properly orient many of their monuments so that the rays of the sun would enter them through narrow openings only on the morning of the summer solstice. To understand the immensity of this architectural feat, one has to imagine a hole about one centimeter in diameter and several meters long drilled in solid rocks from the external surface of the Great Pyramid of Giza to the King's Chamber. I inserted my little finger in that hole. It was a tight fit, and I could feel the breeze coming through it. The guide informed me that the rays of the sun still pass through it on the morning of the twenty-second of June. Neither years nor abuse have been able to alter the position or the direction of this opening. The alignment served as an excellent marker that ancient Egyptians used to correct their calendar whenever corrections were needed. Similar structural alignments have been found at Stonehenge in England and in a number of structures of native Americans.

The advanced state of ancient Egyptian mathematics also points to the ability of the Egyptians to apprehend astronomical phenomena, make correct observations, and plot the positions of heavenly objects. The Ahmes Papyrus, the oldest mathematical treatise known, dates between 2000 and 1700 B.C. It contains information that must have been gleaned several hundred years earlier, and is a striking example of the ability of ancient Egyptian mathematicians.

After the Persian conquest of Egypt and later under the leadership of the Ptolemies, Mesopotamian treatises of astronomy, astrology, and the signs of the zodiac were transplanted into Egypt where they found a fertile field. All viable evidence indicates that they were imported from Mesopotamia to be later exported to Greece.

The first known Egyptian zodiac decorated the temple of Esna. The circular zodiac that formed the ceiling of the temple of Hathor at

Denderah in Upper Egypt-now in the Louvre-is a magnificent representation of the Egyptian sky superimposed upon the Mesopotamian signs of the zodiac (26).

After visiting Egypt in 460 B.C. Herodotus wrote (Book II, p.82):

> They (the Egyptians) assigned each month and day to some
> god; they can tell what fortune and what end and what
> disposition a man shall have according to the day of his
> birth.
> This has given material to Greeks who deal in poetry. They
> have
> made themselves more omens than all other nations togeth-
> er;
> when an ominous thing happens they take note of the out-
> come...,
> and if something of a like kind happen again they think it
> will have a like result.

In general terms, it can be said that the ancient Greeks received their early knowledge of astronomy directly from Mesopotamia, by having their youths visit the educational centers of Babylon and through their frequent commercial contacts with their Near Eastern neighbors. The land of the Nile provided the rest of the known world with much of the astrology that was transplanted from Mesopotamia into Egypt.

---

(1). W. Hartner, "The Earliest History of the Constellations in the Near East and the motif of the Lion-Bull Combat." Journal of Near Eastern Studies. Vol. 24 (1965) pp. 1–16.

(2). On the seventh day of the lunar month at sunset, the moon stands directly overhead like a tiara.

(3). Shapatu is the Babylonian day of rest "for the heart." At first it probably meant the day of the full moon, as this verse indicates. The Hebrew word "sabbath" is also used in the Old Testament to indicate full moon; 2 Kin. 4:23, and Isa. 1:13.

(4). Waerden, B. L. van der, "Dictionary Of Scientific Biography" (1978). Vol. XV, Supplement I. New York, Charles Scribner's Sons. p. 674.

(5). Breasted, James Henry. (1935:213).

(6). Before the ascension of Marduk, Anu was the supreme god, and the three gods Anu, Ea (Marduk's father), and Enlil shared power as a triad.

(7). Herodotus, Histories II, 108.

(8). Schaumberger, J. Zeitschrift fur Assyriologie, Vol. 47. p. 127. (1941), and Vol. 50. p. 42. (1942).

(9). The Chaldeans were Semitic tribes that moved from Arabia into southern Mesopotamia and built an empire that lasted from about 612 B.C. to 539 B.C. They left an indelible mark on astronomy, astrology, and mathematics.

(10). Martin, Thomas R. (1996:91).

(11). Selin, Helaine, Ed. (1997:275).

(12). Swerdlow, N. M. (1998:174).

(13). Swerdlow, N. M. (1998:31).

(14). Ptolemy erroneously ascribed these planetary periods to Hipparchus (Almagest IX, 3).

(15). Breasted, James Henry. (1935:214).

(16). Glashow, Sheldon. (1994:17).

(17). Waerden, B. L. van der "Dictionary of Scientific Biography" 1978. Vol. XV, Supplement I. New York, Charles Scribner's and Sons. P. 679

(18). Swerdlow, N. M. (1998:32).

(19). Ptolemy lived in the second century A.D., did most of his work in Alexandria (Egypt), and wrote Almagest, for the most part a compilation of the work of earlier astronomers. Almagest became a widely respected astronomical treatise.

(20). The geocentric model, also known as the Ptolemaic model, was included in the famed Almagest, and accepted by all astronomers until the early years of the sixteenth century.

(21). Malville, J. McKim, Fred Wendorf, Ali A, Mazar, and Romauld Schield; Nature, Vol. 392, No. 6675; 2 April 1998. PP. 448–490.

(22). Parker, Richard A. Dictionary of Scientific Biography, Supplement 1. 1978, p. 719.>

(23). The fact that Sirius is a double star was not recognized until A.D. 1844. The bright star became known as Sirius (A) and its companion Sirius (B), observed in A.D. 1862.

(24). Selin, Helaine, Ed. (1997:98).

(25). Breasted, James Henry. (1935:59).

(26). Krupp, E. C. (1977:216).

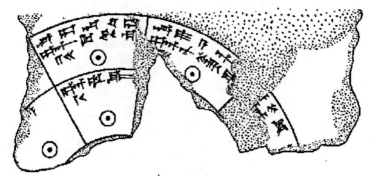

Fig. 9-1. A fragment of a circular Babylonian astrolabe.

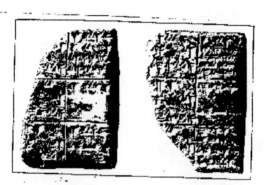

Fig. 9-2. Both sides of a Chaldean astronomical tablet. On the front (left-hand side) are lists of observations of the moon, planets, and some fixed stars. The right-hand side reads,

"On the first mercury rises,
On the third the equinox,
Night of the 15th, 40 minutes after
 sunset, an eclipse of the moon begins.
On the 28th occurs an eclipse of the sun.

The dates of these two eclipses have been calculated as october 9th and 23rd of 425 B.C.

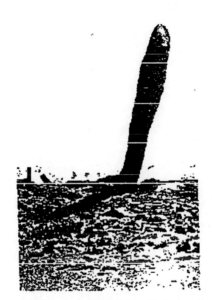

Fig. 9-3. One of the standing megalith of the stone circle
of Nabta, Egypt.

Chapter Ten

The Calendar

Keeping records and knowing the times of events must have interested human beings before the dawn of recorded history. In various localities, such record keeping could have depended on seasonal variations, such as the flowering of trees and shrubs, the migrations of birds, the ripening of crops, or seasonal rain.

Seasonal variations, generated by the fact that the earth is tilted relative to the plane of its orbit around the sun, provide for the timely growth of vegetation and the ripening of various fruits and nuts. These, being the main sources of nutrition for hunter-gatherers, motivated those early dwellers to measure time and formulate calendars.

Although time-keeping could depend on a variety of terrestrial changes, celestial observations must have also played a prominent role. The most obvious, and as a result the most widely adopted by ancient civilizations, were the changes in the phases of the moon. These offer a unique and a convenient scale for the measurement of time.

Early on, with distant travel being slow, difficult, and dangerous; and communication among societies, rare, slow, or non-existent, each of the various communities formulated its own method of time keeping. But with improved method of communications and the ease and safety of travel, civilized nations felt the need to adopt a single workable calendar.

The road that led to our present-day calendar is long and tortuous and forms a part of our heritage. Its formulation is a great achievement that required a great deal of work over an extended period of time and involved astronomers, mathematicians, heads of states, and clergy. The events that led to its completion form an integral segment of the history of our civilization.

As western civilization has its roots in the Near East, this will be the proper place to start a search for the roots of our calendar. The ancient people of the Fertile Crescent, like many others, adopted the lunar scale for their early calendars. This is attested to, primarily, by the origins of some time-related words that are still in use: the Akkadians worshipped the moon as the god Sin-the word is the origin of the Arabic word "sanat" and the Hebrew word "shanah" meaning year; the Arameans and the ancient Arabs worshipped their moon god and calling him "Sahr" and that gave rise to the Aramaic and Arabic word "shahr" (month); the Arabs also worshipped "'Amm" their moon-god and that gave rise to the Arabic word "'am" (year) (1). Finally, the old Babylonians and later the Hebrews called the crescent moon "Terah" (2). In modern Semitic languages, the word is still used to mean history or record. Such relations between the word for "moon" and words related to time-keeping appear in many other languages; as an example, the English word "month" came from the Anglo-Saxon word "monath", which originated from the word "moon" (3).

Recalling that to most ancient peoples celestial objects were perceived as gods, they deduced that these gods move about in the heavens to provide them with correct information one of which is the proper way to keep time. In the Babylonian creation story, Enuma Elish (When Above), composed early in the second millennium B.C. the fifth tablet reads;

He (Marduk) (4) ordained the year and marked its section.
Twelve months he divided by three constellations.
And the days of the year he fixed according to the stars.

Of the various calendars used through out the ancient world, the three most common are those based on the apparent motions of the sun, the moon, or the combined motions of both. Lunar calendars are based strictly on the changes in the phases of the moon. The best known strictly lunar calendar is the Muslim Calendar. The solar calendar is based on the length of the solar year. A calendar based on the motion of both the sun and the moon is termed lunisolar. To bring the lunar calendar to correspond to the motion of the sun and to be in agreement with the seasons, the ancient peoples of the Near East and China irregularly inserted an additional month into their lunar year. In 2357 B.C. the Chinese emperor Yao devised a calendar in which he synchronized the moon months and the solar year by intercalating two additional month every five years. Finding that it was not adequate, this method was later revised by intercalating seven months in each nineteen year cycle, bringing the length of the year to an acceptable value of about 365 days (5).

In the Orient, irregular intercalation continued until the Neo-Babylonian Period-sixth century B.C. (6), when the astronomers of Chaladea (Neo-Babylon) developed a 19-year cycle having twelve years of twelve months each and seven years of thirteen months each. It is not well established whether the Chaldeans devised this calendar on their own, or were aware of the Chinese earlier achievement.

The insertion of the thirteenth month was made according to a fixed pattern that kept the moon calendar adequately synchronized with the sun cycle and therefore with the seasons. This calendar with minor variations was soon adopted by the various groups of the ancient Near East, and still forms the basis of today Hebrew calendar.

Well into the fifth century B.C. at which time the Egyptians were using their almost accurate solar calendar, developed a few thousands years earlier, the Greeks were still content with a moon-month calendar. They approximated the solar calendar by inserting an extra month every third, fifth, and eighth year.

In spite of fixed cycles, the idea of having twelve-month and thirteen-month years, although an improvement upon irregular intercalation, proved to be rather complicated: people, clergymen, and kings usually forgot to properly add days or months to their year, and when they did, the addition was often more or less random and not based on scientific methods.

The Week

A unit of time longer than a day and shorter than a month is needed for humans to conduct certain affairs that need to be routinely performed, such as worship and marketing. For that purpose, different societies devised units of times of varied length. This unit that we call "week" is the most arbitrary of all calendaral units; it has no relation to the changes of the phases of the moon or to the motion of the sun.

Probably as a matter of convenience, ancient peoples of the Near East adopted a time-unit that was four days long. This could also be the result of ancient Sumerian and Egyptian cosmology. The Sumerians viewed the earth as a rectangle with its corners pointing in the direction of the four winds, the south, the north, the east, and the west wind. The ancient Egyptians also viewed the earth as a rectangle with a high mountain on each corner and the havens rest on the peak of the four mountains. If the earth has four corners then four must be a special number to be honored by a time-unit four days long.

But a four-day unit of time was neither unique nor universal; later both Babylonians and Egyptians divided their 30-day months into three equal units of ten days each. The ten-day week was later adopted by the Greeks. On the other hand, Native central Americans had a five-day unit, while Assyrians had a six-day unit, and the Romans, for some-time, had an eight-day unit (7). Up to the time of Julius Caesar (100–40 B.C.), the days of the eight-day marketing week were repre-sented by the letters A through H, which were repeated unbroken and independent of monthly divisions. But regardless of the designation of the last day of the year, The first day of the following year was always assigned the letter A.

The ancient and ardent astronomers of Mesopotamia were able to identify five planets: Mercury, Venus, Mars, Jupiter, and Saturn. They are listed here in the reverse order of their perceived distances from the earth, (See Diagram). These five celestial bodies, together with the sun and the moon became seven important divinities. As the seven-planet-divinity cult spread into the Near East, it became customary to pray for and chant the praise of one of the seven gods on a given day. A seven-day cycle of worship was thus established, and in time the name of the god was bestowed on the day of his worship. A seven-day week came into being (8). Ever since the sequence of the days of the week remained unchanged. Later, the Babylonians tried to divide each month into six time-units of five days each; but the mysticism of the seven was too powerful and dislodged the more convenient time units of both Babylon and Egypt.

The Egyptians began their week with Saturday, but the Jews, after the exodus to spite their oppressors, made Saturday the last day of the week. The Christians accepted the Jewish tradition but changed the day of rest from Saturday to Sunday. The Muslims, to distant them-selves from pagan gods, gave numerical designation to the first five days of the week, beginning their week with Al-Ahad, (the first or the one). The sixth day of the Muslim week, al-Jum'a, as its name indicates, is the day of communal prayer, and for the last day they retained the Hebrew name, al-Sabet.

Roman soldiers stationed in the Near East became accustomed to the seven-day week, and introduced it into the Roman society. Roman Emperor Octavian (Caesar Augustus) and succeeding emperors tolerated the practice and eventually, the seven-day week replaced the Roman eight-day marketing week. Finally, in A.D. 321, Emperor Constantine made the change official. Constantine's declaration was a major step in establishing the seven-day week as a universal unit of time.

Practically in all calendars, neither the month nor the year has to end on a given week-day, and the length of the week has no effect on the accuracy of either Lunar or solar calendars.

The Lunar Months

The period required by the moon to complete its orbit depends on the method used for its measurement, or more precisely on the frame of reference in which the measurement is performed. Only one of these measurements have historically been used in determining the length of the lunar month adopted in lunar calendars.

The moon takes approximately 27.32 days to complete its orbit around the earth and returns to the same position in the sky. This is the length of the sidereal moon month. To early astronomers, the precise length of the sidereal month was not easy to determine and therefore the length of the sidereal month was never used as a unit of time.

The earth and the moon orbit the sun in the same direction. Because of this motion the apparent time needed for the moon to complete its orbit is longer than the sidereal moon month, and it is known as the synodic month, whose length can easily be measured. As a matter of fact it was measured to better than one second over two thousand years ago.

The earliest good values of the lengths of the lunar months were calculated by the Greek astronomer Hipparchus (c. 190–125 B.C.), who, based upon information obtained from Chaldean astronomical records, determined that in 126007 days and 1.0 hour there are 4267 synodic months and 4612 sidereal revolutions less 7.5 degrees. This gives the length of the lunar synodic month as 29.530593 days. This is longer than today's best known value by less than half a second. Hipparchus' calculations of the length of the sidereal lunar month gave a value of 27.3217 days, which is also in good agreement with the correct value.

Once the length of the synodic month is known, the length of the sidereal month may be readily calculated. The new moon occurs when the sun, moon, and earth are aligned, but as we have already stated the moon and the earth orbit the sun in the same direction. Thus during the period between two successive new moons, the earth rotates $T/365.24$ of a complete circle, where T is the length of the synodic month, and the ratio of the length of the synodic month to the length of the sidereal month, T/t, is greater than unity by this fraction,

$$T/t = 1 + T/365.24.$$

Putting $T = 29.53$ days in this relation, gives the value of the length of the sidereal month as $t = 27.32$ days. For a more accurate value of t, the precise values of the length of the year and of the synodic month should be inserted in this relation.

The best known present day value of the length of the synodic month is 29 days, 12 hours, 44 minutes, and 2.8 seconds and this is equal to 29.530588 days, making a lunar year of twelve synodic months equals to 354.36706 days. This is 10.875143 days shorter than the tropical solar year, hence the needed correction if the lunar year is to keep up with the seasons.

Most ancient peoples kept their records based upon a lunar calendar and measured time by lunar months or moons. This was true of ancient Egyptians who, before their superior solar calendar, divided the year into three seasons: "Inundation", "Coming Forth", and "Harvest" and each season into four lunar months. On the opposite side of the globe, the native Americans measured times by moons, that is the time from one new moon to the next.

The Solar Year

As early as 4236 B.C. that is before the first union of the people of the Nile valley, the Egyptians had an acceptably accurate solar calendar. The ancient Egyptians worshipped Sirius, the brightest star in the heavens, as the god Sothis. The appearance of this bright star in the pre-dawn glare of the sun signaled the life-giving annual flooding of the Nile. This makes it a very important date particularly to Egyptian farmers. As a result it played a fundamental role in the development of the Egyptian calendar. Based on the helical rise of Sirius, Egyptian astronomers determined that the number of days in a year is 365. They retained the twelve-month year, which they adopted from the Babylonian lunar calendar but assigned 30 days to each month, leaving five days to be designated feast days, a sort of a holiday, at the end of each year. This addition brought their year into harmony-although not a perfect harmony-with the inundation of river Nile and the apparent motion of the sun.

For added convenience, the Egyptians divided each of their months into three "weeks" of ten days each. Through the years, the Egyptian calendar started to fall behind the seasonal calendar. But Egyptian astronomers, who were able to measure the length of the solar year almost accurately, neglected early on to make any corrections to their calendar. There are indications that at one time, the Egyptians adopted but soon after dropped the idea of a leap year; they might have felt that the addition of a day to their calendar every four years was somewhat cumbersome.

Based on their knowledge of the length of the solar year, the Egyptians built many of their monuments with narrow openings allow-ing the sun rays to enter them only on the morning of the summer solstice. To understand the enormity of this architectural feat one has to imagine a hole about one centimeter in diameter and several meters long drilled in solid rocks from the external surface of the Great Pyramid of Giza to the King Chamber. The rays of the sun still enter through this hole into the King's Chamber on the morning of the summer solstice-the twenty-second of June, the longest period of daylight. Such an alignment could have easily be used to correct the calendar, if corrections were desired.

The alignments of ancient monuments with the position of the sun are not unique to Egypt, and have been found, although not with the same architectural precision, in several ancient structures such as the Stonehenge in England and in a number of monuments built by Native Americans. Thus indicating that peoples of various cultures put enormous effort and built hugh monuments to determine the position of the sun and the length of the solar year.

The first good value of the length of the solar year was obtained by the great Chaldean astronomer Nabu-rimanu, who, early in the fifth century B.C. studied the astronomical records which were available to him and which were obtained from continuous observations made by several Babylonian astronomers over a period of more than two hundred and fifty years. His calculations gave the length of the solar year as 365 days, 6 hours, 15 minutes, and 41 seconds (9), that is 365.26091 days. This is only 26.958096 minutes too long, a deviation of less than 0.005 per cent.

About a century after Nabu-Rimanu performed his work, another great Chaldean astronomer named Kidinnu determined that the length of the tropical year-the length of the year as measured from Spring equinox to Spring equinox-is shorter than the sidereal year-the time it takes the sun to complete a circle relative to fixed stars. The sidereal year, as we know now, is about 20 minutes longer than the tropical year. This difference is due to the fact that the direction of the earth's axis is changing, slowly tracing a cone relative to the fixed stars.

This precession is so slow, it takes about 26 thousand years to complete that imaginary cone (10).

Seasons vary in accordance with the tropical year, and people, being interested in such variations, construct their calendars on the basis of the length of the tropical year whose length has been measured to a high degree of accuracy.

The approximate value of the length of the tropical year, obtained by ancient astronomers and by Sosigenes of Alexandria underwent several improvements in more recent years. One such good measurement was made in the ninth century A.D. by the Arab scholar and astronomer Mohammed Ibn Jabir al-Battani, who came within 22 second of the correct value. Yet, better results were obtained by 'Umar al-Khayyam [the tentmaker] of the Ruba'iyat fame. While working as the director of the astronomical observatory in Isfahan, al-Khayyam (c. A.D. 1020–1110) performed most of his work in astronomy, of which probably the most renowned is his almost accurate measurement of the length of the tropical year. Based on a cycle of thirty-three years, he calculated the mean length of the solar year and obtained a value of 365.2424 days. This is only 0.000201 days or 17.34 seconds longer than the best known value (11), which is 365.242199 days. This odd number of days per year is an average value, which is not the precise length of any given year. The earth is not a solid or a perfect sphere; it totters and wobbles in its elliptical orbit around the sun and it is pushed and pulled by the moon travelling in its own elliptical orbit. As a result the length of the year varies by a few seconds, oscillating about this average value.

To synchronize the calendar year and the solar year, a calendar should be devised such that the length of its year averaged over a certain number of years, is equal, or is acceptably close to 365.242199 days. This is definitely not a simple matter and this is why it took millennia to come up with such a calendar.

With the present close connections among the various parts of the world and the great mobility of many people, many human activities will be significantly simplified if the nations of the world adopt a single calendar with a definite starting date from which to count the years and the centuries (12).

The Roman Contribution

It has been said that the mythical Romulus, the founder of Rome, devised a calendar in the middle of the eight century B.C. composed of only ten lunar months-the number of fingers on both hands. From the Romulian calendar we inherited many of the present-day names of the months: Marius, from Mars, the god of war, Aprilis, probably for the goddess of love, Junius, for Juno, the queen of the gods…Then Romulus fell back on numbers, Quintember (five) through December (ten).

Around 700 B.C. Pompilius, the supposed successor of Romulus, added two months: Janiarius for the two faced Janus and Februarius after the name of the Roman festival of purification. This made the Roman calendar as good as the four millennia older Mesopotamian lunar calendar.

In 48 B.C. Julius Caesar arrived in Egypt to settle a score with Pompey, his rival in the Roman civil war. While attending a lavish feast given in his honor by the highly sophisticated and exotically beautiful Cleopatra, her court scholars informed him about the Egyptian calendar. The Caesar then called upon Sosigenes of Alexandria, the Egyptian mathematician/astronomer, and asked him to come up with a good workable calendar.

The length of the year available to Sosigenes, either from his own measurements or from older Egyptian records, was 365.25 days. Accordingly, he devised a 365-day calendar year, with an extra day added each fourth year. This became known as the Julian calendar. For his effort, Caesar was granted the honor of having his first name bestowed on the month of Quitember, which was renamed July.

To bring the calendar in alignment with the seasons, Caesar further ordered that the year 46 B.C. be lengthened to 445 days. Needless to say the extra days caused so much disruptions through out the Roman Empire that the year 46 B.C. became known as the Year of Confusion.

Although Caesar named it the last year of confusion, it was not meant to be; the Roman priests misunderstood Sosigenes' instructions and leaped every third year instead of every fourth, throwing the calendar back in disorder.

This remained the case until Caesar's nephew Augustus became emperor. He corrected the error by abolishing a few days and ordering the priests to follow Sosigenes' recommendation giving February an extra day every four years, not every three.

Emperor Augustus decided that he also deserves the timeless honor accorded to his uncle and ordered that the month that followed July be named August. He also reasoned that if the month named after his uncle has 31 days, his month should have 31 days also. For reasons unknown, the extra day was taken from the shortest month, February.

When Emperor Constantine embraced Christianity, he adopted the Babylonian seven-day week, which was earlier introduced into the Empire by Roman soldiers, and designated Sunday instead of the Jewish Saturday as the day of worship. This was the big event that eventually led to the world wide establishment of the seven-day week. Constantine further introduced into the calendar a number of Christian holidays and festivals. This action had great detrimental effect on the calendar; it changed it from being astronomically-based to a calendar dominated by religion. It became a system of dates ordained by God, sacred to the Christian Church, not to be altered by humans.

Matters were further complicated by when to celebrate Easter, the day of Christ's resurrection. The Catholic clergy attempted to celebrate the Resurrection according to the Jewish Lunar calendar. As the

Gospels fail to give a specific date, only sating that it occurred on a Sunday during the Jewish Passover (13).

In A.D. 325, Constantine convened the council of bishops in Nicaea and asked them to establish a method for determining the day of Christ's resurrection. The council, after lengthy and sometime heated discussions, agreed on a solution that placed Easter on the first Sunday after the first full moon after the spring equinox. This complicated method did not satisfactorily solve the problem, and the Catholic Church and the Eastern Orthodox Churches still celebrate Easter on different dates.

With the fall of the Roman Empire, the heads of the Church assumed much of the secular authority of the state, and work on the calendar began to be performed under papal guidance.

In 525, Pope John I asked an abbot-mathematician by the name Dionysius Exiguus (Dennis the Little) to calculate the dates on which future Easters should be celebrated. Dennis studied the position of the sun and the moon and devised a chart containing the dates on which futures Easters will fall. He completed his chart in 532, calculating his dates from the birth-date of Christ. He probably miscalculated that date as modern biblical historians believe that Jesus Christ was born the year Herod died, and that is most probably 5 B.C. Error in Christ birth-date is of no great importance in formulating a workable calendar, and Dennis unwitingly made a great contribution; he unified the Roman calendar.

In those days to the Romans the years was either 1285, counting from the founding of Rome, or 248 starting with the reign of Emperor Diocletian-a persecutor of Christians (14).

On Dennis' chart, the year 532 appears as Anno Domini Nostri Jesu Christi DXXXII, which since then has been shortened to A.D. 532.

Some of the many non-Christians using present day calendar prefer the designation C.E. and B.C.E. for common era, and before common era instead of the christian designation A.D. and B.C.

Sosigenes' 365.25-day year is about 11.25 minutes too long, and year after year, the dates in the Julian calendar began to fall behind their true dates. And devout Christians discovered, to their horror, that they were celebrating their holy days on the wrong dates.

In 1265, Pope Clement invited a distinguished English friar named Roger Bacon and asked him to work for the Church. Bacon accepted the appointment and by 1267 devised a highly successful calendar. Bacon's calendar was not put to use until Pope Gregory XIII decided to bring the calendar into proper alignment with the sun. He eliminated 10 days from the old calendar and Thursday October the 5th was followed by Friday the 15th.

The confusion that followed disrupted Work in shipyards, banks, and government offices, and the eighty-year-old pope risked being lynched as a thief of time. To avoid future confusion, scientists came up with several ideas to keep the calendar synchronized with the solar year. The simplest and neatest idea was presented by a physician-astronomer named Aloysius Lilius, according to which centennial years would be leap years only if they were divisible, not by 4, but by 400. Pope Gregory accepted Lilus' approach, and the Gregorian calendar came into being.

The Catholic states of Europe: Italy, Spain, Portugal, France, Belgium, and Poland accepted the papal mandate almost immediately. But protestants resisted the change leaving Europe with two calendars. Kelvin and Luther attacked the change as the work of the devil, "We do not recognize this Draco, whose laws were said to have been written in blood."

When the Gregorian calendar was finally adopted by the British in 1732, citizens were outraged and rowdy demonstrations with placards reading "Give us back our eleven days" marched in most cities and towns, endangering lives and disrupting businesses, and leaving several people dead in Bristol.

In the Julian Calendar the new year began the day following the completion of the Roman census, which happened to be towards the end of March. When Pope Gregory XIII moved the first of the year to January first, those who refused to accept the change became the object of ridicule, and this may have given rise to the April fool pranks.

Revolts not withstanding, the Gregorian Calendar is accurate to within 17 seconds a year; that is it will take us a little over 5000 years to fall behind by one day. Within a couple of centuries most European countries adopted the Gregorian calendar. Later the republic that followed the French Revolution generated its own calendar, but that was short lived. The Russians did not adopt the calendar until after World War One. By then they had to drop 13 days. The Orthodox Church of Antioch eliminated 13 days from its calendar soon after the end of World War II.

And in 1949, chairman Mao Tse-tung stood upon the Gates of Heavenly Peace, announced the formation of People's Republic, then declared that the Chinese, "Would once and for all, use the Gregorian calendar."

That left the tiny semi-autonomous area of mount Athos, the site of a number of orthodox monasteries, at the East end of the Acte peninsula in north-east Greece. Here the monks dominated society still uses the Julian calendar, with its dates 13 days behind the rest of the world.

The Muslim Calendar;

The Muslim or Hijrah Calendar was established by the Righteous Caliph 'Umar. Its starting date is July 16th, A.D. 622, the day the Prophet Mohammed entered Yathrip, later renamed Medinat al-Rasul(The City of the Messenger), or simply al-Medina (The City). This marks the end of the celebrated Hijrah of the Prophet and the establishment of the first Islamic state.

The Muslim calendar is strictly lunar, requiring no correction and has never been adjusted to correspond to the seasons. As a matter of fact, the Holy Month of Ramadon could fall in the middle of winter where the faithful, living in the northern hemisphere, and fastening from day brake to sun down, have to endure that state for only several hours. On the other hand, when Ramadan happens to fall in the summer time, fastening could be as long as fourteen or even fifteen hours.

The lunar year, designated in the Muslim calendar as A.H. for Anno Hegirae, is almost 10.875 days shorter than the solar year, but the ratio of the lengths of the two years that is 354.36706 divided by 365.242199 is very close to 32/33, thus making the following simple relation,

$$A.D. = 622 + (32/33) \text{ A.H.},$$

adequate in converting dates from the Muslim calendar to the Gregorian calendar and vice versa (15).

---

(1). 'Abbudi, Henry S. 1991. pp. 26–28.

(2). Terah is also the name of Abrahim's father-a moon worshipper.

(3). Krythe, Maymie R. 1996. p. 60.

(4). Marduk is the supreme god of Babylon.

(5). Duncan, David. Smithsonian, Vol. 29, No. 11. 1999. p. 52.

(6). Bickerman, Elias Joseph. 1968. pp. 22-23.

(7). Probably this is the origin of the phrase "A week of eight days" still used in many isolated communities in Lebanon.

(8). See the Chapter titled, "THE SANCTITY OF SEVEN."

(9). Breasted, James H. 1935. p. 214.

(10). Glashow, Sheldon. 1994. P. 17.

(11). Al-Andalusi, Sa'id. 1991. p. 89. ,

(12). For example the starting date of the Muslim calendar is A.D. 622, while the Hebrew calendar has 3761 B.C. as its starting date, and the old Chinese calendar begins at 2637 B.C.

(13). "Now upon the first day of the week (Sunday), very early in the morning, they came unto the sepulchre, bringing the spices...And they found the stone rolled away from the sepulchre." (Luke:24,1,2).

(14). Duncan, David Ewing. Ibid. p. 50.

(15). Al-Andalusi, Sa'id, Ibid. P. XXVI.

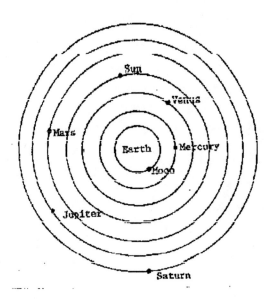

Fig. 10-1. The solar system as viewed by ancient Mesopotamian astronomers.

Chapter Eleven

The Development of Mathematics

"A mind that does not know accounting, is it a mind that has intelligence?" Thus says an ancient Babylonian proverb. The reverence portrayed to the field of mathematics in this proverb equates mathematical dexterity to the exclusion of other disciplines with mental capability. It is certainly true, to say the least, the study of mathematics is an intellectual activity that calls for both imagination and intuition.

The word mathematics was originally used to mean arithmetic; then simple algebra was introduced into its domain to be followed by plane geometry and other related concepts. Here the word mathematics is used in a most general sense, derived from its development into a world wide language having a particular kind of logic, to encompass arithmetic, algebra, trigonometry, and plane and solid geometry. Let us think of mathematics in these broad terms, as a concise and meaningful definition is virtually impossible.

We know of no ancient society that had no method of tallying and counting. One may easily associate the process of counting with finger and toes; such connection must have been the first step in the long road of the development of mathematics. When this process was extended to involve a word which codes for a finger, a more complex but much more useful code resulted. The new word does not reflect the idea of a finger or a toe; rather it designates a position in a progression. And early mathematicians began to count without the use of their fingers or toes.

The next giant but simple step was to represent each word in the numerical progression by a written symbol, thus making it possible to keep written records. In most ancient societies, a straight line, which has the shape of an extended finger, scratched on a stone or a bone, stood for the number "one". Higher numbers were represented by additional straight-line scratches. Among the societies that used this system were the Egyptians, the Hittites, the Indus, the Phoenicians, the Aramaeans, and the Lydians. Present day Roman numerals are a good example of this representation, where one, two, three…are represented by I, II, III…. The five (V) is two connected scratches and the ten (X) is two intersecting scratches (1). Another popular form of representing numbers used dots instead of straight lines, and this was adopted by the Aztecs, the Mayas, and the ancient Greeks. Although these two simple representations were the most widely used, other shapes are known to have existed.

From the need to count and record numbers arose the study of mathematics. As this need is universal, so is the development of mathematics, and every known society has developed some form of counting and tallying to recall the number of objects in a common collection such as livestock, agricultural produce, or people. That such development took place in all societies is attested to by the variety of counting systems used over the centuries and around the world. Our base-ten counting system, although the most common because of its association with the number of fingers of both hands, is just one of many.

The necessity to record the passage of time created a close link between mathematics and astronomy. This link played an important role in the development of both fields and gave rise to the formulation of early calendars.

In exploring ancient mathematical advances, it becomes evident that most ancient cultures dealt not only with applied mathematics, which was needed to conduct basic transactions and facilitate business dealings, but also with recreational mathematics, which may be viewed as a pure mental exercise and the origin of what is presently referred to as pure mathematics.

MESOPOTAMIAN MATHEMATIC:

The oldest mathematical records uncovered in Mesopotamia belong to the early Sumerian period (c. 2700 B.C.). In these records, Sumerian mathematicians used the following numerical signs: ⚊ for 1, ⬤ for 10, ⬭ for 60, ⬤ for 60 X 60. To add numbers they simply put them next to each another and figured out their sum. To subtract one number from another, they separated the two numbers by a minus sign ⌐ or ⌐ ; nine is written as 10 - 1, thus ⬤⌐⚊ or thus ⬤⌐ . To multiply two numbers, they inscribed one inside the other, for example ⬤ is 10 X 60 or 600, and ⬤ is 10 X 60 X 60, and so on.

With the advent of cuneiform, the old Sumerian numerals were replaced by wedge-shaped signs; ⲧ stood for 1, and ⲧⲧ became a 2. To write 3, they arranged three symbols for 1, either next to each other, ⲧⲧⲧ or two above and one below, ⲧⲧⲧ . To add two numbers,

This was the first step in the development of a place-value numeration system. There was no further need for a distinct sign for 60 as its position denotes its value. The place-value numeration system was, without a doubt, a giant step in the annals of mathematics, and it was conceived of by the mathematicians and astronomers of Babylon towards the beginning of the second millennium B.C. This system of numeration is far superior to any other system used in the ancient world.

The Babylonian place-value system has a sexagesimal base and is strictly positional (3). For example the number 65 is no longer written as ▽ 𒁹𒁹𒁹 but as 𒁹 𒁹𒁹𒁹 , and to write say 4815, one writes

𒁹   ⪤⪤ ⪤𒁹𒁹𒁹

1 , 20 , 15, which is $1 \times 60^2 + 20 \times 60 + 15 = 4815$. The system is not free from ambiguities that could result in errors; the following three group of numbers may easily lead to confusion.

⪤⪤ 𒁹𒁹𒁹   is 25

⪤ ⪤𒁹𒁹𒁹   is $10 \times 60 + 15 = 615$

⪤ ⪤ 𒁹𒁹𒁹   is $10 \times 60^2 + 10 \times 60 + 5 = 36605$

To avoid such a confusion, the mathematicians of Babylon inserted one of the following signs into the empty spaces, to indicate separation between two numbers:

𒐖 or 𒐕 or 𒐖

Another imperfection of with the Babylonian place-value system was the absence of a sign to represent zero. For some time, Babylonian scholars were unable to come up with a sign to represent nothing. By about one thousand B.C., to overcome this difficulty, Babylonian scribes began to leave an empty space to indicate that a power of sixty was missing. To express, say, 3615, they wrote

$$𒐖 \quad 𒌋 𒐈 = 1 \times 60^2 + 0 \times 60 + 15$$

This did not completely alleviate the problem, as careless scribes often failed to leave such a space.

Over a period of more than one thousand years, Babylonian mathematicians and astronomers performed several sophisticated calculations in spite the shortcomings of their numerical system. At a time not precisely determined, but probably towards the end of the fifth century B.C. the mathematicians of Babylon developed a true sign to indicate the absence of a sexagesimal unit. This is the first known genuine representation of the zero. And the people of Mesopotamia, who planted the early seeds of civilization, continued their scholarly contributions especially in the fields of astronomy and mathematics; first they developed a place-value system and later they invented a genuine symbol for zero. By the fifth or fourth century B.C., Babylonian scribes began to use symbols similar to their separation signs to denote zeros; instead of blank space, they wrote one of the following signs:

𝗧𝗧 or 𝗙𝗙 or 𝗧

To express, say, 3612, they wrote either

𝗧𝗧𝗧 ◀𝗧𝗧 or 𝗧 𝗧 𝗧𝗧◀𝗧𝗧 or 𝗧𝗧 𝗧 ◀𝗧𝗧.   (4).

The mathematicians of Babylon true to their sexagesimal system wrote all their fractions as numbers divided by sixty, which was implied and did not need not to be explicitly written. This is similar to our use of the decimal system; when we want to write one and one half, we do not write 1 + 5/10, but simply 1.5. To write the same number, the Babylonians wrote

𝗧 ; ◀ which is 1;30 = 1 + 30/60 = 1.5

The Babylonian way of writing fractions is still in use today; we still say the time is half past one or 1:30. In certain rare cases, Babylonians used higher powers of sixty for their denominator, such as 60^2 or 60^3, and retained some of the old Sumerian symbols such as: ● = 1/120, 𝓖 = 1/60, ·◌· = 1/30, ❱ = 1/5. ●● = 1/10

Babylonian Algebra

For our knowledge of Babylonian mathematics we are indebted primarily to the work of Otto Neugebauer, who between 1935 and 1937 published all the then-known mathematical cuneiform texts in three volumes entitled Mathemattische Keilschrifttexte (MKT). In these volumes he included photographs, transcripts, and translations into German. He also wrote a good commentary, and for an extended period he continued to translate and publish articles about Babylonian mathematical texts.

Neugebauer indicated that Babylonian algebraists were mainly concerned with the solution of equations of various types; they worked with linear equations of one unknown and systems equations having two or three unknowns. They also worked on the solutions of quadratic equations.

To solve for x and y from the following equations,

$$x + y = a$$
$$bx - cy = d,$$

they did not eliminate one of the unknown between the two equations as it is done today, but wrote x and y in term of a third unknown, thus

$$x = a/2 + s$$
$$y = a/2 - s.$$

This method became known as "plus and minus" substitution. When these values are substituted in the second equation, the value of s is calculated, then the values of x and y are obtained.

In addition, the Babylonians worked out the solutions of the following standard types of equations:

(I). $x + y = a$ $xy = b$
(II). $x - y = a$ $xy = b$
(III). $x + y = a$ $x^2 + y^2 = b$
(IV). $x - y = a$ $x^2 + y^2 = b$

All four types were worked out by the "plus and minus" substitution method.

They also worked out solutions of quadratic equations of the form

$$x^2 - x = 14,30,$$

which they viewed as the area of a square minus one of the sides. One cuneiform tablet reads, "I have subtracted the side of the square from the area, and the result is 14,30. [British Museum 13901]. The rules for solving such an equation were stated as follows:

"Take 1, the coefficient (of the linear term).

Take one-half of 1 (result 0;30).

Multiply 0;30 by 0;30 (result 0;15).

Add 0;15 to 14,30, result, 124,30;15.

The square root of this is 29;30.

Take the 0;30, which you have multiplied by itself

and add it to 29;30.

Result, 30: this is [the required value of the side

of the] square (5).

This method, which continued to be used during the Hellenistic period, is a step-by-step procedure equivalent to the modern formula for solving quadratic equations of the type

$$ax^2 - bx = c,$$

whose solution is

$$x = [-b + (b^2 - 4ac)^{(1/2)}]/2a.$$

In several cuneiform tablets, one finds cubic equations of the type

$$x^3 = a.$$

For the solutions of such equations, Babylonian mathematicians composed tables of cube roots. And for equations of the type,

$$x^2(x + 1) = a,$$

they prepared tables giving the values of the expression $x^2(x + 1)$ in the first column and the corresponding values of x in the second column, with values of x ranging from 1 to 60. The neo-Pythagorean mathematician Nicomachus of Gerasa expressed great interest in the mathematical expressions $x^2(x + 1)$ and $x^2(x - 1)$, calling them arithmoi paramekepipedoi.

Babylonian mathematicians were certainly familiar with the rules of elementary algebra, such as

$$(a + b)(a - b) = a^2 - b^2$$
$$(a + b)^2 = a^2 + 2ab + b^2$$
$$(a - b)^2 = a^2 - 2ab + b^2,$$

which they probably derived by drawing rectangles and squares, a method later used by Greeks and Arabs.

In one Babylonian text (Neugebauer, MKT, I, 96–107), the following summation of the geometrical progression is written

$$1 + 2 + 4 + \ldots 2^9 = 2^9 + 2^9 - 1,$$

as well as the sum of the squares of the integers from 1 to 10,

$$1^2 + 2^2 + 3^2 + \ldots n^2 = 1/3(1 + 2n)(1 + 2 + 3 + \ldots n).$$

Babylonian Geometry

Babylonians used the correct formula to calculate the areas of triangles:

$$A = hb/2$$

where h is the height and b is the length of the base. They also used the correct formula to calculate the areas of trapeziums;

$$A = h/2(a + b),$$

where a and b are the lengths of the two parallel sides.

Probably as a result of their interest in dividing farm land equally among inheritors, early mathematicians of both Mesopotamia and Egypt worked on dividing various geometrical shapes into equal segments. One such shape is a trapezium, divided into two equal parts by a line parallel to its base. The length of the dividing line was given by Babylonian mathematicians as

$$x = [(a^2 + b^2)/2]^{(1/2)} \quad \text{[Neugebauer, MKT, I, 131]}$$

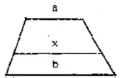

They also used the same relation to divide the area of a triangle into two equal parts by a line parallel to the base. The length of the dividing line is

$$x = [a^2/2]^{(1/2)}$$

where a is the length of the base (6).

In several Babylonian texts, the volumes of frustums of cones and pyramids were incorrectly calculated by the relation

$$V = (h/2)(A + B),$$

where h is the height and A and B are the areas of the bottom and of the top.

At about the same time, the Egyptians were using the correct relation to calculate the volume of a frustum of a pyramid having a square base,

$$V = (h/3)(a^2 + ab + b^2).$$

Several texts belonging to the Old Babylonian period clearly show that Babylonian mathematicians were familiar with the relation

$$a^2 = b^2 + c^2,$$

where a, b, and c are the sides of a right triangle. They calculated the hypotenuse, a, as the square root of $b^2 + c^2$ [Neugebauer, MKT, II, 53; and MKT III, 22.] A cuneiform tablet also belonging to the Old

Babylonian period contains extensive values of a, b, and c that satisfy the above relation.

This relation is traditionally referred to as the "Pythagorean Theorem"; the triangles obeying such a relation are called "Pythagorean Triangles"; the numbers a, b, and c satisfying this relation are known as "Pythagorean Triples or Triads".

Greek tradition states that Pythagoras, like many Greek students of his generation, visited Mesopotamia and probably learned about his theorem during his visit. He also learned the science of numbers, the science of music, and the other sciences from the magi.

This is one such instance where tradition needs to be corrected, and the right of the discoverer should be recognized, honored, and preserved. This theorem should be referred to as the "Babylonian Theorem" and not as the "Pythagorean Theorem".

In addition to this theorem, it is well established that the Babylonians greatly influenced the mathematics of the Greeks, and through them that of the Western World. Here are a few examples to prove the point. As we mentioned earlier, the numerical values of the expression $x^2(x +/- 1)$ were appropriated by Nicomachus; the "plus and minus" method of solving equations was later used by Diophantus of Alexandria; the four Babylonian standard types of pairs of equations, listed earlier, appear in Euclid's Elements as theorems 5 - 6 and 9 - 10 in Book II. And as Neugebauer pointed out, the Greek geometrical solutions of these equations are the same as algebraic solutions of the Babylonians; whenever the Babylonians wrote, "Take the square root of A.", the Greeks changed it to read, "Take the side of the square of area equal to A."

Egyptian Mathematics

We will consider the mathematics developed in Egypt between the end of the fourth millennium B.C., when learned Egyptians began towrite and preserve their writings, and 332 B.C. when Alexander of Macedon conquered Egypt and the Greek and the Egyptian cultures began to share many of their elements. During these three millennia, mathematics played a central role in Egyptian education and culture, and was geared primarily at producing mathematicians who could survey the land and could calculate areas of various geometrical shapes as well as the quantities of grain the tracts produced.

As a result of this emphasis, many critics claim that Egyptian mathematics was of a purely practical nature and was developed simply by trial and error. True as that might be, the ancient Egyptians, as we shall see, were also the originators of many important mathematical concepts. Like most ancient civilizations, Egyptian mathematicians were not interested in generalities but in the solutions of specific problems.

Some ten ancient papyri have been recovered and are preserved in various universities and museums: four in London, two in Cairo, and one in each of the following cities: Ann Arbor, Berlin, Boston, and Moscow. Various minor mathematical documents are also housed in Berlin, cairo, London, and Manchester.

Egyptian Numerals And Fractions

Over a period of three thousand years, Egyptian numerals underwent some changes, but not in their fundamental forms. The Egyptians had a special sign for each of the first seven powers of ten, which enabled them to write whole numbers up to and greater than 1,000,000.

A vertical straight line stood for one; and ten was represented by an upside-down U; for 100 they drew a spiral; and for 1000 a lotus flower. A raised finger slightly bent stood for 10,000; for 100,000, they used a tadpole; and for 1,000,000, a kneeling genie with upraised arms. This figure also stood for a genie holding up the sky and later came to mean eternity, a million years, a multitude, or a very large number (7).

But the Egyptian had a special set of symbols for measuring length; their unit of length was the cubit, which was equal to seven palms, and each palm was equal to four fingers. A length of, say, fifteen fingers would be written as three palms and three fingers (8).

The Egyptian numerical system is based on the principle of addition: to represent a number the sign for each power of ten was repeated as many times as it was necessary. This is obviously a cumbersome way of writing, as it took, for example, twenty-seven signs to write 999. To simplify the process of reading these repeated signs, the scribes arranged them vertically in groups of three or four.

The Egyptian numerical system is not a perfect decimal system; it lacks a symbol for zero, which it does not need. It is also not a place-value system and thus, not like a functional decimal system, requires a large number of symbols to write big numbers. In spite of these shortcomings, the Egyptian numerical system is considered by many historian of mathematics as the origin of the decimal system of the Western World.

In general, to write fractions, Egyptian scribes drew the form of an open mouth and wrote the denominator beneath it. This came to mean "a part of", thus;

$$\text{☂} = 1/3 \quad \text{☂} = 1/5 \quad \text{☂} = 1/10 \quad \text{☂} = 1/100.$$

When the denominator was too large to fit under the sign of the open mouth, they did not enlarge the sign. Instead, they wrote part of the number after the sign. Reading from right to left, they wrote 1/240 as:

$$\text{☐☐☐} = 1/240$$

Egyptian mathematicians had special signs for some common fractions such as 1/2, 2/3, and 3/4, which were written as:

$$\text{⊃} \quad \text{or} \quad \text{⊃} \quad , \text{ which stood for } 1/2$$

For simplicity, the open mouth has been replaced by a dash.

As the Egyptians used special symbols for their units of length, they also had special notations to designate fractions of their unit of volume. The 'hekat' (9), estimated at about 4.8 liters, was their unit of volume. To denote fractions of a 'hekat', Egyptians used special and curious notations; they divided the eye of the god

᚜ or ᚜᚜ or ᚜, which stood for 2/3

᚜᚜ , which stood for 3/4

All fractions were viewed by the Egyptians to have 1 for numerator, thus 2/3 and 3/4 were not regarded as fractions. In writing a given number, for unknown reason, they avoided the use of any fraction more than once; to write 3/5, for example, they did not write 1/5 + 1/5 + 1/5, but wrote 1/2 + 1/10, and the result of multiplying 1 + 1/5 by 2 was never written as 2 + 1/5 + 1/5 but rather 2 + 1/3 + 1/15. Several Egyptian papyri contain tables of addition of fraction. They are usually written as follows:

$$\overline{4} + \overline{12} = \overline{3}$$
$$\overline{5} + \overline{20} = \overline{4}$$
$$\overline{9} + \overline{18} = \overline{6}$$

etc.,

Horus into six parts and assigned each part to one of the common fractions, 1/2, 1/4, 1/8, 1/16, 1/32, and 1/64 (10). The right part of the cornea stood for 1/2, the iris for 1/4, and so on (11).

This strange way of designating fractions probably has its origin in the legend describing the violent struggle between Horus and his uncle Set. In one of their battles, Set gouged out Horus's eye, cut it into six pieces, and scattered the pieces throughout Egypt. These pieces were later collected by Thoth, who put them together to create a complete and healthy eye. Horus's eye later became the most important talisman in Egypt, bringing light, knowledge, abundance, and fertility to the people of the Nile.

Multiplication, Division, And Square Roots

The Egyptians devised a simple process to multiply numbers; it is based on the principle of doubling, and on the fact that every integer can be expressed as the sum of powers of two;

$$13 = 2^0 + 2^2 + 2^3$$

and

$$15 = 2^0 + 2^1 + 2^2 + 2^3.$$

To multiply say 15 X 28, one starts with unity on the left hand side and double the numbers until their sum is 15. At the same time one begins with 28 on the right hand side and double the numbers as shown in the table. When the sum on the left is 15, the sum on the right is the desired result; 28 + 56 + 112 + 224 = 15 X 28 = 420.

Egyptian notation		Modern notation	
I	IIII / IIII ∩∩	I	28
II	III ∩∩∩ / III ∩∩	2	56
IIII	II ∩ 9	4	112
IIII / IIII	IIII ∩∩99	8	224
IIIIΠ	∩∩ 9999	15	420

The same method may be used to multiply say 13 X 28

\ 1	28 /
2	56
\ 4	112 /
\ 8	224 /
13	364

The numbers marked with \ in the left column add up to 13, and the sum of the corresponding numbers, in the right column, marked with /, is the desired result; 28 + 112 + 224 = 13 X 28 = 364. The 2 and the corresponding 56 are not included in these calculations as they correspond to the missing number, 2^1, in the expansion of 13. If the 2 is included, the sum of the numbers in the left column will be greater than 13, in violation of the rules of multiplication (12).

This method of multiplication was widely used in Egypt and neighboring countries and provided the foundation of most Egyptian calculations. It entered into Greece and later into most of Europe where, with some variations, it was used well into the Middle Ages. Until recently, it was popular in some rural Russian communities, and in the West, it became known as the Russian Peasant method.

Several Egyptian papyri contain multiplication tables, which are also tables of addition of fractions. In general, they have no heading or title, and no statements about the methods of calculations that help understand the use of their entries. For the sake of simplicity, the sign of the mouth over the numbers to denote fractions is omitted. In one such very concise table, the entries read as follows:

Generators (1, 3, 6)

3	9	18 = 2
6	18	36 = 4
9	27	54 = 6
12	36	72 = 8

and so on. In present day notations, the entries in this table are equivalent to,

line 1   1 X 3 = 3, 3 X 3 = 9, and 6 X 3 = 18,
line 2   1 X 6 = 6, 3 X 6 = 18, and 6 X 6 = 36,
line 3   1 X 9 = 9, 3 X 9 = 27, and 6 X 9 = 54,
line 4   1 X 12 = 12, 3 X 12 = 36, and 6 X 12 = 72.

And the sums of the fractions to the left of the equal signs are equal to the fractions at the right. Thus,

line 1   1/3 + 1/9 + 1/18 = 1/2,
line 2   1/6 + 1/18 + 1/36 = 1/4,
line 3   1/9 + 1/27 + 1/54 = 1/6.
line 4   1/12 + 1/36 + 1/72 = 1/8

Egyptian mathematicians viewed division as the inverse of multiplication; instead of saying "divide 297 by 11," they would say "by what number would you multiply 11 to get 297?" and proceeded accordingly.

$$
\begin{array}{ll}
\backslash 1 & 11\,/ \\
\backslash 2 & 22\,/ \\
4 & 44 \\
\backslash 8 & 88\,/ \\
\backslash 16 & 176\,/ \\
\hline
27 & 297
\end{array}
$$

Numbers in the right column marked with / add up to 297, and the corresponding numbers in the column to the left add up to 27, which is the desired result. When the division of two integers does not produce an integral quotient, the procedure, although similar to the one discussed above, becomes truly involved.

In one of the Cairo papyri, the square roots of certain numbers are calculated as follows. The square root of 345 is written as

$$(345)^{1/2} = (18^2 + 21)^{1/2}$$
$$= 18 + 21/36$$
$$= 18 + 1/2 + 1/12$$

Better results are obtained using this same method to calculate the square root of, say, 105;

$$(105)^{1/2} = (10^2 + 5)^{1/2}$$

$$= 10 + 5/20$$
$$= 10 + 1/4$$

10.25 is very close to being the correct value of the square root of 105, which is 10.247.

These calculations are mere examples of the approximation

$$(a^2 + b)^{(1/2)} = (a + b/2a)^{(1/2)},$$

whose Egyptian origin has, for a time, been forgotten and is usually attributed to Archimedes or Hero.

To calculate the square roots of certain fractions, Egyptian mathematicians came up with an ingenious approach; to determine the square root of, say, 1/2, they calculated the square root of 18/36.

$$(1/2)^{(1/2)} = (18/36)^{(1/2)} = (4 + 2/8)(1/6) = 4.25/6,$$

which is close to the correct value.

Geometry And Algebra

The annual inundation of the Nile obliterates boundaries and renders the subdivision of Egypt fertile land unrecognizable. To overcome this vicissitude, Egyptian scholars educated a class of surveyors, whose function was to retrace and rebuild these boundaries year after year. In time, these surveyors acquired the ability to determine the areas and the perimeters of various geometrical shapes and divide such areas into several equal parts. Their ability led many modern scientists to believe that the Nile Valley is the birth-place of plane geometry.

Egyptian mathematicians performed outstanding work on the parameters of circles; although in some papyri, the ratio of the circumference of a circle to its diameter is given as 3, Egyptian mathematicians often used 256/81 as a value of this ratio. This gives the area of the circle the elegant form, $[(16/9) R]^2$. The value of 256/81 is 3.16049383 and is larger than today accepted value of 3.14159265 by only 0.6 %. An improvement that required over 4000 years to accomplish.

In this field, the Egyptians worked out problems such as: "the area of a circle is 100 find its diameter." And they gave the answer as 2R = 11 2 20, which is 11.55. Using present day method, we find 2R = $2(100/3.14)^{(1/2)} = 11.287$.

Egyptian mathematicians also arrived at the correct relation for the area of the surface of a hemisphere, which they wrote as,
$$A = 2 [(8/9)d]^2,$$
where d is the diameter of the circle.

Another common problems in Egyptian plane geometry is the one encountered in Babylonian geometry, and discussed earlier. It asks, "To divide the area of an isosceles trapezium with a line parallel to the top and the bottom and to determine the length of that line."

Using the same notations given in the Babylonian examples, the Egyptian solutions to this problem was written as:
$$x = a^2 - 1/2(a + b)(a - b).$$
A relation that can easily be reduced to the simple Babylonian formula, $x = (a^2 + b^2)/2$, stated earlier.

One Cairo papyrus, dated from about 300 B.C., or probably a little earlier, contains nine similar problems related to "Pythagoras theorem". One such problem reads; "A ladder of five cubits has its foot three cubits from a wall. To what height will it reach?" With only one exception, the answers given are those of the "Pythagorean triads" (3, 4, 5), (5, 12, 13), (20, 21, 29)...

Another interesting problem dealing with the area of a rectangle reads, "A rectangle having an area of sixty square cubits and a diagonal of thirteen cubits. What are the length of its sides?" Using modern notations, the problem was worked out as follows:
$$x^2 + y^2 = (13)^2 = 169$$
$$xy = 60, \qquad 2xy = 120$$
$$(x + y)^2 = 169 + 120 = 289$$
$$(x - y)^2 = 169 - 120 = 49$$
$$x + y = 17, \qquad x - y = 7$$

$$2x = 24, \qquad x = 12 \text{ cubits, and } y = 5 \text{ cubits.}$$

The Egyptians were also interested in determining the volumes of various geometrical objects. For example, in calculating the volumes of frostrums of cones, they averaged the top and the bottom diameters and used that average to determine the area of a circle,

$$A = [(8/9)d]^2.$$

Then multiplying this value by the height. The results obtained in this fashion are closer to the correct values than those obtained by averaging the areas of the top and bottom circles and multiplying by the height.

One of the problems found on a papyrus that dates back to about 2000 B.C. has mystified mathematicians since it came to light; they could not apprehend how did the scholars of ancient Egypt arrive at the correct solution to such a complex problem. In that 4000 year old papyrus, the volume of a truncated pyramid is calculated as follows:

"If it is said to the, a truncated pyramid of 6 cubits in height,

of 4 cubits of the base by 2 cubits of the top.

Reckon thou with this 4, its square is 16.

Multiply this 4 by 2. Result 8.

Reckon thou with this 2, its square is 4.

Add together this 16 with this 8 and with this 4. Result 28.

Calculate then 1/3 of 6. Result 2.

Calculate then with 28 twice. Result 56.

Lo! It is 56! You have correctly found it" (13).

Designating the height by h, the length of the side of the base by a and the length of the side of the top by b, the above statement gives the volume of the truncated pyramid as

$$V = (h/3)[a^2 + ab + b^2],$$

which as stated earlier, is the correct relation whose apprehension eluded mathematicians for millennia.

Another problem with an intriguing solution deals with the volume of cylindrical granaries, where using modern notations, Egyptians mathematicians, without any explanation, began the solutions either with the relation,

$$V = [(8/9)d]^2 \, h \text{ cubic cubits}$$
$$= [(8/9)d]^2 \, h(3/2) \text{ khars}$$

or with the relation,

$$V = (2/3)[(4/3)d]^2 \, h \text{ khars.}$$

Obviously obtaining the same results,

$$V = (128/27) \, r^2 \, h \text{ khars. (14).}$$

Several Egyptian papyri contain equations that require simple algebraic reasoning. Here are a few examples of such equations and their solutions;

$$x + \bar{7}x = 19; \qquad x = 16\ \bar{2}\ \bar{8}$$
$$x + \bar{2}x = 16; \qquad x = 10\ \bar{3}\ \bar{3}$$
$$x + \bar{2}x + 4 = 10; \quad x = 4$$
$$x - \bar{2}x - \bar{4}x = 5; \qquad x = 20$$
$$x + \bar{3}x + \bar{4}x = 2; \qquad x = 1\ \bar{6}\ \overline{12}\ \overline{144}\ \overline{228}.$$

Egyptian mathematicians also worked with second order algebraic equations. A papyrus, now in Berlin, contains a few examples;

$$x^2 + y^2 = 100$$
$$4x - 3y = 0.$$

and

$$x^2 + y^2 = 400$$
$$4x - 3y = 0$$

The Kahun papyrus (London) contains the following relations,

$$xy = 12$$
$$3x = (3/4)y$$

The solutions of these relations have all been worked out by Egyptians as well as other mathematicians.

Several of what may be termed recreational problems may be found in Egyptian literature; they are presented as a series of exercises designed to teach the use of an algorithm. A typical example and its solution are here presented as they appear in their original form (15).

A quantity; its (1/4) added to it. It becomes 15.

(1) Calculate starting with 4; you will make its 1/4; 1.

(2) Total 5.

(3) Calculate starting from 5, to get 15.

\1	5
\2	10

3 is the result.

(4) Calculate starting from 3.

1	3
2	6
\4	12.

The quantity: 12. its 1/4: 3. Total 15.

Another problem that belongs to the same series, but a little more involved, reads: "A quantity, its half, and its quarter, added together, become 10. What is the quantity?

The problem is solved by changing it to read; by what number would you multiply 1 $\overline{2}$ $\overline{4}$ so as to obtain 10? The problem has thus been reduced to a simple exercise in multiplication. The answer given is 5 $\overline{2}$ 7 $\overline{14}$, which is correct to six significant figures.

The Alphabetical Numerical System

The date when the letters of the alphabet began to be used to designate numbers is not precisely known. As we have stated earlier, some believe that the signs of the alphabet were originally devised and used as a number system. Equally shrouded in ambiguity is the originator or originators of this system.

Except for the place-value numerical system, the alphabetical numerical system was the most efficient and the least cumbersome of all its contemporary systems; it was fully comprehensible and avoided the troublesome repetition found, say, in the Egyptian numerical system.

The attractiveness of the alphabetical numerical system is the result of its simplicity, and its natural use for educational purposes; a student, while learning to read his alphabet, also learns the use of numbers. In its simplest from, the signs of the alphabet are assigned numerical values in the following manner: a = 1, b = 2, c = 3…j = 10, k = 20, l = 30…s = 100, t = 200, u = 300…up to z = 800. Higher numbers were usually designated by adding a small distinguishing mark at the upper left side of the letters; 'a = 1000, 'b = 2000, 'c = 3000, and so on.

Who were the people who came up with this highly simplified numerical system? A series of contemporary authors have repeatedly stated that the people who invented the alphabet were the first to use its letters as numerical signs (16). Plausible as this may be, it lacks the support of any concrete evidence. Although both the Phoenicians, the bold seafarers and great traders, and their cousins, the Aramaeans, the skilled land traders, have, in all probability, used this numerical systems, they left no known inscriptions that reveal such use.

A few authors conjectured that the Greeks were the first to allocate numerical values to the letters of the alphabet, and that the Phoenicians simply took it over (17).

We may never know who made this significant contribution to the development of mathematics, nor when it was precisely made, but what we are sure of is that it was used by many peoples from the Indus to the Nile and from South Arabia to Greece and other Mediterranean countries. Thus it was extensively used by to the Aramaeans, the Greeks, the Phoenicians, the Arabs, the Hebrews, and the Syriacs. And in many areas, its use endured well into the twentieth century.

(1). The change in the system at 5 is a matter of convenience, as it is difficult to read at a glance number such as IIIII, IIIIII...

(2). Ifrah, Georges. (Trans. from the French by Lowell Blair) (1985: 374–375).

(3). Babylonian mathematicians used the decimal system from 1 to 59 and the a sexagesimal system for numbers greater than 59.

(4). Ifrah, Georges. Ibid. pp. 379–381.

(5). Waerden, B. L. van der, Dictionary of Scientific Biography. Vol. 15. Supplement I. 1978. p. 668.

(6). Huber, P. "Zu einem mathematischen Keischrifttext," Isis; Vol 46, (1955). pp 104–106.

(7). These are hieroglyph signs. Different signs were used in hieratic writings, and to avoid confusion, they are not mentioned here.

(8). Selin, Helaine. (1997:630). The Egyptian royal cubit is about 52.3 cm. and the short cubit is about 45 cm.

(9). The word 'hekat' was also used in many parts of the Middle East as a unit of weight until it was displaced by the metric system.

(10). When a student pointed out to his master that these fractions do not add up to unity, the master replied that Thoth would always supply the missing 1/64.

(11). Ifrah, Georges. Ibid. p. 208.

(12). Nelson, David; Joseph, George G. and Williams Julian. (1993: 99).

(13). Gillings, R. J. Dictionary of Scientific Biography, Vol. 15 Supplement I. 1978. P. 697.

(14). A cubic cubit is equal to 1.5 khars, and is also equal to 30 hekats.

(15). Selin, Helaine. (1997:630).

(16). Ifrah, Georges. Ibid. p. 276.

((17). Fleg, Graham. (1983:63).

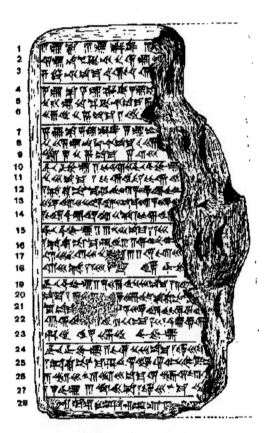

Fig. 11-1. This mathematical clay tablet was uncovered in Uruk. It was dated from either the late third or early second century B.C. It contains the earliest known signs of the babylonian Zero. (Musee de Louvre, Paris).

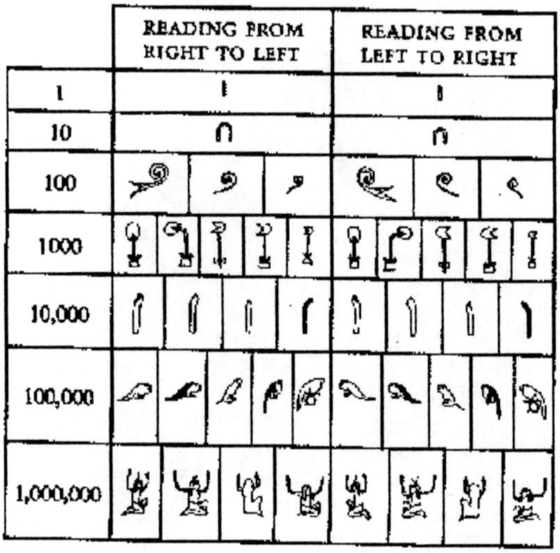

Fig. 11-2. The Egyptian numerals. Notice the slight variations. Most of the symbols face the direction in which they should be read.

Chapter Twelve

Laws and Societies

The biggest and most magnificent step that a society takes on the ladder of civilization is an adequate code of law that provides its citizens with a sense of equality, security, and protection. A ruler, who promulgates such a code, provides his people with a protective shield, and leads them on the road to stability, civilization and ultimately to democracy.

To safeguard their very existence, people living as a group, primitive as they might be, must agree to some practices and adhere to some customs. They must acquire some knowledge and reach some understanding as how to deal with one another and avoid lawlessness. A band that knows no rules and practices no common customs tends to blow over and vanish.

The roots of laws must be as old as the formation of the first band of human hunter-gatherers, and codes of laws must have existed in every group regardless of its locality or the period of its formation. Ancient European dwellers must have had some social customs or regulations prior to being introduced to the laws of Near Eastern civilizations. These arrangements, with some minor changes, must have endured for hundreds of thousands of years, from the formation of the first band of

hunter-gatherers until the advent of statehood where governments prepared and publicized written laws and were able to enforce them.

The first such state was formed in Mesopotamia around 3500 B.C.
and the oldest known code of laws was written in Sumer-southern
Mesopotamia-about 1500 years later. Older codes must have existed,
but we have no record of them; they either have not been written, or if
they were, they have deteriorated or have not yet been unearthed.

Civilized societies govern themselves and their citizenry with a body
of laws designed to fit their needs, regulate their affairs, and protect
their rights and properties. A system of laws, to be effective, must con-
form to the needs of the society and should reflect the customs of that
society. It should also provide answers to the everyday problems of the
people. A simple tribal community needs simple direct laws, and an
advanced, highly developed society requires a rather complex code.

The earliest known code of laws was written in Sumerian and was
promulgated about 2070 B.C. by Ur-Nammu, the first king of the Third
Dynasty of the city of Ur (the Biblical Ur of the Chaldees). The first
code of laws, written in a Semitic language was uncovered in an obscure
mound called Tell Abu Harmal located near Baghdad. It dates back to
the old Babylonian kingdom of Eshnuma. This code was written on two
clay tablets, and in its brief prologue, it mentions a king by the name of
Bilalama, hence the name Bilalama code. This code must not have
gained popularity as Sumerian remained the language of the law until
the time of the great king Hammurabi. Other cuneiform law-codes
include the Lipit-Ishtar, the Hittite, and the Middle Assyrian.

Thus by the middle of the first half of the second millennium B.C.
codes of laws were formerly established in most Near Eastern states;
whereas, there is no reference to any laws in Greek literature prior to
the end of the eighth century B.C.

Most Near Eastern codes were buried and forgotten for centuries,
until they were unearthed and translated during the first half of the
twentieth century, when the western powers began excavating the

mounds and ruins of the Near East. The only code that did not suffer this fate is the Mosaic code as it was written mostly on animal skin, and Hebrew scribes kept making new copies as older ones deteriorated. Thus, it is through this code that the modern West became acquainted with the laws of the ancient Near East.

At the dawn of human history, in the highly civilized state of Sumer, interests went beyond the promulgation of laws, and into their practical application and enforcement. A record of a murder trial was inscribed on a clay tablet that dates back to about 1850 B.C. It was uncovered in 1950 and subsequently translated by S. N. Kramer and Thorild Jacobsen. A fragment of another tablets that deals with the same case was uncovered earlier.

The case involves the murder of a temple official by three men. The murderers, for an unknown reason, informed the victim's wife, who failed to inform the authority. But the sure arm of the law uncovered the case and brought the criminals to King Ur-Ninurta, who turned their case over for trial to the Citizens Assembly at Nippur.

Nine Members of the assembly argued that the three accused murderers as well as the wife should be executed. They considered her an accessory after the fact because she had remained silent after being informed of the crime.

Then two members of the assembly spoke up in the defense of the wife; stating that she took no part in the killing of her husband, and she was justified in her silence, since her husband was not supporting her. Then concluded their argument stating that, "The punishment of those who actually killed should suffice." As a result only the three killers were executed (1).

The complexity of the case and the existence of an assembly that acted as a court of law having prosecutors and defenders are proofs of a highly civilized society. That was Sumer some four thousand years ago where law and justice were fundamental concepts that govern the social and the economic life of the citizens. This was further demonstrated by the thousands of Sumerian clay tablets inscribed with a variety of legal documents. The uncovered tablets proved that in ancient Sumer the study of the law was seriously undertaken by most students. This was the civilization that shaped the characters of all the Near Eastern civilizations that followed.

The Babylonians, the Akkadians, and the Assyrians translated all the knowledge of Sumer into their Semitic languages and that certainly included the codes of Sumerian laws. In Babylon, the promulgation of the law reached its zenith in the middle of the eighteenth century B.C. when at the order of Hammurabi, the far-famed Semitic king who began his rule around 1750 B.C. a code of laws was inscribed in Semitic "so that the people have the laws in their mother-tongue." We shell see later that, through the Bible, the Hammurabi code had tremendous influence on the laws that were later promulgated in the Western World.

We are not certain if the laws in pre-Roman Europe were affected by the ancient codes of Mesopotamia. Although, as we have stated the civilization of the Fertile Crescent did reach into Europe in pre-historic times, there no indication that the adoption of the law was similarly disseminated. There are some similarities between what was customary in Greece during the City-State Period and the regulations of the Hammurabi code, but there is no proof that the ancient Greeks were familiar with or adopted some of the cuneiform laws.

Sacred prostitution was accepted in the temple of Aphrodite in Corinth as it was in the sacred temple of Ishtar in Mesopotamia, and in both temples the earnings of the sacred prostitutes helped support the sanctuary. On the other hand adultery in both Greece and Mesopotamia carried harsh penalties.

In Greece as well as in Mesopotamia, a woman brought with her a dowry and her husband was legally obliged to preserve that dowry and return it to her in case of a divorce, and a wife, on her initiative, could leave her husband and return to her guardian (her father, uncle or brother) (2).

These similarities could be accidental as most codes contain parallel regulations. As most of the codes of the ancient Near East are based on the old Sumerian regulations, variations in these codes, when they exist, reflect the needs of the diverse societies for special laws; a land-locked country with no navigable rivers, needs no regulations to govern its shipping activities; and a tribal society of tent dwellers requires no laws to regulate the construction of houses or temples.

Similarities among all these codes abound; there is little doubt that the authors of the later codes were influenced by those who preceded them, and the older codes had collectively influenced many of the regulations of the Mosaic code, which was promulgated over a thousand years later. A point that will be looked into with some scrutiny, as through the Bible, the legal and moral pillar of Western Civilization, the West was introduced to the laws of the ancient Near East.

There are those who believe that the Mosaic laws were handed to Moses by Yehwah and therefore are unique in character and bear no dependence on any other earthly code. It suffices to say that all the law-givers of antiquity claimed to have received the law from their gods; the Hammurabi code was handed to him by the Sun god Shamas, and the god Ashur provided the Assyrian king with the Assyrian code, and king Minos of Crete received the Minoan code of law from his god also. Common people find no difficulty obeying the law if they believe it was handed down to their king by their god.

In comparing the Hmmurabi and the Mosaic codes, it is reasonable first to compare the two societies for which these codes were promulgated.

The Babylonian laws presuppose a much more highly organized and much more advanced social community than the Hebrew code, and thus provide for a much greater variety of cases (3). To regulate the complex and sophisticated Babylonian society, the code of Hammurabi provides for a greater variety of cases than the Mosaic code. But in spite of these differences, the two codes exhibit great similarities in the ordinances that deal with every day disputes or injuries to humans and livestock, or property damage. For these cases, it is believed that the Hebrew laws were drawn from the code of Hammurabi, or the author or authors of the Mosaic code were familiar with the cuneiform regulations (4).

The code of Hammurabi antedates the Mosaic code by at least several hundred years. The Pentateuch, although handed to Moses in the middle of the thirteen century, vas not canonized until about 530 B.C., that is after the return form the Exile. But despite its early date, the Hammurabi code, in many areas, is considerably more detailed, more advanced, and definitely better organized than the Mosaic code; it refers to written documents, monetary compensations, physicians, wages, and taxes. All are essential characteristics of a developed society. It is divided into sections each of which deals exhaustively with various aspects of a given problem.

According to the Old Testament, the Pentateuch, the main source of biblical laws, was dictated by Yahweh to Moses. In the Pentateuch, the conversations between Yahweh and Moses are reported verbatim. On the other hand, although the great god, Shamas, gave the law to Hammurabi, later on Hammurabi declared that he was the one who established the law. In the introduction to the code, Hammurabi is quoted as saying, "When Marduk (the supreme god of Babylon) sent me to rule the people and to bring help to the land, I established law and justice in the language of the land and promoted the welfare of the people." Hammurabi, a powerful king, could impose the law on the citizens of his vast kingdom and could punish those who broke it. Moses did not have such an authority over his free-spirited tribesmen.

Before Hammurabi issued his code of laws probably each of the various communities in the vast Babylonian empire had its own laws and customs. Hammurabi must have foreseen that a single code for the entire empire would bring judicial uniformity to the empire and may serve as a desirable unifying force. To be obeyed, a code of law, even if handed down by a god and issued by a god-king, should not run contrary to established and practiced customs. The Mosaic code served a similar purpose and must have been influenced by Hebrew established practices; it organized the various Israeli tribes into a union where the clans could live together under the same code and worship Yahweh and no other gods.

The Hammurabi code was inscribed on a large block of black diorite and housed in Esagila (E Sag Ila), the temple of Marduk (5). It remained in the temple until the twelfth century when Babylon was overrun by the Emalites, who took it back with them as a war trophy. In January of 1902, a French expedition excavating at Susa uncovered the great pillar broken in three pieces, with some of its regulations missing. What remains of Hammurabi code, and it is believed that only a few of its ordinances were lost, is some two hundred and sixty regulations. They cover practically all human activities from witchcraft to surgery and from theft to slavery; they regulate marriage and divorce, adoption and inheritance, business and partnership and the responsibilities of boatmen and physicians.

While the code of Hammurabi refers to judges and judicial decisions, and even how such decisions may be reversed, the biblical code mentions no organized court (6). Often, the suspect was brought before the Lord, the priests, and rarely judges and his guilt or innocence were usually determined by some religious test, such as "an oath of the Lord". Both the Hammurabi code and the biblical laws often contain terse dogmatic statements that presuppose that guilt or innocence may be easily established."Whosoever lieth with a beast shall surely be put to death." (Exc. 22:19); and the Hammurabi code states, "If a man practices brigandage and is caught, that man shall be put to death."

Both the Hammurabi and the Mosaic codes of law claim divine authorship rendering them complete, sacred, and requiring no revision.

While the regulations in the cuneiform code are organized in sections each of which deals with a given subject matter, the biblical laws are not. They are interspersed in five books of the Old Testament: Genesis, Exodus, Leviticus, Numbers and Deuteronomy, with Exodus and Deuteronomy containing the largest number of regulations. These five books became known collectively as the Pentateuch (a Greek word meaning five scrolls). As presented, these laws lack the harmony of thought and the uniformity of style; they also lack the proper arrangement and the systematic approach found in the Babylonian code. Based on this discord, many scholars doubt the single authorship theory of the biblical laws (7).

The laws found in the book of Deuteronomy (the word is a Greek translation of a Hebrew phrase, meaning "the second law" or "the repeated law") represent a recapitulation of previously given laws. Although the author or authors of this book quote Moses verbatim (Deut.1:5; 4:8), biblical scholars are of the opinion that Deuteronomy contains both revisions of, and additions to earlier Pentateuchal laws and interpret this to mean that it was written after the time of Moses (8).

To provide for the complex Babylonian society, the code of Hammurabi contains many ordinances that have no parallel in the Old Testament. They include the duties and privileges of soldiers, constables and tax-collectors, the laws dealing with commerce, bankruptcy, agents, merchants and grain storage, the laws of adoption, renunciation and foster-mothers, the laws regulating the duties and privileges of physicians and veterinarians, the laws of branding and selling of slaves, the responsibilities of house-builders and boatmen, the wages of laborers and how much to pay for renting an animal.

These laws were simply not needed in the Israeli society where most of these functions were not practiced or known; among the Hebrews, there were no boatmen, no physicians, no veterinarians, no policemen and no tax-collectors.

In the religion-dominated Israeli society, there are many laws in which religious, moral and civil obligations are interwoven in a mixture of rituals that have no parallel in the Babylonian code. Most of the book of Leviticus falls into this category. Other Israeli laws with no parallel in the Hammurabi code are the laws governing the duties and responsibilities of priests (Lev. Chap. 21), the laws protecting the poor (Lev. 19:9,10; Deut. 24:19-21 and Exc.23:10,11) and the laws prohibiting homosexuality and bestiality. These regulations had tremendous influenced on western morals and civilization. To people who were brought up and who lived under these moral and religious doctrines, their treatment of morality and religion may appear superior to that of the other codes.

Similarities Between the Two Codes

In an effort to present the biblical Laws as the product of the Near Eastern culture and civilization, comparison of some of the Hammurabi regulations (HR) and biblical laws are presented and the similarities between their ordinances are pointed out.

False Witness, From HR:

"If in a case a man has borne false witness, or accused a man without proving it, if that case is a capital case, that man shall be put to death."

"If he has borne witness in a case of grain or money, the penalty of the case he shall himself bear."

The laws given in Deut. 19:18,19 are similar to these regulations: "And the Judges shall make diligent inquisition: and behold, if the witness be a false witness, and has testified falsely against his brother; then shall ye do unto him, as he thought to have done unto his brother: so shalt thou put the evil away from among you."

Theft, From HR:

"If a man has stolen ox, or sheep, or ass, or pig, or boat, either from god (temple) or a palace, he shall pay thirty fold. If he is a poor man, he shall restore ten fold. If the thief has nothing to pay, he shall be put to death."

A similar law is found in Exo. 22:1,4: "If a man shall steal an ox, or a sheep, and kill it, or sell it; he shall restore five oxen for an ox, and four sheep for a sheep..... If the theft be certainly found in his hand alive, whether it be an ox, or ass, or sheep; he shall restore double."

Lost objects, From HR:

"If a man who has lost anything, finds that which was lost in a man's hand, and the man in whose hand the lost thing was found says: 'A seller sold it to me; I bought it before witnesses'; and the owner of the lost thing says: 'I will bring witnesses who know that the lost thing is mine'; if the purchaser brings the seller who sold it to him and the witnesses in whose presence it was bought, and the owner of the lost thing brings witnesses who know that the lost thing is his, the judges shall examine their testimony. The witnesses before whom the purchaser purchased it, and the witnesses who know the lost thing, shall give their testimony in the presence of a god. The seller is a thief; he shall be put to death. The owner of the lost thing shall take that which was lost. The purchaser shall take from the house of the seller the money which he has paid."

This law was oversimplified, judges and witnesses eliminated, and was recast in Lev. 6:3-5: "...have found that which was lost, and lieth concerning it, and sweareth falsely; in any of all these that a man doeth, sinning therein: then it shall be, because he hath sinned, and is guilty, that he shall restore that which he took violently away, or the thing which he hath deceitfully gotten, or that which was delivered to him to him to keep, or the lost thing which he found, or all that about which he hath sworn falsely; he shall even restore it in the principal, and shall add the fifth part more thereto, and give it unto him to whom it appertaineth, in the day of his trespass offering."

The HR goes on and discusses all other possibilities pertaining to this case and passes judgement on each. These details are not found in the Old Testament.

Stealing a Person, From HR:

"If man steals a man's son who is a minor, he shall be put to death."

The ordinance in Exo. 21:16. is parallel to this law: "He that stealth a man selleth him or if he be found in his hand, he shall surely be put to death."

Guilty Not Caught, From HR:

"If a robber is not caught, the man who is robbed shall declare his loss, whatever it is, in the presence of a god, and the city and governor in whose territory and jurisdiction the robbery was committed shall compensate him for whatever was lost. If it is a life, that city and governor shall pay his relatives one mina (9) of silver."

Deut. 21: 1-6. is somewhat similar to this regulation: "If one be found slain in the land which the Lord thy God giveth thee to possess it, lying in the field, and it be not known who hath slain him: then thy elders and thy judges shall come forth, and they shall measure unto the cities which are round about him that is slain: and it shall be, that the city which is next unto the slain man, even the elders of that city shall take a heifer, which hath not been wrought with, and which hath not drawn in the yoke; and the elders of that city shall bring down the heifer unto the rough valley, which is neither eared nor sown, and shall strike off the heifers neck there in the valley."

Laws of Agriculture, From HR:

"If a shepherd causes his sheep to eat vegetation and has not made an agreement with the owner of the field, and without the consent of the owner of the field has pastured his sheep, the owner of the field shall harvest that field, and the sheperd who without the consent of the owner of the field caused his sheep to eat the field, shall pay the owner of the field in addition twenty Gur of grain for each Bur of land."

This law is parallel to the biblical law given in Exo. 22:5: "If a man shall cause a field or vineyard to be eaten, and shall put his beast, and shall feed in another man's field; of the best of his field, and of the best of his own vineyard, shall he make restitution."

Damage to Neighboring field, From HR:

"If a man has opened his sluice for watering and has left it open and the water destroys the field of his neighbor, he shall measure out grain to him on the basis of that produced by neighboring fields."

No such law is needed in arid Palestine, but similar damage may be caused by a careless man's fire, hence the law given in Exo. 22:6: "If fire break out, and catch in thorns, so that the stacks of corn, or standing corn, or the field, be consumed therewith; he that kindled the fire shall surely make restitution."

Laws on Deposits, Form HR:

"If a man continually travelling has given silver, gold, precious stones, or property to a man and has brought them to him for transportation, and that man does not deliver that which was for transportation at the place to which it was to be transported, but has appropriated it, the owner of the transported goods shall put that man on trial concerning that which was to be transported and was not delivered, and that man shall deliver unto the owner of the transported goods five times as much as was entrusted to him."

"If a man has grain or money deposited with a man and without the consent of the owner he takes grain from the heap or granary, they shall prosecute the man because he took grain from the heap or granary without the consent of the owner, and the grain as much as he took he shall return, and whatever it was he shall forfeit an equal amount."

Similar laws are found in Exo. 22:7-11: "If a man shall deliver unto his neighbor money or stuff to keep, and it be stolen out of the man's house; if the thief be found, let him pay double. If the thief is not found, then the master of the house shall be brought unto the judges, to see whether he hath put his hand unto his neighbor's goods.... If a man deliver unto his neighbor an ass, or an ox, or a sheep, or any beast, to keep; and it dies, or be hurt, or driven away, no man seeing it: then shall an oath of the Lord be between them both, that he hath not put his hand unto his neighbor's goods; and his owner of it shall accept thereof, and shall not make it goof. And if it is stolen from him, he shall make restitution unto the owner thereof."

Laws on Debts, From HR:

"If a man is subjected to an attachment for debt and sells his wife, son, or daughter, or they are given over to service, for three years they shall work in the house of their purchaser or temporary master; in the fourth year they shall be set free."

Exo. 21:2, although requiring longer period of servitude, is similar: "If thou buy a Hebrew servant, six years he shall serve; and in the seventh he shall go out free for nothing." and Deut. 15:12 states: "If thy brother, an Hebrew man, be sold unto thee, and serve thee six years; then in the seventh year thou shalt let him go free from thee." Both verses deal with Hebrew slaves and offer no time restriction on gentile slaves, and give the time of service as six years instead of the three year-period given in HR. This has direct bearing on the meaning of the sentence: "...for he hath been worth a double hired servant to thee, in serving thee six years, (Deut. 15:18)". Without this comparison, the Deuteronomy verse is incomprehensible (10). According to the Priestly Code, the liberation should await until the year of jubilee, (Lev. 25:40).

Laws on Adultery, From HR:

"If the wife of a man is caught lying with another man, they shall bind them and throw them into the water. If the husband of the woman would let her live, or the king would let his subject live, he may do so."

There is a regulation in the Hittite code that is almost identical to this regulation. The same law is found in Lev. 20:10: "And the man that committeth adultery with another man's wife, even that committeh adultery with his neighbor's wife, the adulterer and the adulteress shall surely be put to death." and in Deut. 22:22: "If a man be found lying with a woman married to an husband, then they shall both of them die...." The Bible, unlike the HR and the Hittite code, mentions no clemency.

From HR:

"If a man forces the betrothed wife of another who is living in her father's house and has not known a man, and lies in her loins and they catch him, that man shall be put to death and that woman shall go free."

An identical law is found in Deut. 22:25: "But if a man find a betrothed damsel in the field, and the man forced her, and lie with her: then the man only that lay with her shall die."

From HR:

"If a man after his father's death lies in the loins of his mother, they shall burn both of them. If a man after his father's death is admitted to the loins of his chief wife who has borne children, that man shall be expelled from the house of his father."

Lev. 20:11 is similar: "The man that lieth with his father's wife hath uncovered his father's nakedness: both of them shall surely be put to death."

The laws prohibiting incest, which are just touched upon in the HR were practiced in the early days of Israel; Reuben, the firstborn son of

Jacob, lost his firstborn rights (Gen. 49:4) because he defiled his father's bed with Bilhah, the father's concubine (Gen. 35:22). These laws receive extensive and detailed coverage in Lev. 18:6-18; Lev. 20:19-21, and Deut. 22:30.

From HR:

"If the wife of a man is accused by her husband, and she has not been caught lying with another man, she shall swear her innocence and return to her house."

"If the finger has been pointed at the wife of a man because of another man and she has not been caught lying with the other man, for her husband's sake she shall plunge into the sacred river."

These laws are similar to the laws of jealousy found in Num. 5:12-31; both codes impose trial by ordeal; Num. 5:27 reads: "When he (the priest) hath made her to drink the water,.... if she be defiled, and have done trespass against her husband, the water that causeth the curse shall enter into her, and become bitter, and her belly shall swell, and her thigh rot."

Laws Dealing With a Slave-Girl, From HR:

"If a man takes a priestess and she does not present him with children and he set to take a concubine, that man may take a concubine and bring her into his house. That concubine shall not rank with his wife."

"If a man takes a priestess and she gives to her husband a maid-servant and she bears children, and afterward that maid-servant would take rank with her mistress; because she has borne children her mistress may not sell her for money, but she may reduce her bondage and count her among the female slaves."

"If she has not borne children, her mistress may sell her for money."

There are no laws parallel to these laws in the Bible, although a few of the patriarchal accounts are in striking conformity with these laws.

Sarah gave her Egyptian handmaid, Hagar, to Abraham so that she "may obtain children by her" (Gen. 16:2), and the slave girl, although she conceived, did not rank with her mistress (Gen. 16:6,9). Also Rachel gave her maid, Bilhah, to Jacob and she conceived and bore two sons (Gen. 30:1-8). Similarly, Leah gave her maid, Zilpah, to Jacob to wife (Gen. 30:9-13). The Patriarchs and their wives acted in accordance with Babylonian laws. Were the Hebrew patriarchs familiar with the Hammurabi code and acted accordingly?

Laws on Divorce, From HR:

"If a man would put away his spouse who has not borne him children, he shall give her silver equal to her marriage gift, and the dowry which she brought from her father's house he shall restore to her and he may put her away."

"If she had no dowry, he shall give her one mina of silver for a divorce."

"If he belongs to the laboring class, he shall give her one-third of a mina of silver."

"If the wife of a man who is living in the house of her husband sets her face to go and act the fool, neglects her house and belittles her husband, they shall prosecute that woman. If her husband says: "I divorce her," he may divorce her. On her departure nothing shall be given to her for her divorce. If her husband does not say: "I divorce her," her husband may take another wife; that woman shall dwell as a slave in the house of her husband."

"If a woman hates her husband and says: "Thou shalt not hold me," they shall make investigation concerning her into her defects.

If she has been discreet and there is no fault, and her husband has gone out and greatly belittled her, that woman has no blame; she may take her marriage portion and go to her father's house."

"If a woman does not choose to live in the house of her husband, he shall make good to her the dowry which she brought from her father's house and she may go away."

"If a man takes a wife and she is attacked by a disease, and he sets his face to take another, he may do so. He may not divorce his wife who was attacked by disease. She shall live in the house he has built and he shall support her as long as she lives."

The biblical laws on divorce (Deut. 24:1–4) lack the development found in HR; they provide no alimony for the divorcee, and the husband can divorce his wife because he has found some uncleanness in her. "When a man hath taken a wife, and married her, and it come to pass that she find no favor in his eyes, because he hath found some uncleanness in her; then let him write her a bill of divorcement, and give it in her hand, and send her out of his house (Deut. 24:1).

According to HR, a woman, although she is not accorded the same rights as the man, may initiate divorce proceedings. She may take her dowry and return to her father's house. In the Old Testament, the woman has no such rights. Furthermore the biblical laws make no provisions for a diseased woman.

Laws On Inheritance, From HR:

The laws on inheritance in the HR comprise twenty-three regulations dealing with all eventualities which may be encountered in a complex, commercially oriented society. By comparison, the biblical laws are considerably simpler. The two codes present some similarities when dealing with the cutting off of a troublesome son.

From HR:

"If a man set his face to cut off his son, and says to the judges: 'I will cut off my son,' the judges shall make investigation concerning him; if the son has not committed a grave crime which cuts off from sonship, the father may not cut off his son from sonship."

"If he has committed against his father a grave crime which cuts off from sonship, he shall pardon him for the first offense. If he commits a grave crime the second time, the father may cut off his son from sonship."

The Old Testament has no regulations for cutting off a son from his inheritance, but a son that rebels against his parents may be put to death; "They (his father and his mother) shall say unto the elders of his city, this our son is stubborn and rebellious, he will not obey our voice; he is a glutton, and a drunkard. And all the men of his city shall stone him with stones, that he die." (Deut. 21:20,21).

Preferred Son, From HR.

"If a man has presented to his son, the first in his eyes, field garden, or house, and written for him a sealed deed, and afterward the father dies; when the brothers divide, he shall take the present that his father gave him, and over and above they shall divide the goods of the father's house equally."

In the Old Testament, the father does not choose "the first in his eyes", as he has to give his firstborn son, even if he is the son of the hated wife, "a double portion of all that his father hath: for he is the beginning of his strength; the right of the first born is his." (Deut. 21:17). In the Old Testament, the firstborn son is the first in the eyes of his father.

A Daughter's Inheritance, From HR:

"If there is a wife of a god, priestess, or sacred harlot, whose father has given her a dowry and written a record of gift; and in the record of gift he has written: 'after her she may give it to whomsoever she pleases,' and has granted her full discretion; after her father dies she may give it after her to whomsoever she pleases. Her brothers have no claim on her.

"If a father does not give a dowry to his daughter, a priestess living in an appointed house, or a sacred harlot, after the father dies she shall receive from the goods of her father's house the same share as one son, and as long as she lives she shall enjoy it. After her it belongs to her brothers."

"If the father of a priestess, sacred harlot, or a temple maiden gives her to a god and does not give her a dowry, after her father dies she shall receive from the goods of her father's house a third of the portion of a son and shall enjoy it as long as she lives. After her it belongs to her brothers."

"If a father does not give a dowry to his daughter, a priestess of Marduk of Babylon, and does not write a record of gift for her; after her father dies she shall receive from the goods of her father's house one third of the portion of a son, and shall pay no tax. After her death, a priestess of Marduk may leave it to whomsoever she pleases."

"If a father presents a dowry to his daughter who is a concubine, and gives her to a husband and writes a record of gift; after the father dies, she shall not share in the goods of her father's house."

"If a father does not present a dowry to his daughter who is a concubine and does not give her to a husband; after her father's death her brothers shall give her a dowry according to the value of the father's estate and shall give her to a husband."

The biblical laws dealing with a daughter's inheritance are over simplified; If the father has sons and daughters, they provide no inheritance or dowry for the daughters; but "if a man die, and have no son, then ye shall cause his inheritance to pass unto his daughter." (Num. 27:8). But "if they be married to any of the sons of the other tribes of the children of Israel, then shall their inheritance be taken from the inheritance of our fathers, and shall be put to the inheritance of the tribe whereunto they are received." (Num. 36:3). This provision was probably intended to keep the tribe's property within the tribe. In matter of inheritance, in both codes, the female offsprings are shortchanged.

Repudiation of Parents, From HR:

"If a son of a temple servant or the son of a sacred harlot says to his father that brought him up or to his mother that brought him up, "Thou art not my father ," or "Thou are not my mother," they shall cut his tongue."

"If the son of a temple servant or the son of a sacred harlot has identified his father's house and hated the father who brought him up or the mother who brought him up and goes back to his father's house, they shall pluck out his eyes."

These two classes of people were not allowed in Israel, but an almost identical law is given in Deut. 21:18-21, according to which a disobedient, stubborn and rebellious son shall be stoned "that he die."

Laws On Assault And Battery, From HR:

"If a son strikes his father, they shall cut off his hand."

A similar law in the biblical code reads, "And he that smiteth his father or his mother, shall be surely put to death." (Exo. 21:15).

From HR:

"If a man destroys the eye of the son of a patrician, they shall destroy his eye."

"If he breaks a man's bone, they shall break his bone."

"If a man knocks out the tooth of a man of his own rank, they shall knock his tooth out."

These laws were summed up in Exc. 21:24; "Eye for eye, tooth for tooth, hand for hand, foot for foot."

From HR:

"If one destroys the eye of a man's slave or breaks the bones of a man's slave, he shall pay half his value."

Exc. 21: 26 portrays some similarity to this law: "If a man smite the eye of his servant, or the eye of his maid, that it perish; he shall let him go free for his eye's sake."
Causing Miscarriage, From HR:

"If a man strikes a man's daughter and causes a miscarriage, he shall pay ten shekels of silver for her miscarriage."

"If that woman dies, they shall put his daughter to death."

The law in Exo. 21:22,23 is similar: "If a man strike, and hurt a woman with child, so that her fruit depart from her, and yet no mischief follow: he shall be surely punished, according as the woman's husband will lay on him; and he shall pay as the judges determine. And if mischief follow, then thou shalt give life for life."
In A Quarrel, From HR:

"If a man strikes a man in a quarrel and wounds him, he shall swear, 'I did not strike with intent,' and shall pay for the physician."

The regulation in Exo. 21:18,19 is similar: "If men strive together, and one smite another with a stone, or with his fist, and he die not, but keepeth his bed. If he rise again, and walk abroad upon his staff, then shall he that smote him be quit: only he shall pay for the loss of his time."
Laws Concerning Cattle, The HR contains sixteen regulations dealing with cattle: the hiring of cattle, injuries caused to cattle and injuries caused by cattle. Of these regulations the ones with biblical parallel are:
From HR:

"If an ox when passing along a street gores a man and causes his death, there is no penalty in this case."

Exo. 21:28 reads: "If an ox gore a man or a woman, that they die, then the ox shall be surely stoned." No penalty to the owner.
From HR:

"If the ox of a man has the habit of goring and they have informed the owner of his fault and his horns he has not protected not kept his ox in, and that ox gores a man and causes his death, the owner of the ox shall pay a half mina of silver."

The law in Exo. 21:29,30 is similar: "But if the ox were wont to push with his horn in time past, and it hath been testified to his owner, and he hath not kept him in, but that he hath killed a man or a woman, the ox shall be stoned, and his owner shall be put to death. If there be laid on him a sum of money, then he shall give for the ransom of his life whatsoever is laid up him."

From HR:

"If an ox gores the slave of a man, the owner shall pay a third of a mina of silver."

The law in Exo. 21:32 bears striking resemblance to this law: "If the ox shall push a manservant of a maidservant; he (the owner) shall give unto their master thirty shekels (half a mina) of silver, and the ox shall be stoned."

From HR:

"If a man hires a herdsman to tend his cattle or sheep, he shall pay him eight Gur of grain per year." "If he loses an ox or a sheep that is intrusted to him, he shall restore ox for ox and sheep for sheep."

"If a herdsman who has had cattle of sheep intrusted to him receives his full pay and is satisfied, and he causes the cattle or the sheep to diminish in number or lessens their birth-rate, he shall give increase and produce according to his contracts."

"If a sheperd to whom cattle or sheep have been given to tend is dishonest and alters the price or sells them, they shall persecute him, and he shall restore to their owner ten times the oxen of the sheep which he stole."

"If in a fold there is a pestilence of a god, or a lion has slain [some animals], the sheperd shall before god declare his innocence, and the owner of the fold shall bear the loss of the fold."

"If the sheperd is careless and causes the loss of the fold, the sheperd shall make good in cattle or sheep the loss which he caused in the fold and shall give them to the owner."

The laws given in Exo. 22:10–15 bear some similarity to these laws.

A general look at the two time-honored codes reveals that the Hammurabi code is a purely civil code brought forth to regulate a highly advanced society and to unify the legislation of a cultured commercial people. On the other hand, the Pentateuch is basically an amalgamation of religious and moral laws set to guide a far less socially advanced community and to protect a tribal people engaged in cattle raising and agriculture. Two such societies do not need similar laws. And except where the two societies have similar legal requirements, their two codes, as expected, are different.

This could explain why the two codes have so many unrelated regulations. Even though the Hammurabi code was available to the biblical authors, many of its laws were useless and even meaningless to them and to their tribal society. Where the needs of the two communities were alike, as in settling daily disputes and personal infractions, the two codes, as we have seen, exhibit marked parallelism. One may presume that in these cases, the Hebrew legislators adopted the Babylonian regulations, often simplified them, and incorporated them along with customs that they themselves have established, thus formulating their code of law. Many of the Hebrew commonly practiced customary laws, like many of their historical traditions and religious lore are unmistakably of Mesopotamian origin.

It is surprising that for the same offense, the punishment ordered in the highly religious Mosaic code is often harsher than the one found in the Babylonian code; clemency, forgiveness and women rights were not practiced in the Hebrew society, and found no place in Hebrew laws.

Establishing the dependence of the Mosaic regulations on the Hammurabi code proves that the biblical laws are the product of Near

Eastern civilizations and their roots go as far back as the Sumerian period. Thus, the influence of the cuneiform ordinances on the laws of the Western world becomes clear. Since the time of the Roman Empire, the Bible has been the major factor in the shaping of Western civilization. It is the foundation of the laws and the political systems of the Judeo-Christian world. It is the resource book that cultured the Western mentality, providing guidance for Western leaders, thinkers, and reformers.

---

(1). Kramer, S. N. (1981:56).

(2). Martin, Thomas R. (1996:68,69).

(3). Barton, George A. (1937:380).

(4). Wigoder, Geoffrey (1986:615).

(5). According to the Old Testament, "He (Joshua) wrote there upon the stones a copy of the law of Moses." (Jos. 8:32). And Moses commanded the people saying: "Thou shalt write upon them all the words of this law." (Deu. 27:3). With these stones an altar was built on Mount Ebal (Deu. 27:1–8); (Jos. 8:31–35). Neither the altar nor the stones bearing the inscriptions have been found.

(6). At times, the towns' elders got together and passed judgement on certain cases. King Jehoshaphat (c.850 B.C.) is also credited with the appointment of judges in the "fenced cities of Judah" (2Chr. 19:5).

(7). Smith, John M. Powis (1931:173,174).

(8). Wigoder, Geoffrey (1986:278).

(9). One mina is equivalent to sixty shekels, and is approximately equal to 500 grams.

(10). It is interesting to note that "A six year term of service," has been translated into "a double hired" and is most probably in reference to being twice as long as the three-year period given in the HC regulation. This provides strong indication that the author is well acquainted with the Babylonian code. A six-year period of service also gives the slave his or her freedom on the sacred "seventh" year.

Bibliography

1. 'Abbudi, Henry H. 1991. Encycloepedia of Semitic Civilizations (in Arabic), Tripli, Lebanon: Jarrus Press.

2. Alexander, Pat. Edit. 1986. Encycloedia of the Bible. Icknield Way, Tring, Herts, England: Lion Publishing.

3. Aldington, Richard and Ames, Delano. Trans. 1959. New Larouse Encyclopedia of Mythology. London, New York, Sydney, Toronto: Prometheus Press.

4. al-Andalusi, Sa'id. 1991. Science in the Medieval World (Book of the Categories of Nations); Trans. from Arabic by S. I. Salem and A. Kumar. Austin: University of Texas Press.

5. Barton, George A.1937. The Archaelogy of the Bible. 7th Ed. Philadelphia: American Suday-School Union.

6. Bickerman, Elias Joseph. 1968. Chronology of Ancient World. Ithica, N. Y. Cornell Univesity Press.

7. Black, Jeremy and Green, Anthony. 1992. Gods, Demons and Symbols of Ancient Mesopotamia. Austin: University of Texas Press.

8. Bloch, Raymond. 1958. The Etruscans. New York: Fredrick A. Prager Inc. Pub.

9. Breasted, James Henry. 1935. Ancient Times: A History of the Early World, 2nd Ed. Boston: Gin and Company.

10. Bulfinch, Thomas. 1979. Bulfinch's Mythology, New York: Crown Publishers, Inc.

11. Collier, P. F. 1994. Collier's Encyclopedia, New York, Toronto, Sydney.

12. Curtis, Adrian. 1985. Ugarit (Ras Shamra), Grand Rapids, Michigan: William B. Eerdnans Publishing Company.

13. Diamond, Jared. 1997. Guns, Germs, and Steel, New York and London: W. W. Norton & company.

14. di Neuhoff, Sonia. 1970. The Minoan Civilization And the Knossos Palace, Fokionos Negri 52, Athens: E. Tzaferis A. E. Publishers.

15. Durant, Will. 1935. The story of Civilization: Our Oriental Heritage. New York: MJF Books.

16. Ellison, Jhon W. 1984. Nelson's Complete Concordance of the Revised Standard Version Bible, 2nd. Ed. Nashville-Camden-New York: Thomas Nelson, Publishers.

17. Frazer, James G. 1981. The Golden Bough, The Root of Religion and Folklore. New York . Avenel: Crown Publishers, Inc.

18. Frazer, R. M. 1966. The Poems of Hesiod. Norman and London: University of Oklahoma Press.

19. Freyha, Anis. 1992 3rd. Printing. A Dictionary of the Names of Towns and Villages in Lebanon (in Arabic), Beirut: Librarie du Liban.

20. Freyha, Anis. 1991. Risalate fi al-Tarikh (Essays in History), Tripoli, Lebanon: Jarrus Press.

21. Garraty, John A. and Gay, Peter. 1972. The Colombia Histroy of the World. New York: Harper & Row.

22. Glasgow, George. 1923. The Minoans. New York/London: Kennikat Press.

23. Glashow, Sheldon, 1994. From Alchemy to Quarks. Pacific Grove CA. Brooks/Cole Publishing Company

24. Gordon, Cyrus H. 1957. Common Background of Greek and Hebrew Civilization, New York: W. W. Norton & Company Inc.

25. Gordon, Cyrus H. 1957. The Ancient Near East. New York: W. W. Norton & Company Inc. and Toronto: George J. McLeod, Limited.

26. Gordon, Cyrius H. 1966. Ugarit and Minoan Crete, New York: W. W. Norton & Company Inc.

27. Graham, Lanier. 1997, Goddesses, New York, London, and Paris: Abbeville Press, Publishers.

28. Gray, Jhon. 1965. The Lagacy of Canaan; The ras Shamra Texts and Their Relevance to the Old Testament, the Netherlands: E. J. Brill, Leiden.

29. Green, Peter. 1996. The Greco-Persian Wars, Berkeley, Los Angeles, and London: Universtiy of Californian Press.

30. Hopkins, Adam. 1977. Crete, Its past, present and people, London: Farber and Farber Limited.

31. Hutchinson, Richard Wyatt. 1968 Rev. Ed. Prehistoric Crete, Beltimore, Maryland: Penguin Books.

32. Ifrah, Georges; Translated from the French by Bair, Lowell. 1985. From Zero to One. [The Original French Title is Histoire Universelle des chiffres]. Harrisonburg, Virginia: R. R. Donnelley & Sons Company.

33. Inwood, Brad. 1985. Ethics and Human Action in Early Stoicism, Oxford, Oxford University Press.

34. James, Peter and Thorpe, Nick. 1994. Ancient Inventions, New York: Ballantine Books, A division of Random House, Inc. And Toronto: Random House of Canada.

35. Jastrow, Morris, Jr. 1915. The Civilization of Babylonia and Assyria, Philadelphia and London, J. B. Lippincott Company.

36. Jidejian, Nina. 1968. Byblos Through the Ages, Beirut: Dar El-Machreq, Publishers.

37. Kilmer, A. D.; Brown, R. R.; Crocker, R. I. 1986. Sounds from Silence: Recent Dscoveries in the Ancient Near Eastern Music, Berkeley: Bit Enki Publications.

38. Kramer, Samuel Noah. 1961. Sumerian Mythology, New York, Evanston, and London: Harper and Row, Pulishers.

39. Kramer, Samuel Noah. 1981. Histroy Begins at Sumer, Philadelphia, The University of Pennsylvania Press.

40. Krumbhaar, E. B. 1958. A History of Medicine, 2nd Ed. New York: Alfred A. Knopf.

41. Krupp, E. C. 1977. In Search Of Ancient Astronomie, Garden City, Nrew York: Doubleday & Company Inc.

42. Krythe, Maymie R. 1996. All about the month, New York, Evanston, and London: Harper and Row, Publishers

43. Lucian. 1913. The Syrian goddess, Trans. Herbert A. Strong, London: Constable & co., Ltd.

44. Marinatos, Spyridon and Hirner, Max. 1960. Crete and Mycenae. New York: Harry N Abrams, Inc.

45. Martin, Thomas R. 1996. Ancient Greece, from Prehistoric to Hellenistic times, New Haven & London: Yale University Press.

46. Moscati, Sabatina, 1968. The World of the Phoenicians; Translated from the Italian by Hamilton, Alaster. New York, Washington: Fredrick A. Prager, Publisher.

47. Murray, Oswyn. 1983. Early Greece, Stanford, California: Stanford University Press.

48. Nelson, David; Joseph, Geirge G. and Williams, Julian. 1993. Multicultural Mathematics, Oxford and New York: Oxford University Press.

49. Nemet-Nejat, Karen Rhea. 1993. Cuneiform Mathematical Texts as a Reflection of Everyday Life in Mesopotamia, New Haven, Connecticut. American Oriental Society.

50. Neugebauer, Otto. 1927. Zur Entstehung des Sexagesimalsystems, in Abhandlungen der Akademie der Wissenshaften Zu Gottingen, n.s. 13.

51. Oppenheim. A. Leo. 1964. Ancient Mesopotamia, Portrait of a Dead Civilization, Chicago & London. The University of Chicago Press.

52. Pettinato, Giovanni. 1981. The Archives of Ebla "An Empire Inscribed in Clay, Garden City, New York: Doubleday & company, Inc.

53. Pfeiffer, Charles F. 1962. Ras Shamra and the Bible, Grand Rapids 6 Michigan: Baker Book House.

54. Porter, Roy, Editor. 1996. The Cambridge Illustrated History of Medicine, Cambridge: Cambridge University Press.

55. Redford, Donald B. 1992. Egypt, Canaan, and Israel in Ancient Times, Princeton, New Jersey: Princeton Universtiy Press.

56. Richardson, Emeline Hill. 1964. The Etruscans, theri art and Civilization. Chicago: University of Chicago Press.

57. Al-Rihani, Ameen. 1986. Qalib Lubnan (Heart of Lebanon). Beirut, Lebanon: Dar al-Jeil.

58. Saggs, H. W. F. 1962. The Greatness that Was Babylon, A survey of Ancient Civilization of the Tigris-Euphrates Vally, New York and Washington: Frederick A. Praeger, Publisher.

59. Sarton, George. 1930. Introduction to the History of Science, Vol. 1. Baltimore:

60. Scullard, H. H. 1967. The Etruscan Cities and Rome, Ithaca, New York: Cornell University Press.

61. Schmandt-Besserat, Denise. 1996. How Writing Came About, Austin: the University of Texas Press.

62. Selin, Helaine, Ed. 1997. Encyclopaedia of the History of Science, Technology, and Medicine in Non-Western Cultures, Dordrecht / Boston / London: Kluwer Academic Publishers.

63. Smith, Jhon M. Powis. 1931. The Origin of th History of the Hebrew law. Chicago: The University of Chicago Press.

64. Strange, J. 1980. Caphtor/Keftiu: A New Investigation, the Netherlands: E. J. Brill, Leiden.

65. Swerdlow, N. M. 1998. The Babylonian Theory of the Planets. Princeton, New Jersey: Princeton university Press.

66. Varisco, Daniel Martin. 1994. Medieval Agriculture and Islamic Science-The Almanac of a Yemeni Sultan. Seattle and London: University of Washington Press.

67. Waddell, L. A. 1924; re-printed 1983. The Phoenician Origin of Britons, Scots & Anglo-Saxons. Howthorn, CA: The Christian Book Club of America.

68. Weill, Raymond. 1940. Phoenicia and Western Asia to the Macedonian Conquest. London, Toronto, Bombey, Sydney: George G. Harrap & Co. Ltd.

69. Wigoder, Geoffrey (Gen. Ed.). 1986. Illustrated Dictionary and Concordance of the Bible. Jerusalem; G.G. The Jerusalem Publishing House, Ltd.

70. Zohary, Daniel and Hopf, Maria. 1988. Domestication of plants in the Old World. Oxford: Clarendon Press.

Index

W
Wind Flower; 124

Y
Yahweh; 23, 40, 173, 292–293
Yamm; 133, 135
Yathrip; 255

Z
Zagros Mountains; 9, 14
Zero; 263, 271, 315
Zeus; 38, 75, 94, 113, 141, 163, 182
Zigzag Function; 227
Zodiac; 79, 101, 225, 233–234
Zoser; 15, 198–199

About the Authors

Sema'an I. Salem is professor emeritus at California State university, Long Beach, where he taught and did his research since 1961. He has published three books and over 100 scientific papers, mostly on atomic physics. He made some forty presentations in the United States, Europe, and the Middle East.

He is the recipients of several research and educational grants and many awards and recognitions, among them the Outstanding Professor of the Year (1981–1982) and the Scholarly and Creative Achievement award (1983).

Lynda A. Salem received her Master of Science in Library Science degree from the Catholic University of America and is working as a librarian in the city of Long Beach. The two authors are a father-daughter team.